Notions on Emotions

Notions on Emotions

◆ ◆ ◆

Re-Viewing their nature and function

L. Hade

Artwork by Kamea Hadar

ISBN: 0692997814
ISBN 13: 9780692997819
Library of Congress Control Number: 2017919076
L. Hade, Haleiwa, HI

Contents

Introduction and Summary

The Puzzling Nature of Emotions

We talk about our emotions, study them, and feel we know a lot about them, and yet we are far from having an agreed-upon definition or even a common understanding of emotions as a whole phenomenon. We particularly do not have clarity about what emotions actually are or how they should be seen. Why do they develop? What unique functions do they fulfill? What special advantages do they give us (other than heart break)? Considering the puzzlement over this topic and the confusion regarding its location in our conceptual universe, this essay aims to offer an innovative, helpful perspective that can resolve some of this mystification.

Prior to writing this essay, I undertook extensive research on the topic of emotion, covering scientific, philosophical, popular, and self-help literature, as well as artistic expressions. In addition to a wide examination of the literature, I asked hundreds of people in an informal survey to give some basic notion, idea, concept, view, definition, function or even a mental association regarding emotions as a category or general phenomena. This group included many experts—psychologists, therapists, psychoanalysts, philosophers, and theorists of emotions, as well as educated, knowledgeable non-specialists.

Many of the respondents were well-versed in various philosophies and psychological theories, had studied specific emotions (such as fear and anxiety or happiness), were familiar with emotional dynamics, pathology, and therapy, or had studied various components of the phenomenon of emotion, such as neurological, cognitive, physical, social, and cultural aspects. However, when asked for a general view of emotions, the majority had difficulty coming up with a clear, specific formulation; they noted that emotion is "an experiential phenomenon," "a personal non-rational reaction," "a subjective experience," "a cognitive construct," "an appraisal-motivational-relational process," "adaptive reactions or techniques," or "neuro-chemical processes or substances."

When asked "What are emotions?" or "What is their function?" most people (including scientists) typically offer examples, descriptions of emotional incidents and associated behavior, and finally conclude that "we all know what they are and how they feel, so why bother with all these extra-hard questions?"

Accordingly, emotions are often restricted to, confused with or reduced to other phenomena, such as behavior (anger is when we shout and act mad), thoughts and evaluations ("fear is an evaluation of risk," "it is all in your head"), sensations ("I feel it in my heart or stomach"), or neuro-chemical processes (as psychiatry or medicine often describe them).

Readers of this essay are welcome to join in and contemplate this question right now. They can judge whether they feel that they have a satisfactory definition or understanding of what emotions are, or how they should be seen, what their main function is, and so forth.

There are endless writings which discuss emotions in some form or another, but very few philosophers or psychologists have actually concentrated on emotions as a general category or phenomenon or considered their place in philosophy, psychology, and/or biology.

It is even less common to find emotions considered in political or structural social studies. Even today, in most areas of life, emotions continue to be seen as a personal phenomenon which compromises rational behavior (for example, the legal system, business, government operations, science, and technology).

The discussion that follows will mention a few philosophers (who up until the last century often wrote about psychology as well), prominent psychologists, and other thinkers who discussed emotion and contributed a great deal to the general subject. Today, a comparatively small number of very valuable psychologists and neuropsychologists and a few philosophers continue to focus on this question and provide extensive, helpful research. However, most psychologists and psychoanalysts, as well as the majority of thinkers, writers, theologians, philosophers or artists still shy away from discussing emotions as a general phenomenon. They often discuss particular emotions, emotional behavior, emotional development, pathology and therapy, artistic emotional expressions, and the role of emotions in technology (or lack of it). However, rarely do they try to explain the category as a whole.

This is rather surprising, considering that emotions are one of the topics most talked about in common discourse, and that they draw and direct much of our energy. They also play a central role in fiction and poetry, are depicted frequently in the arts, and are the focal point of a number of scientific fields. Emotions obviously occupy much of our attention and influence most of our actions. We all seem to have a good sense of how they feel and affect behavior, and whether they are "normal" or have become pathological or destructive. However, most times we treat them as something mysterious that cannot be fully understood or managed. This essay is designed to help us move further in understanding the perplexing phenomenon of emotions.

What This Essay Hopes to Accomplish

This essay will not attempt to resolve all the questions about emotions or come out with the "ultimate" definition. However, *it will propose a new way of looking at emotions, their overall function, a few of their main essential characteristics, and the way they relate to vital concepts.* Not only do emotions take place between a person and his or her environment, or have a relational aspect, as some of the leading contemporary theories claim, but their primary function is relational. They are in fact a special *relational method* with a number of unique characteristics which distinguish them from other relational practices and experiences. This is why we should move beyond the typical questions of whether emotions are cognitive or not, or rational or irrational. Instead, we might view them through a novel analogy—as our personal domestic and foreign policies, and as such, study their special mental requirements, processes, and implications. They give us specific, flexible, and powerful relational capabilities, and they improve our relational skills to cope with our unique survival, parental engagement, and social needs, as well as our cultural, intellectual, and artistic yearnings.

This new perspective will provide the basis for some possible distinctions and for a typology, as well as offering a new way of viewing the interactions between the concept of emotion and other key concepts such as cognition and rationality. The way of perceiving or categorizing emotion offered in this essay is not necessarily the best or the only way to treat the topic. Instead, it is a rather original and, we hope, helpful way to think about emotions as we search for a better understanding of their function, unique workings, and conceptual position. With these fresh perspectives, distinctions, and questions, this essay hopes to rejuvenate, widen, and accelerate the discussion and study of emotion as a general phenomenon in psychology, philosophy, and even social, political science, technology, and the arts.

Somewhat analogous to some of the practices of advanced physics, this essay offers a theoretical hypothesis waiting to be tested by future empirical research. In theoretical physics, scientists often maintain a productive cooperation between the theoreticians who advance new theories and the empiricists who later test them. This essay could be tested soon by existing psychological methods, or it could await future development of more advanced knowledge and techniques that offer a better understanding of the brain. In the meantime, like many other conceptual theories, it can best be judged in terms of its heuristic value, its usefulness with regard to other explanations, further research, predictions, and practical goals, such as therapy, technology, the arts, and social and political improvements.

Thus, though extensive scientific and philosophical research has gone into the writing of this essay, and though it has been written by a scientist, it is not presented as an empirical psychological study or as a typical philosophical investigation.

Instead of offering another typical but limited empirical or philosophical study for the benefit of a few experts in the field, it seems more beneficial at this point to engage in long- overdue conceptual reconfiguration of the basic understanding of emotions and closely related key concepts. Since emotions are central to all people and are of primary interest to so many disciplines and communities, as well as to those in non-scientific professions, the hope here is to reach a wider and more diversified, interested audience. We hope such readers will benefit from these fresh views as well as participate and contribute to the future development of an improved but accessible view of emotions. Therefore, this essay is written for a diversified readership, including a broad range of professionals, artists, creative people, and all other persons who find the understanding of emotions central to their work or life. As an essay, this work presents a multidisciplinary discussion of philosophical and psychological notions designed to engage a wide swath of experts as well as non-specialists.

With this view in mind, this essay begins with an introductory summary to present key ideas, and an initial clarification of some central concepts. These ideas will then be taken up in depth in the body of the essay, which consists of three major sections. First, it explores and analyzes the unique function of our emotions, and their special advantage or contribution. Second, it looks at particular dimensions of emotions and the necessary conditions for their occurrence. To sharpen and clarify our view, we compare emotional to non-emotional styles of relating. This outlook is then tested on a few relevant emotional phenomena, such as short-term vs. long-term emotions and intense emotional events vs. calm ones. Last but not least, we see how this new relating theory helps resolve some of the age-old, enigmatic connections between emotion and closely linked concepts such as drives, values, cognition, rationality, objectivity, self, and relationships.

A Roadmap

The following summary offers a preview of ideas that will be explored in the body of the essay. It is designed to serve as a kind of roadmap for the more detailed discussions to come. Considering the topic's complexity, the current flood of information (not necessarily wisdom), the growing impatience of our culture (this writer included), and the wide variety of interest levels, the strategy here is to provide a comprehensive, thorough summary in the beginning. For some, this summary will be sufficient and will save them from the long, detailed journey that led to these conclusions. For others, it will offer a concise, initial overview and a good point of reference for the rest of the reading. The hope is that it will also function as a comfortable summation to return to after struggling through the intricate discussions and ideas in the body of the essay. A novel approach to a complex subject often requires recurring alternative and complimentary presentations, and a few reiterations that may seem somewhat repetitive. Reading a full summary in the beginning also contributes to this impression. Unfortunately, a certain amount of repetition is inevitable, and the author apologizes for this in advance.

As the discussion of key concepts suggests, this exploration of emotion calls for a seemingly odd assortment of emotional components and processes that mandates an interdisciplinary approach in which psychological, philosophical, practical, and even political considerations are combined. As a result, the approach in this essay is somewhat eclectic, and some of the discussions may seem disconnected. However, rather than thinking of the structure as sequential, like floors in a high-rise building, consider it as analogous to the creation and modification of a very complex 3-D map or model constructed by different team members.

This multifaceted and diverse collection of discussions and approaches is essential for constructing a new view of emotions, and the author hopes it will not interfere with the key insights and the fuller picture that emerges in later sections. Each section of the essay makes a unique contribution to the creation and establishment of this new perspective. Nevertheless, with the exception of Part A, which might be critical to understanding the overall outlook, readers are welcome to pick and choose from the rest of the sections, depending on their interest.

Summary Preview

Obstacles to Clarity Regarding the Phenomenon of Emotions

Not only are emotions a very complex and unique phenomenon, but their overall function has traditionally been viewed as problematic or secondary. Historically, they have been seen as rather private, unpredictable phenomena that contradict rationality, cognition, and common sense. Accordingly, the number of scholars and studies pondering this category as a whole has been very limited, and the situation is not much different today. Because the topic is not a typical philosophical focus, only a few philosophers have studied it in depth, and it has rarely been central to the discipline. Most of our psychological efforts have been, and still are, aimed at specific emotions, various emotional processes, problems, improvement, and therapy (perhaps starting with Freud himself). The small number of psychologists and philosophers who have looked at emotions as a whole have given us good insights into different emotional components and their inner-workings (see sources cited in the essay and the bibliography). The popular appraisal theories, in particular, provide a good indication of the main aspects of emotions, including some relational ones. Nevertheless, even the few scholars and approaches that do look at emotions as an overall phenomenon are still primarily busy figuring out particular emotional components, what constitutes them, and how they work.

Therefore, while they improve understanding about some of the parts and inner processes of emotions, most theories are still not clear about the overall and primary function of emotion in our lives. The broad recognition that emotions contribute to our adaptability, rely heavily on cognition or other mental or somatic processes, along with most of our common emotional definitions (for example, "subjective experiences"), remains far too vague. These concepts are so general that they are typically insufficient, and frequently confusing or even misleading.

This might be one of the main reasons for the lingering diversity of definitions and confusion surrounding emotion. That is also why somewhat of a "disconnect" exists between the limited and often complex studies of the emotional phenomenon and the larger public, including most psychologists. Most are still puzzled and would rejoice to have a clearer overall view of emotions and their place in our life.

A New Way to View Emotions

The simple but critical recognition fundamental to this essay is that emotions actually are, or should be seen as, *a special way of relating and the unique body/mind dynamics that facilitate it*. From a developmental point of view, their primary function could be said to enhance our relational capacity and provide us with extremely powerful but highly refined, flexible, customized, sophisticated, forceful, and dynamic relational and commitment capabilities. The emotional aptitude enables us to relate, commit, connect, empathize or conceptually interact with individual and specific elements of life beyond relating generically or indistinctly to categories or groups of items. With our emotional capabilities, we can relate in a unique manner to each of thousands of different elements and change these orientations quickly as needed. We contemplate our interdependence with various elements in our environment and accordingly are motivated by them and care about their destiny (for better or for worse). Thus, emotions enhance human adaptability and social connectivity, and provide us with high-performance but flexible and dynamic relational abilities. These capabilities are particularly necessary for organisms such as mammals with a long and intricate care trajectory for offspring (for both parents and offspring), complex social systems, and a highly diversified geographical environment. They constitute and function as a crucial part of our personal "domestic and foreign policy," and could be viewed as a unique and critical aspect of our interface with the physical, social, and conceptual environment. In other words, to present an idea that will be developed further, emotions can be considered analogous to the foreign policies or positions countries take in relation to other countries and various issues, including the preparation and organization necessary to facilitate those policies, whether in times of peace or military tension. Cognition, which we will discuss further, could be seen as analogous to the processes which analyze, design, and manage these policies.

Emotions are not just individual, internal, subjective experiences or cognitive processes as many common definitions propose, but rather relational methods, techniques, capacities, skills, and orientations with particular configurations and modus operandi which we partially experience. They also do not merely influence our relationships, nor are they merely affected by them; but instead, they can be viewed as an actual, specific, type, category or portion of relationships. This family of distinctive methods of relating includes special body/mind organizations, preparations, configurations, modes, and motivations formed by our body/mind when relating in this manner.

Though highly directed by our cognition or our mental capacity (like many other human functions and activities), emotions are not solely cognitive or mental, and should not be limited to appraisals, judgments, evaluations, or any other cognitive or mental processes in our minds. They are also not "just feelings" or senses in the body or even the simple combination of evaluations and feelings, as often suggested. They are better viewed as an actual, integral, synergic, body/mind relational process and configuration. Any attempt to separate them from, or include them in, cognition or sensation risks the age-old dualism of Descartes and reflects a basic misunderstanding of their relational function. In a sense, they are *felt relationships* or *a manner of relating which we sense or experience.* In other words, we literally feel how we perceive and relate, sense these special relationships and configurations, and experience our position vis-a-vis various elements! They are not something we "have," but something we are, or a mode of being and relating at one time or another. This is why we **are** angry or **in** love, and don't just have angry thoughts or a perception of love.

Special Emotional Dimensions

Emotions require and possess special qualities which differentiate them from purely cognitive functions and from other ways of relating to objects, people, and ideas. These qualities, or emotional dimensions, can be divided into four main groups: interdependence, motivational force, specificity, and feeling.

To start with, we tend to develop an emotional relationship with elements with which we perceive a physical, perceptual or emotional *interdependence*. Namely, we believe that we will be somehow affected (or that we have been affected) by what happens to these elements or by our relationships with them and vice versa. This perceived connection or intertwined destiny is usually why we care about these individuals or situations or focus our attention on them.

We tend to have these relationships only with *specific* irreplaceable objects, people or groups—and not with generic categories or exchangeable items. In other words, emotions are *item-*, *person-*, *or community-specific.* For example, we typically will not have an emotional relationship with a cashier, a customer service person, or a generic tool if we perceive them to be completely interchangeable with another person, tool, or an automated service. However, once they become somehow special, memorable, and interconnected (nicely or badly), we tend to relate to them emotionally—with anger, fondness or in some other way.

These relationships also tend to include **motivation** or a sense of force with a particular direction. Emotions express our motivations or motivate us, pull and push, and connect us in a specific way to particular circumstances, people, and much that matters to us. That is, not only do we care about what happens to these elements of our lives or our relationship with them, but we feel a push for action or for a specific development in one form or another (even if we end up not acting on it). This is also why emotions have an intensity that more purely cognitive constructs or processes typically lack (for example, concepts or evaluations). Emotions (and perhaps life in general) could be said to manifest certain mental configurations which are expressed in and guide physical energy (our sensations, motivation, and actions).

The last and most familiar dimension is the element of physical changes and sensation. Typically, the level of significance of the situation and our interdependence with it influences the intensity of the emotional relationship and, accordingly, if and *how it feels.* Thus we actually *feel* the way we relate or sense our relationships. Feelings also act like pain and pleasure and give us a positive or negative incentive or feedback for the way we relate to people or circumstances. We therefore are often aware of our relations and are motivated by them, even if we are not always clear on what we feel or aware of why we feel it. Awareness does not guarantee clarity.

For instance, hate is the common name we give today to ways of relating in which we typically see a reverse correlation between our well-being and that of a specific individual, group, idea or situation. Thus, we wish the worst for this object and are motivated to act on it, which means that typically we want to distance ourselves from it and/or are driven to hurt or destroy it.

Among its million descriptions, love could be seen as the popular, current name for the ways we relate to particular people, objects or ideas when we perceive a positive correlation of our mutual destinies. Accordingly, typically, we empathize, wish the best for those, are pushed to help them, and want to get closer or commit to stay connected to them.

These four components—interdependence, motivational force, specificity, and feeling—seem necessary for an emotional relationship to develop, and ultimately they determine what kind of an emotion we will have and how strong it will be. Future discussions might question, add to or change some of these emotional essentials, but the ones suggested here offer a good start for a fresh debate about emotion.

It could be argued that these dimensions are gradations and should be viewed in terms of degrees rather than as an on/off switch. Namely, as noted, the stronger the perceived interdependence and accordingly the significance and motivational force, the higher the intensity, the sensations, and how passionate we feel.

Non-emotional Relationships or Ways of Relating

Emotions are a special modality of relating, but not the only one. This essay distinguishes two or possibly three more complementary styles of relating or types of relationships: "utilitarian," "reflective," and "pre-emotional." These can stand apart from or be combined with emotional modes of relating. Nevertheless, they are qualitatively different methods or strategies for relating. There are many ways to dissect our vast relational pool, but this distinction is helpful in that it shows by contrast what is unique about emotions and thus sharpens our understanding of them.

As hinted above, when we relate to elements of our lives which we perceive to be generic or interchangeable, we typically have only utilitarian or instrumental relationships with them. This is how we usually relate to a customer service person, the chicken we ate yesterday, or a common screwdriver. Unfortunately, this is also how many cultures traditionally related to the environment as a whole. These relationships might be based on certain needs (we want the function or service), but because the object is replaceable, these relationships lack interdependency and specificity, and therefore evoke no particular care regarding the future of the object or our relationship with it. In other words, the object's identity is incidental instead of essential. Accordingly, we typically lack any specific motivation regarding this relationship (except the desired utility) or any physical sensations or feelings about it.

"Reflective" relationships include the ones we have with elements of our lives we know about, but do not rely on for service or feel interdependent with. For instance, a piece of trivia, anonymous people we handle with indifference for a large company or government, or items we see on TV or on the street when we pass by. We are aware of them and can reflect on them, but like a reflection in a mirror, we do not necessarily feel connected to them. Accordingly, we commonly do not care about them, feel any inclination toward action in their direction, or have sensations related to them.

It is also possible to distinguish "pre-emotional" ways of relating for non-emotional or less emotional organisms (according to received standards). These relationships may resemble emotional ways of relating. For example, they might include the way some birds or even social insects relate to their offspring, to other community members or to danger. However, on the whole, these ways of relating seem to be more instinctive and categorical, less individual, and less customized and dynamic.

Human beings seem to combine most, if not all, the above relational styles and use them together or separately.

If we choose to view the emotional dimensions in terms of degrees as suggested above, the difference between our various methods of relating could also be seen as a matter of gradated distinctions instead of a clear cut sharp separation.

Evolutionary Speculations: Organisms and Machines

It is clear that most organisms have several ways of relating to their environment. One interesting question is how these ways have developed or diversified through the evolutionary process, and why and how we ended up with emotional ways of relating.

A possible hypothesis is that, in order to survive, most organisms initially developed some simple form of recognition of elements in their environment, and some process by which they either decided or were instinctively programmed to relate to them in order to utilize, protect, avoid or ignore their presence. Some of these earlier and more instinctual ways of relating could be considered similar to the reflective and utilitarian ones described above. A few of those relationships, for example, could be seen as pre-emotional patterns of relating similar to our notions of fear, parental care, and aggression. Some even include expressions of social cohesiveness, and could be described as instances of duty or loyalty to offspring and community, such as we see among some organisms like social insects.

Nevertheless, these ways of relating differ from our typical emotional methods in that they tend to be instinctive and thus applied categorically and inflexibly. They often lack the dimension of specificity, the complex process of appraising interdependencies, elements of long- term commitment (such as empathy, affection or animosity), the specific, "customized" capacity, the diversity, the dynamic nature of human emotions that allows for quick adjustments, and so forth.

It could be assumed that as new forms of life developed, as mental capacity increased in certain organisms, and as life and society became more complex, extra relational needs developed as well as additional techniques and skills. Some studies claim that in mammals, and particularly in people, new relational capabilities and methods developed in response to growing needs, such as the new necessities of long-term, individual, affectionate parental care, complex and diversified social interactions, and varied geographical requirements.

Thus, over time, some basic ways of relating, relationships or interactions might have evolved to become what we now consider and call "emotions," such as human fear, hatred, and love. In some cases and contexts, emotional methods of relating replaced previous relational styles, but it seems that in many instances, they were combined with earlier ways of relating or enhanced them.

What portion of our relational system is emotional, what part of it is instinctual and universal, and what portion is cultural or personal? These are highly complex and controversial questions today. Definitive answers are beyond the scope of this essay, but hopefully these questions will direct our attention to interesting, fresh, and helpful studies in the future.

All in all, we always relate, but if we have more developed social needs and brains, we have to relate to more things in more ways, and we are able to, which is another way of saying that we have a more complex relational and emotional repertoire, skills, and capacity. It is important to emphasize that we don't only have more shades of relationships or better relational skills, but we seem to have more and better-suited, types, styles or methods of relating, and this may explain the function of emotional development and the reason for it.

Most of what is said above can also be applied to our ongoing efforts to develop machines and Artificial Intelligence. If our aim is to make machines and programs "more human" we may benefit from utilizing many of the insights presented in this essay. For instance, we would need to consider the machines' values, drives, and particular preferences which their emotions are supposed to express and enhance. We also have to ensure their ability to form and change endless specific ways of relating to a multitude of elements based on scenarios of interdependence (instead of on pre-programmed relational categories). Similar challenges will arise regarding their commitment to various relationships, motivation for action, specific behavior, or their use of rationality to sort through endless options.

Intensity, Time, and Focus

In examining this new perspective on emotions, it seems helpful to view it in the context of actual emotional relationships along three different spectrums—intensity, time, and focus.

Calm vs. Intense Emotional Episodes. The element of force in our emotions varies in intensity. This intensity is partially dependent on our arousal level and the varying significance of the object of our emotion. The arousal level and significance are also associated with the fluctuating perception of our interdependence with this object. This intensity could be seen as another dynamic dimension of our whole emotional system.

During calm times, we seem to have the ability to practice multiple emotional relationships with many elements of our lives almost simultaneously ("emotional multitasking"). We tend to narrow our relational interactions when the intensity rises. Our modes of operation vary, somewhat like a nation or a military organization with levels of alert or states of emergency. The higher the alert, the more our attention and all our other resources (not just mental focus) are concentrated and mobilized. However, this focus typically comes with a rise in the cost of resources, a decrease in flexibility, and a lower consideration for other concerns and courses of action. This is commonly interpreted as having a one-track mind, being less rational, and exhibiting a lack of control, as in cases of extreme infatuation, anger or fear. The intensity and concentration of being "on high alert" can overshadow other relationships, coloring our mood or resulting in a "spillover" effect. Clearly, the higher the intensity, the more we feel the increase in mobilization and motivation.

Thus, the recognition is that we have emotions most of the time and toward multiple elements, but many of them are not necessarily intense or felt strongly. However, if one of these emotions becomes highly forceful, we tend to concentrate, mobilize further, and feel more of what we traditionally have considered "emotional."

Long-Term vs. Short-Term Emotions. The issue of long-term vs. short-term emotions is another puzzling question which is often discussed but rarely understood. Why do we seem to have mixed and changing feelings toward the same person? Do we actually have long-term emotions, or only emotional evaluations of prolonged periods?

Recently the United Nations and many other experts have been debating similar questions in their attempt to better understand and measure happiness. Long-term emotions seem to be more cognitive and can be viewed as an evaluation of a personal history, or a collection of short-term emotional episodes. Alternatively, long-term emotion can be seen as a pattern of similar short-term emotional experiences with coherence and consistency that is nevertheless surprising flexible and penetrating, somewhat like a beam of light. Thus, long-term emotions can change slightly according to particular momentary circumstances or be incorporated with other emotions which interchange with them periodically (depending on our preferred view). If emotions are considered as a way of relating, we do not necessarily "feel" them all the time unless the intensity goes up. Nevertheless, whenever we encounter the same object of our emotions and find that it acts in familiar ways, we tend to relate in a similar manner. Though frequently of lower intensity, long-term emotions should not be misinterpreted as having less strength or significance, as our relationships with our children, spouse or country often prove. They don't disappear in calm times, as some might think, but keep on shaping the biases of our universe, including our unique perceptions, preferences, and goals.

Focused vs. Diffused Emotions. All the way from the writings of Plato, and particularly in Brentano's philosophy (Solomon 1977, 2003, Reisenzein 2006), emotions have been said to have "intentionality," which means that they are *about* something. However, when it comes to more diffuse emotions like happiness, depression, and various moods, it is often not so clear what we are relating to or have a relationship with (what de Sousa and others call "objectless emotions" in the *Stanford Encyclopedia of Philosophy*/Emotion 2013).

Even though emotions have certain common denominators, they are a highly-diversified group. Thus, the first option is that we can create different subgroups within the category of emotions to identify those which share some dimensions in common (for example, interdependence and sensations), but are different in other ways.

While some emotions are about relating to something specific, others might have to do with the way we relate to more general, more spread-out circumstances, like a person's overall environment, situation or life as a whole. This means that we have the ability and tendency to also relate emotionally to "diffused" situations like our condition or circumstances (beyond specific people and objects).

It is important to realize that even though we usually do not form emotional relationships with generic notions or categories (for example, wives), it is clear that we can relate emotionally to cumulative concepts, such as country, and to abstract ideas. As long as we consider these "integrative ideas" to be somewhat cohesive and unified, we can also relate emotionally to a family, an ethnic group, a nation, humankind, the "environment," our overall history, or even a specific situation.

Thus, it is not hard to assume that at times we can also relate to our life as a whole or to an evaluation of our general state of affairs (over a period or for a moment). This is relevant to the "spillover" effect described previously in which a specific emotion affects our general emotional state. It helps to explain how music, smells, drugs, and other such triggers can influence our overall mood. Our happiness could be said to rise out of such a relational orientation to life and our environment, as we subconsciously assess our circumstances and sense a desirable equilibrium and/or progress (see Hade's forthcoming essay on happiness).

Emotion and Important Related Concepts

As indicated earlier, when presenting a novel and unorthodox view of an established phenomenon, it is important to examine, and possibly reestablish, its connections to key, closely related concepts. Unfortunately, beyond their own highly complex nature, ideas about emotions are closely related to other complicated and controversial concepts, such as values, cognition, rationality, the self, and so forth. This complexity is compounded by the need to summarize everything here in a few brief paragraphs. Therefore, while the condensed summary so far may not have been easy to comprehend, the following few sections are even more complex and may be hard to digest at first reading. Although these sections are not totally essential for understanding and utilizing the new view of emotions suggested here, as said above, they help with the reconceptualization of the emotional phenomenon. Thus, those who are sufficiently interested and dedicated may venture into the corresponding sections in the essay to help clarify some of the ideas abbreviated here.

Emotions and Drives, Values and Beliefs

Many of the associations between emotions and drives, values, and beliefs (called "directives" here, for short) are well-researched in psychology. However, these connections are mostly studied to inform therapy in individual pathological cases, and the conclusions are rarely applied on a large scale, or for social or political analysis and policies. Bridging this gap leads to some of the more interesting public consequences that arise from the new relational view of emotions, suggested here and in our conclusions.

Emotions seem to represent our entrenched subconscious directives more than our stated ones. This is why we might be aware of many of our emotions but feel little or no control over them. Put differently, emotions tend to reflect more of what we actually want and believe in, rather than what we *want* to believe in.

Emotions are the way we relate to elements in our lives to facilitate or advance our directives. They manifest or express the actual execution of these directives in shaping and directing their particular forces to specific objects, people or situations. For instance, we are afraid of the elements that endanger our survival, we hate the people that compromise our drive for social position, and we love the paintings that expresses our values of beauty and esthetics.

Therefore, if we want to bring about social or emotional change, it is often preferable to alter our beliefs and values. This tends to be more effective and longer lasting than simply asking for direct emotional changes such as "more love" or "less hatred," as many of our songs and speeches call for. (The same is true if we want to change foreign policy.)

At the same time, emotions also contribute to our values and affect them. Many philosophers propose that they enable humankind to develop empathy and morality. However, the extent and particular direction of this ethic are still determined by our beliefs and values, and can vary dramatically between great care and horrifying hatred. Accordingly, our emotions can be a good window into our "real/true" values. For example, by observing closely how, and how strongly, we actually feel about different issues, people and objects, such as far-away wars and the people who are dying there, we can learn more about our actual values and how important these elements really are in our constellation of priorities.

Emotions and Cognition

Perhaps one of the more important outcomes of this essay's new relational outlook is a clarification of the age-old problem of the complex relationships between emotions and cognition. If emotions are seen as a special method of relating, including the particular body/mind configuration that comes with it, they are better *not* seen as part of cognition or in opposition to cognition. Rather, cognition simply participates in their initiation, formation, processing, and termination, as it does in many other body/mind processes such as athletic performance or sleep. Clearly, the interaction is mutual, and cognition also adapts and changes to facilitate these special configurations and relationships. For example, it formulates and changes perceptions and priorities, widens or narrows its focus according to intensity (like a camera), mobilizes resources, and so forth.

Thus, cognition and emotion are closely interconnected but could be seen as two non-parallel categories that do not operate on the same continuum. Cognition can be viewed more as a mental subsystem which participates in many of our activities, while emotion can be seen as a relational method and avenue which reaches beyond cognition. Following the foreign policy analogy, cognition can be seen as the main part of our decision-making process and apparatus (for example, government and bureaucracy), while emotion can be viewed as an aspect of our actual foreign and domestic positions and policies, and as the way we prepare for and relate to organizations, countries, and so forth. This view of the two functions offers, for our purposes, a better explanation of their unique qualities and differences while clarifying the role which they play in each other's operation as well as their mutual contribution and influence. It avoids the traditional competition between cognition and emotion, hierarchy, or the collapse of one phenomenon into the other.

Emotions and Rationality

Like cognition, rationality is a highly intricate term with multiple and confusing interpretations. Nevertheless, most of the traditional interpretations agree that emotions compromise rationality.

Rationality is primarily used to judge cognitive efficiency and quality, even when evaluating actions and behavior. If cognition is seen as a separate, facilitating subsystem, instead of as a competing or all-inclusive category, rational evaluations can be applied to cognition, but not necessarily to emotions. Emotions might be based on mistaken or "faulty" assumptions and beliefs, which can compromise their cognitive or appraisal process. However, emotions themselves are neither rational nor irrational thoughts or judgments. Emotions are rather types of relationships or relational configurations which promote and express our basic drives and values. As such, they represent our end goals and directions, and preferably should not be assessed for rationality. Criticizing an emotion is primarily a value judgment. Is the love of the ocean or poetry rational? Is being sad about a lover irrational?

Though emotions themselves cannot be judged for rationality, their interaction with cognition might lower our capacity for rational performance. When emotional intensity goes up, we tend to concentrate on fewer relationships, our priorities change, and the leading ones seem highly urgent and vital. This appears to affect what experts call "instrumental rationality" (that is, the efficient match of means and goals). If we are madly in love, getting close to a loved one or caring for them becomes extremely important. Accordingly, we are ready to give up other, longer-term economic, social, and even survival considerations and goals. This often seems irrational to outsiders since it is frequently out-of-character behavior and at odds with typical social goals. However, it is not necessarily irrational as much as it is unpopular, atypical, and unproductive for common social goals. This is why society might consider such emotional sacrifices irrational when considering an "inappropriate" lover, but highly noble and rational when saving a child.

Intense emotions are also said to affect what is often called "procedural rationality," namely our ability for calm and complete analysis of all options. Again, much of this process is relative to contextual situations. For example, if we are deeply afraid and running away from a bear, it is not surprising that we do not go through a complete analysis of all the possible reactions before acting. This response has more to do with urgency than with the effect of our emotions; similar reactions might occur even in non-emotional situations that call for quick decisions, such as operating in the stock market, performing surgery, or engaging in sports.

Emotions and Objectivity

Similar to rationality, objectivity has been assumed to be directly opposed to emotions. Objectivity is often viewed as a practice or an ideal that prevents personal considerations and biases, with the goal of ensuring an unbiased judgment and outcome. In a more general and theoretical sense, it could be viewed as a search for a common view, either communally or universally (for example, evaluating whether a scientific or political article is "objective" or not). Practically speaking, objectivity could be seen as a cognitive or a social technique or norm devised to guarantee equal and non-discriminatory treatment in order to ensure an impartial judgment (judging impartially in court, sport or science). Similar principles are expected to be used in getting a comparatively clearer, more correct or more socially agreed-upon picture of "reality," which is associated with another connotation of rationality (does one have an "objective," realistic picture of reality?). However, this understanding of objectivity or rationality can reflect aspects of social and political conformity (is a political prisoner delusional or simply critical of the status quo?) that are unrelated to typical psychological or pathological dimensions of emotions.

Because emotions, as specific ways of relating, incorporate a "force" or motivation with a particular direction, they enhance certain biases in normative orientations and intentions that can make the practice of objectivity harder.

It is clear today that no person ever has a purely unbiased reading of reality, and rising emotional forces only intensify or alter an existing, personally or communally selective, biased picture. We have emotional biases in calm times as well as in intensely emotional times, but the biases differ. The effects of emotions on rationality and objectivity are qualitative and graduated in proportion to rising intensity and significance. They are better evaluated in terms of style and degree of reciprocal interaction, rather than as an "off/on switch" or in opposition to one another. When the impacts of emotions are extreme and prolonged, therapists may consider these effects "irrational" or even "erroneous," which is another way of saying that they are pathological or dysfunctional according to typical social norms.

A good analogy for this is the image of Einstein's curved space. Our conceptual universe is always biased or "curved" by our emotions. However, similar to entering a very strong field of gravity, intense emotions bend our space in such a manner that they tend to "toughen" the practice of socially acceptable objectivity or rationality. This perspective contradicts with widely accepted interpretations of reality that assume the possibility of a "flat" space with few or no emotions and thus no biases and preferences. Thus, people could be said to be always emotional and never totally objective. Nevertheless, they can be partially or comparatively more objective in certain contexts in which they are less emotionally involved and emotionally aroused.

All in all, this relational view suggests that rationality and objectivity do not contradict emotions, nor are they mutually exclusive. Rather, they have a mutual influence which is more pronounced or noticeable during intense emotional events. Rationality and objectivity do not operate *without* or despite emotions, but *within* a personal or collective universe shaped by them.

The Notion of the Self

The relational view of emotions can also provide a possible fresh look at our notion of "Self." Similar to Kahneman's theory in *Thinking, Fast and Slow* (2011), a relating theory of emotions suggests a distinction which avoids the confusion between our biological selves and our conceptual selves. Many of us think of the biological self as our "live body," which is served by most of our basic unconscious drives, values, and emotions. This is the self that we worry about and try to preserve when we are afraid of a shark while swimming. If we opt for the view that there is no discrete self (such as a Buddhist one), we might think of the biological self as the personal "nexus of relationships" where most of our interactions intersect. On the other hand, the conceptual self commonly denotes our conscious narrative and picture of who we think we are or would like to be. This is the self we are concerned with when we are worried about our self-image. It can nevertheless be as important as other closely related "selves" that indirectly affect us, such as those of our spouse or our children.

This new perspective might help to ease the ongoing tension among such views as the Freudian Ego, the Cognitive Behavioral Theory sense of self, and the Buddhist idea of no self.

An Additional Relational Ontology

The overall advantages of a relational view can possibly lead us to undertake an additional, much deeper and wider philosophical and psychological transition. The idea is to consider and utilize a supplementary or alternative view of reality called "relational ontology," along with our ontology of entities (see Hershock 2013). Traditionally, we view reality as primarily consisting of entities (atoms, objects, people, stars) which might or might not have relationships with other entities. An alternative view gives priority to the relationships which constitute and make these entities. Thus, entities could be seen as temporary, dynamic interactions, manifestations or nexuses of these relationships or processes. In other words, we can see entities as a combination or intersection of these specific formations in time and place (for example, a wave, a storm, or a person).

This perspective can help our understanding of emotions and emotional problems, our various notions of the "self," as well as many other psychological mysteries and phenomena.

A Number of Possible Applications

Clearly, some of the main contributions of this essay will derive from its relational perspective on emotions. A new understanding of their function, unique characteristics, contrast with other, non-emotional ways of relating, and their relocation vis-a-vis concepts such as values, cognition and rationality could be particularly helpful.

As a theoretical discussion of emotions, this essay cannot cover more practical and therapeutic applications extensively. However, the essay itself includes some examples that show the possible effects of the relational model on general emotional difficulties, therapy, research, and even public policy. Nevertheless, most of this insight will have to come in the future, from psychological and therapeutic experts, who will hopefully find applications for some of the perspectives offered here.

Most importantly, the relational approach emphasizes the sophistication and flexibility of our emotional system while demonstrating its complexity. This is particularly apparent when the emotional system is compared to other ways of relating, such as utilitarian or pre-emotional, instinctual modes of relating. Unfortunately, more intricate systems often have more problems and pathology, are harder to understand and fix, and are difficult to balance, as we see with our common emotional difficulties and our eternal search for happiness. In addition, at the same time that emotions have made morality, empathy and love possible, they have also enhanced hatred, aggression, envy, sorrow, and anxiety.

Non-emotional styles of relating might appear simpler and easier to handle and amend. However, they can also lead to growing detachment, alienation, and indifference. For instance, the relational view draws more attention to the growing tendency to replace emotional relationships with utilitarian ones. This seems to be an essential part of the convenience of treating people with indifference as *generic* consumers, workers, citizens, or tools in an exploding population with larger and larger governments and companies utilizing computerized services. ("The Prisoner" of the 1967 t-v series says "I am not a number, I am a free man.") A better balance of these relational styles presents a complex challenge and will obviously require much more research and discussion.

Seeing emotions as a special relational skill might nevertheless help open new possibilities for social change. For example, no longer do we have to perceive emotions as finite resources (unlike attention, money, and time), and the typical lovers' argument that "loving another person comes at my expense" is probably false, as a mother with many children can easily demonstrate. This is also true on the communal level, where an unfortunate, traditional insistence on hatred for outsiders and the different has often been an essential part of corporate culture, patriotism, and religious or ethnic loyalty. If love is a way of relating and not a finite resource, and if emotions are shown to be expressions of values, a proper change of values could result in more loving relationships instead of competitive, aggressive ones.

As noted earlier, the insight that we form emotional connections with communal concepts such as family, company, institution, and country (for example, patriotism) is often underestimated. We also relate emotionally to abstract concepts, including ideologies, moral principles, political ideas, and spiritual entities like God. At the same time, most of us now work and live in one or more such social structures, such as a company, institution, government body, and nation. These institutions could be viewed as formalized sets of relationships which are embedded with specific values, require particular behavior, and accordingly promote certain emotions. Those might be more obvious in a terrorist organization or a totalitarian nation, but they can be as dominant in democratic countries, governmental offices or aggressive, "all about profit" corporations. Since these communal values and emotions often overpower our personal ones—I have to do my job regardless of my personal preferences—they tend to dominate much of our global behavior and emotional composition.

Part of what is novel and unique about our emotions is the larger mental capacity they are associated with. This is a big portion of what differentiates the more decentralized, adaptable societies of "more-cognitive brained" organisms like human beings from less flexible, more centralized "less-cognitive brained" societies like those of social insects. Unfortunately, enormous, concentrated human populations combined with larger, centralized, homogeneous, and more overpowering institutions, will probably only lower this diversity, individuality, and adaptability.

These kinds of concerns support the immense importance of understanding emotions which, beyond affecting our personal lives, also affect our social and global relationships. As long as we are not veering toward a version of "public emotional engineering," as in George Orwell's *1984*, more research, thought, debate, and public awareness of these issues could help our society move in more desirable and helpful directions.

Rationale Going Forward

As an intricate work of conceptual architecture, this essay risks the possibility that some of its many explanations may be insufficient or even partially incorrect. However, the author's conviction is that at least some of the many ideas presented here could help improve our understanding of emotions, give us insights into key related concepts and their interactions with emotions, and thus help our personal and public emotional well-being. To say the least, the new outlook presented here does seem to have broad explanatory power and should have a similar positive effect on emotional analysis.

Some readers might claim, correctly, that the connection between our relationships and our emotions has been analyzed before. However, we must remember that despite the recognition that they mutually influence each other, emotions and relationships are still viewed as two separate elements or phenomena, and emotions are still commonly viewed as internal cognitive processes (for example, appraisals) or vague subjective experiences. Those who are familiar with appraisal theories will be aware of an initial recognition in that work of the basic relational perspective. Nevertheless, preoccupation with the cognitive aspect, and particularly with the appraisals process, tends toward primarily "cognitive" or "subjective experience" images of emotions.

Viewing emotions as a relational method might seem at first glance to represent only a subtle difference, but in fact this distinction is rather fundamental. It leads our perceptions, attention, research, and culture in a markedly different direction. Without underestimating the excellent research that is going into cognitive or other emotional components, the time has come to leap forward and look at emotions in a wider context. Namely, we must try to view them in the general context of our development, life, and interaction with the rest of our social, physical, and conceptual environment.

The new outlook shifts the categorization of emotions and our attention beyond cognitive issues to include more relational questions, concepts, and theories. It better explains the reasons for emotional development, function, and its unique role and qualities vis-a-vis other non-emotional ways of relating and organisms. It can change our view of cognition, rationality, objectivity, and even global emotional problems and aggression. As in the analogy of Einstein's theory, which calls for the acceptance of new principles, we must realize and accept that space is permanently "curved" by our emotions, and learn to navigate within it. In this sense, emotions could be said to add a third dimension or topography to an otherwise flat, two-dimensional, instrumental universe. More poetically, they could be seen as enhancing a silent movie with a sound track or volume.

The emphasis, and with it the torch light which illuminates our view, can shift to a more interactive, relational sphere instead of the sphere involving just "me, myself, and I." It confirms, strangely enough, that *we are personally affected by the way we perceive, treat, and relate to other people and objects.* Just as "we are what we eat," we can now say "we feel how we think," "we are how we relate," "we feel how we relate," "we are relational beings," or "we are a nexus of our relationships." Similar to some of the relational realizations in Chinese philosophy, this is a big change from "we are individual entities with cognitive, private, internal emotions, which influence external relationships." This is not a religious conviction or a moral teaching. It is rather a recognition of how important relational choices and practices are to us, and how we actually prepare for them, are affected by them, and sense them all. As such, we can perhaps better explain why people are often happier when they help others instead of shopping for themselves all day (frequently stated, randomly practiced).

As said above, like many innovative ideas, the notion of viewing emotions as "ways of relating" or as a "relational style or method" might strike some as odd and confusing; some may think it's a novel approach, while others might find it all together obvious. Amazingly enough, short of a few studies (mentioned below) which hint at this direction, this view is simply unheard of or at least rare.

If it is any consolation, we all need to realize that no matter how confusing and complex the following theories and discussions seem, they are still a far simplified model of our actual, extremely intricate world of emotions and relationships. Besides, when it comes to refreshing and improving our understanding of emotions, reading a good analysis is far easier and cheaper than taking courses at a reputable college or going into therapy.

A more comprehensive, detailed, and hopefully clearer discussion is presented in the chapters that follow.

Preliminary Consideration of Some Elusive Distinctions

This essay's attempt to present a different view of emotions requires the setup of some new basic distinctions and terminology, as well as the introduction of a few rather non-conventional analogies. New understandings often require new terminology or a change of meaning in existing terms like emotions, relationships, and cognition. The preference in this essay is to start by using common associative terms instead of advancing restrictive, delineating definitions, or making up new terms. As a group or family of related words, common understandings are more familiar and easier to keep track of. This review of their partial connotations and overlap is intended to give the reader a better "feel" for the *new* meaning suggested here and an improved indication for its *relocation* in our conceptual universe.

However, commonly used individual terms rarely capture the new, desired meaning in a complete and precise manner. So, it is important at the outset to clarify how this essay works with several central concepts—emotion, cognition, and relationships—and occasionally presents these ideas in a new light.

The Use of Definitions

It is now widely recognized that *delineating definitions* can vary dramatically according to the purpose of the definer and how they are applied theoretically and practically. Therefore, the preference here is to develop a *core definition* rather than a more typical, delineating definition. Namely, our efforts will follow the kind of characterization used for colors in a spectrum or rainbow. In this type of definition, red is identified in the center (core) of its area by what is *most* red, while it gradually changes to other colors on both sides. In exploring some topics, this is a helpful alternative to restrictive definitions with clear borders and sharp delineations[1].

---

1 See a similar idea of a "prototypical" category in Ben-Zeev [2000].

We have started with many overlapping explanations to give readers some basic conceptual tools and an initial orientation to help navigate the complex discussions that follow. However, whenever possible, we will avoid specific definitions all together, and practice more associative discussions in which the topics are described, compared to related terms, and elaborated through examples, analogies, and views. This type of approach will support more flexible practices with longer lasting consequences. Relocating traditional phenomena in a new conceptual context may enable people to see these phenomena differently, as something else, and thus better relate them to other concepts.

This kind of discussion is intended to open the conversation instead of narrowing, restricting, and closing it, as delineating definitions often do. The closest we will get to a traditional definition will be the general working description of emotions offered in the concluding discussion of this essay, or in the beginning summary. Unlike a mystery novel, reading the end of this essay with its concluding notes first, or reorienting oneself by returning to the summary, are not violations of any normative rules. Therefore, if it helps, readers can turn to the definition at the end right away, and come back to it or to the summary again after tormenting themselves through the rest of the essay.

Emotion as a Diversified Category

It is important to note that, as is the case with many other commonly used categories, the various elements which people tend to label "emotions" don't constitute a solid, consistent group. On the contrary, many scholars of emotions agree that this category actually seems to represent quite a diversified collection of phenomena (see Russell 1991, Solomon 2016, and more). Beyond their obvious relational differences (consider love, hate, and anger), we may find even more categorical differences among certain subgroups of emotions which, although they might share some common dimensions, differ in other ways.

Instead of looking for elements which are common to *all* the members of this group, emotions, we will try to concentrate on unique characteristics which act as key differences or distinguish the majority of this category's members from other categories. Therefore, not all of what people designate as "emotional" will be included or fit perfectly.

Thus, the special characteristics described here might fit only some emotions or will fit some better than others. For example, intense emotions differ from calm ones, short-term from long-term, and focused emotions such as love or hatred are different from their diffused counterparts, such as happiness and depression. In addition to internal diversity among emotions, there are many related "cousins" to emotions, such as moods and global dispositions which display some but not all of the characteristics of emotion. Because of the vast extent and complexity of this subject, this essay will primarily deal with specific emotions that are directed at particular elements—people, situations, institutions or concepts—which is to say that they are *about* something, that they have intentionality. It will only briefly touch upon related phenomena such as moods, generic feelings, and emotional evaluations of people and periods of time.

Use of the Term "Cognition"

Traditionally, cognition has referred to "our ability to learn and know" (Latin *cognito*: to get to know, learn) (Oxford Dictionary 2016). In the Western tradition, the term can be traced to Greek philosophy but comes into more common use in the thirteenth century with Aquinas's contrast between the cognitive (how we know the world) and the affective (how we understand the world via feelings and emotions) (Aquinas 2002).

However, throughout the ages and particularly recently, with the vast development of cognitive psychology, philosophy of mind, and cognitive science (see Lakoff and Johnson 1999 and numerous other writings), this concept has been reinterpreted and used broadly with a wide variety of meanings, many of which are quite different from its more limited origin.

A good example of this broad approach appears in the description we find currently in *Wikipedia* regarding cognition: "It encompasses processes such as knowledge, attention, memory and working memory, judgment, and evaluation, reasoning and 'computation,' problem solving and decision making, comprehension and production of language, etc. Human cognition is conscious and unconscious, concrete or abstract as well as intuitive and conceptual. Cognitive processes use existing knowledge and generate new knowledge" (Wikipedia 2016).

While it is obvious that this essay is not the place to fully discuss such a loaded term or attempt to reconfigure its meaning, we will veer away from such a broad definition of cognition. Considering our focus on emotions, our exploration of this term will be limited to a summary examination of the connection between emotions and cognition, and possibly a reformulation of these relations in order to rejuvenate our understanding of emotions. This connection is discussed throughout the essay and particularly in a later section dedicated to this relationship.

The intention at this stage is not to refine our understanding of cognition or cognitive distinctions, but to sharpen our view of emotions and reevaluate their relations with other key terms and concepts. Therefore, we would rather start with a more common, generic, definition of this term, such as the one presented in the Oxford Dictionary: "The mental action or process of acquiring knowledge and understanding through thought, experience, and the senses" (2016).

What is important for our discussion of emotions is to have a notion of cognition that is limited to a certain portion of our overall mental activities, and which primarily includes the common cognitive processes or constructs that are typically either contrasted with emotions, or attributed to them. For instance, thought, appraisals, evaluations, judgments, rationality, objectivity, orientations, concepts, conceptions, knowledge, and pure information. If we need to use a broader term to describe such activities and processes we will use terms such as "brain processes" or "mental activities."

Use of the Term "Relationship" and the Exclusion of Behavior from Notions of Relating and Emotions

The term "relationship" will initially be used in a wide, inclusive manner. Relationships will comprise all the components that take place between two parties: how they interact, think, behave, treat each other, and act toward each other; their mutual attitudes and orientations; the exchange of resources and services; interdependency; and so forth. While the idea of "relationship" will be framed broadly, the concept of "relating," and in this sense the notion of emotions as well, will be applied more narrowly. They will include one's position, orientation, approach, attitude, feelings, stance, and standpoint toward another person, situation, or idea. Relating, and thus emotions, will not extend to behavior or actions, but they will incorporate motivations, and the dynamics and reconfiguration of our body/mind when behaving or acting in a certain manner (for example, the way our body/mind changes in a fit of anger, or the way a nation prepares and gets reorganized in times of military tension). It is clear that our emotions and the way we relate to elements lead to, or are associated with, certain actions and behavior. It is often also a very blurry line as the "behavior" of tears and laughing can demonstrate. Nevertheless, since emotions were mostly seen traditionally as internal cognitive phenomena and didn't include behavior and actions (just led to them), it seemed simpler and more useful to initially somewhat arbitrarily separate the behavior and actions from the way we relate or from our notion of emotions.

We will refer to the more physical and active parts of our relationships as "physical interactions," actions or behavior. These interactions can be short-lived or ongoing (for example, with a stranger on the plane or with one's spouse), solely utilitarian (with a cashier in a store), highly emotional (for example, with our children), one-sided, mutual or a combination of all the above. Thus, if we say that we have an emotional relationship with another person, or that an interaction was very emotional, what we mean here is that these are based on, motivated by, include, or express an emotional way of relating.

This understanding of relationships is of course different from "relations," which typically refer to the more logical, categorical connection or association between elements imposed by an outside view or order, such as the relations between numbers or between roles in a given organization, or between company presidents and their executives. One type of relationship does not exclude the other, and often there will be an overlapping of both. However, we will concentrate most of our discussion on ways of relating and relationships, unless otherwise specified.

We must emphasize again that the term "relationship" has been used in many different ways, and it is a very loaded term. On top of it, because the relating theory offered here is rather new, we lack the appropriate refined "relational" vocabulary. Last but not least, we must always remind ourselves of the obvious but often forgotten "truth" that our distinctions are artificial and often inconsistent impositions on phenomena that are actually continuous processes, and that these distinctions are made primarily for heuristic reasons. For these and other reasons, it is difficult to avoid using the term "relationship" when talking about emotional connections; likewise, it is difficult to use relational terms in a perfectly consistent way. However, the terminology will become clearer as we discuss the idea of emotions more fully. The exact choice of terminology is not so important, as long as we keep in mind the general direction of the underlying metaphor or model.

Part A: A New View of Emotions and their Characteristics

1

Various Theoretical Approaches to Emotions

A survey of contemporary approaches to the subject of emotion in the *Atlantic* argues that there are as many theories of emotions as there are writers or thinkers in the field (Beck 2015). This might be the only claim that scholars fully agree upon. This means that the study of emotion is still a very controversial field with no basic consensus on the function of emotions, what they are, or how they should be seen. This lack of clarity might be partially due to their complexity and multifaceted nature, their confusing and loaded position in Western philosophy, our limited knowledge of the brain, or the surprisingly small number of scholars and studies which concentrate on this category as a whole (and not just in relation to therapy).

Philosophers have typically shied away from the problem of emotion, which was traditionally at odds with reason and thus excluded from mainstream philosophical studies (some exceptions are mentioned later). Today, most philosophers stay out of emotional studies since they are considered to be part of the domain of psychology. Psychologists, as we said, typically concentrate on therapeutic problems and focus less on the philosophy or the general nature of emotions. (This was even true of Freud and most other proceeding key psychologists).

Though the scholars who have treated emotions as a general category are few in number, their approaches and theories are highly diversified. Solomon (2003) organizes the wide variety of emotional theories by dividing them into roughly five groups: the sensational, physiological, behavioral, evaluative, and cognitive. Appraisal theories, which currently dominate much of the field, could be included either in the general cognitive group or the evaluative one (see the next section and the bibliography).

Beyond these main groups, three views are growing in popularity. The first, which often overlaps with appraisal approaches and is described as Social Construction, is held mostly by social psychologists and anthropologists. These theorists argue against the traditional view of emotions as personal, individual expressions, and claim that they are more the product of our cultural, social environment (see Lutz 1986 and Lazarus 1991a). Just as Wittgenstein (1953) argues for the impossibility of a private language, these theories view emotions as more public, cultural phenomena.

Another, radically different, view of emotions comes from some of the Eastern philosophical traditions in which there are no "individual selves" to experience emotions independently. Somewhat closer to this essay's view, a few Eastern philosophical thinkers now locate emotions in relationships, which are seen as more ontologically basic than physical entities or "individuals" (Hershock 1996, 1999a, 1999b, 2004, 2006, 2013). (See a short discussion of this view in our later section on emotions and relationships).

Growing neurological and genetic research has led to a corresponding rise in "biological" and "genetic" theories of emotion. However, with the exception of a few dedicated neurological scholars of emotions (listed below), many of the "genetic/biological" studies seem unfortunately to reduce emotions to neuro-chemical processes and chemicals (or they are misunderstood as doing that). Thus, they often give the general public a somewhat deterministic, mechanical, reductionist perception of our emotional universe (see Harari's [2015] comparison of emotions to algorithms). The misconception is that emotions are basically a number of chemicals or neuro-chemical processes, which is like saying that a person is just a bunch of cells and water, or a computer is only a bunch of wires, silicon, electricity, and metal. These descriptions miss the evolutionary ingenuity and uniqueness in the design of these elements and their ongoing interactions with the environment. On top of it, just because we now partially understand how neurons and chemicals function when we have cognitive or emotional experiences, it does not mean that they are the *cause* of emotions. At best, they only partially show how these types of processes occur biologically. Unless we use psychoactive substances or suffer from a pathological biological problem, chemicals usually do not initiate emotions or thoughts. They may produce them or be included in them, but they do not trigger or instigate them on their own. In most cases, a social, perceptual or cognitive chain of events initiates a thought or an emotion that is performed or executed by the activity of neurons and chemicals. Chemicals are part of the process, or the result, but less commonly the reason. Regardless of the definitional origin of emotions, for most people as well as for most experts of emotions (including biologists), it is probably as useful and interesting to figure out what survival, social, and cognitive constellations initiate emotions, besides the particular chemicals or neurons which participate in the process.

Overall, biological-deterministic views often give people the impression that they can't do much about their emotions and thus are released of emotional responsibility and accountability for actions and behavior (which is what Aristotle [1987] and many later scholars like Sartre [1957], and Solomon [1992, 2003, and 2016] fought so hard to counteract).

As hinted above, many of the leading theories today (for example, appraisal) fall into the evaluative and cognitive groups. These stress the strong connection between cognition and emotions, or even identify emotions as a form of cognition.

Despite the immense progress of the last few decades, our knowledge of the brain's internal working and the way mental processes interact with or constitute emotions is still limited. It is therefore difficult now to reach a conclusive biological or psychological judgment on this issue. It seems that any such argument is at best an educated guess or a well-made hypothesis. Thus, from a philosophical point of view, as suggested in the introductory notes, identifying or characterizing emotions in any specific way can perhaps best be undertaken for the heuristic value of the theoretical, normative, and practical benefits it might generate.

Since the flourishing of Greek philosophy, and particularly with the development of the Stoics' orientation, Western culture has tended to characterize emotions by negation, separating them and setting them in opposition to logical thought processes. Various philosophers have acknowledged the importance of emotions (Aristotle 1987, Epicurus 2005, Hume 1977, William James 1950, Brentano (in Solomon 2003), Heidegger 1962 and a few others cited in the bibliography). However, the most common social or philosophical stance has been to establish the dominance of rationality over emotions, or to exclude emotions all together. This is still apparent today, for instance in the practices of science, business and economics, much of philosophy, and the legal system, where rationality and objectivity have remained the leading values (see Sabini and Silver 1996).

Many of the leading psychological schools still emphasize rational, perceptual processes. They hold that although human psychology is compromised periodically by cognitive imperfections (Alford and Beck 1997, Kahneman 1979, Tversky 1992, Epstein 1999) or emotional interference, the key is to understand and perfect cognition and rationality for better emotional guidance and overall life performance (where Rational Choice Theory and Utility Theory dominate). Thus, although psychology considers many emotional problems, the solutions it provides are mostly rational (see Ellis's 1994 REBT and most of Alford and Beck's 1997 CBT methods). In the same manner, though emotions have been one of the main subjects of study for psychology, psychologists are nevertheless supposed to put their emotions aside and arm themselves with rational objectivity. At best, they are allowed to retain certain "helpful" emotions such as empathy to better connect and relate to the client, not unlike a religious guide or a helpful parent. The traditional duality between emotion and rationality and the dominance of rationality has been retained here, as in most other modern Western thought. On top of it, surprisingly enough, most psychologists rarely discuss the general category of emotions as a whole, and almost never study, compare, and position this unique category in relation to non-emotional psychological processes or other human and social phenomena.

Emotions have been very central in art and literature, where rationality and objectivity take a back seat. They have also been appreciated in Western and Eastern religions and religious philosophies (such as Christianity, Islam, Judaism, Buddhism and Hinduism) when unquestioned belief was necessary, when rational thought seemed insufficient for revelation or enlightenment, and when social, ethical systems had to be developed (Marks and Ames 1995). However, these systems of thought have often taken emotions as an unexplored means to an end, or selectively focused on particular ones according to their contribution to their moral objectives (for example, love in Christianity, compassion in Buddhism, God's anger in Judaism).

Many of the recent psychological studies that make an effort to reemphasize the importance of emotions and attempt to better incorporate them seem to belong to some version of the cognitive view, and particularly to Appraisal theories. One of the main achievements of these kinds of theories is to accentuate the view that emotions are not necessarily just primitive, instinctual, irrational or "bad desires" with a few rare, positive exceptions (such as love and compassion), as they have commonly been portrayed in the past. Accordingly, they cannot be reduced to bare physical sensations (as the Jamesian view seemingly claims, which will be discussed later). Instead, these approaches tend to equate emotions or incorporate them into other mental processes, or show them to be a result of cognition. The choice of which mental element subsumes emotion varies among these theories (for example, emotions were depicted as judgments, appraisals, evaluations, beliefs, algorithms, motives), but most of them are cognitive and most of them retain the traditional bias toward rationality. The differences among them are more typical of the kind we might find within a school of thought, rather than between schools.

The cognitive focus is not surprising considering that its originating scholars have roots in behaviorism. It also makes sense considering the importance of various mental components and processes in the formation and modification of emotions. These are particularly interesting and helpful to psychologists in their quest for better understanding and treatment of emotional processes and pathologies (that is, for therapy).

By incorporating emotions into cognition and/or identifying the cognitive element or process in emotions, these theories seem to eliminate some of the traditional negative stigma of emotions as opposing cognition and/or rationality; they also better explain the wide variety of emotions and their refined articulation (within and between cultures); help therapy by working on emotions through cognitive modifications; and express their importance to human ethics. Though very helpful, these theories still do not explain sufficiently the overall phenomenon of emotions and their unique role or function.

Most contemporary theories of emotions tend to describe them as a sum of components (cognitive, physiological, motivational, social, and so forth). It is not clear whether many of these theories view emotions as a combination of components, and thus tend to miss their overall function, or whether the theories are not clear about the general role of emotions, and thus are left with a component-oriented description. Whatever the reason, the end result is an improved analysis of the *parts and processes,* but one that does not offer adequate clarity about the *sum* or the *whole.*

As we are going to argue repeatedly in this essay, cognition may well be critical in emotional formation, but it has a similar role in most human phenomena. Thus, concentrating on the role of cognition or cognitive processes, such as appraisal, doesn't tell us enough about the specific human phenomenon of emotion and its unique purpose. It often even diverts our attention from what is special about emotion and gives the erroneous impression that it is somewhat a cognitive phenomenon, like appraisals, judgments, or thought. This distortion is evident in most theories that concentrate on any one of the emotional components. Accordingly, these approaches tend to confuse the general public (including psychologists) by underestimating their other mental, non-cognitive aspects, and non-mental dimensions. However, most importantly, they fail to identify the critical and unique relational function of emotions and their underlining relationships with other key concepts such as cognition, rationality, self, and relationships.

Although there have been a number of attempts to offer alternatives to these cognitive approaches, such as Prinz's (2004) more somatic approach, even these works don't clarify what emotions are all about or what their primary and unique purpose is.

Such terms as "experience," "subjectivity," and "evolutionary purpose" that are common in definitions of emotions are so general that they don't tell us much about emotions. They fail to explain how emotions are different from all our other endless "subjective experiences" or from other functions with an "evolutionary purpose" that are common to most organisms (for example, hunger, exhaustion).

Without underestimating the contributions of these theories, it often seems as if they are trying to push a foster child into an unwelcoming family. Perhaps this theoretical problem is not very different from past examples of difficult scientific transitions, such as astronomy prior to the Copernican revolution. Astronomers then made countless attempts to fit the infinite inconsistencies in the "sun's revolution around Earth" into the prevailing theories of the period.

Since most traditional philosophies (and Western ones in particular) have primarily been built around the concept of rationality and logical mental development, emotions have been mostly confined to personal relationships, mental health, art, religious faith, and hysterical women. It is therefore clear that, other than in the therapeutic treatment of personal emotional difficulties and the arts, the majority of our social and formal scientific values, categories, terminology, public systems, and methods have been formulated to either set aside emotions, as an irrational, personal phenomenon, or to somehow associate them with cognition. A small number of thinkers are trying to reverse this tradition and reposition emotions conceptually and socially, but it remains an uphill battle that requires an innovative reconfiguration of many key concepts—one of the tasks which this essay hopes to contribute to.

Contemporary Attempts to Integrate Emotions as a Whole Category

Despite the continuing tension between emotions and rationality mentioned above, the increased importance of psychology, and particularly the rising interest in and analysis of cognitive processes in the second part of the twentieth century, have helped to incorporate emotions into mainstream scientific and public thought. Countless psychological studies have added to the understanding of the general phenomenon of emotions, even though part of this work came through indirect analysis that considers various emotional processes, emotional development, and pathologies.

Appraisal theories, which contributed to the views presented in this essay, offer a promising aspect of emotions as a materialization that takes place in the relationship between a person and his or her environment.[2] These approaches have been consolidated by Arnold (1960), further developed by Lazarus (1991a), and continued by Scherer (2009a, 2013), Smith (1999, 2009), Ellsworth (2009, 2013), Frijda (1986, 2007), Roseman (1984, 2013), Johnson-Laird and Oatley (1989), and others (see a recent survey, *Appraisal Theories of Emotion: State of the Art and Future Development* by Moors, Ellsworth, Scherer and Frijda 2013). These theorists are aware of emotions' multiple components and processes, but the bulk of their attention, as said above, is aimed at cognitive processes, and particularly appraisals (hence the name). Since the unfortunate passing of some of its leading scientists (Arnold and Lazarus died in 2002, Solomon in 2007, and Frijda in 2015), the field seems to continue its focus on appraisals with very little attempt to tackle the broader conceptual question of emotion.

---

2 Recently, the term "environment" has primarily come to signify our physical world (for example, our oceans, land, air, flora and fauna). However, when discussing the relationships people have with their environment, we will refer here to everything that surrounds a person including their social, physical, spiritual, intellectual, and symbolic world.

Another related theoretical angle that is helpful comes from studies such as that of Parkinson, Fischer, and Manstead (2005), which look at emotions as an aspect of social relations. They also view emotions as primarily relational and analyze their function and workings in social situations and interactions.

In philosophy, one of the Western traditions that has given emotions comparatively more attention and importance in the twentieth century is Existentialism, with philosophers such as Kierkegaard, Nietzsche, Heidegger, Sartre, and Merleau-Ponty. Heidegger in particular (1962, 1972) has given emotions a more central role in his original philosophical theory, in his system of moods/emotions, and the centrality of "care." Perhaps this is also why Heidegger, in his later years, went on to look for "better" answers in poetry and drama, where emotions are more central and accepted. Sartre viewed emotions as strategies, a perspective that is in some ways closer to the relational outlook presented here[3].

More recent attempts at carving a new position for emotions are implied in Amelie Rorty (1980), Sousa (1987, 1913), Solomon (1992), and a few others. Those are rather unique attempts to break away from the traditional dichotomy between emotions and rationality. Solomon, for instance, starts with the idea that emotions are a combination of judgments, sensation, and behavioral patterns, though they cannot be reduced to any one of these components. However, he goes on to propose a fresh outlook: ". . . Emotions *situate* us in the world, and so provide not so much the motive for rationality—much less its opposition—but rather its very framework" (Solomon 1992, 610). Different versions of this idea also appear in Sousa 1987, 2013, and Turski 1994a, which refers to even earlier moves in this direction by Merleau-Ponty 1968.

---

3 For details and wider surveys, see the bibliography, particularly R.C. Solomon's [2003] excellent book *What is an Emotion?* and de Sousa [2013] on Emotion in the Stanford Encyclopedia of Philosophy.

However, most contemporary scholars and philosophers do not venture far beyond these previous ideas, and do not offer a clear-enough theory, role or advantage for emotions. In his later papers, Solomon even seems to retreat back to safe ground, where he suggests that emotions are merely a subspecies of judgments and are not much different from any other thought process. Thus the conversation tends to regress back to the cognitive view, to a renewed attempt to "eliminate" emotions, as was argued by Sabini and Silver (1996), reintroduction of somatic theories (Prinz 2004), or shifts to reductionist biological approaches (Harari 2015).

Except for a number of neurological experts who focus specifically on emotions (such as Damasio 1999, 2010, Panksepp 2004, LeDoux 1996, Solms and Turnbull 2002, Barrett and Russell 2015, and a few others), the recent and growing genetic, chemical, and neurological descriptions of emotions mostly explain the biological processes and neuro-chemical compounds associated with emotions. However, they typically do not give us much insight into the social and conceptual workings of emotions, their unique functions in our body/mind, our society or their place in evolution.

This overall puzzlement is also clearly reflected and somewhat perpetuated by most contemporary definitions in our dictionaries and text books (see for example Kazdin 2000, *The Encyclopedia of Psychology*). Again, they define emotions by negation, as a collection of components or experiences, or through some partial cognitive construct. Thus, when trying to grasp an overall idea of the phenomenon (beyond the technical details), most of us are left with either the traditional impression of emotions as "mysterious experiences," or the generic vague "subjective experience" mentioned previously. These could characterize almost any human phenomena, and thus remind us of Hegel's argument about the "night in which all cows are black."

The approach offered here may require more effort and patience on the part of readers at the outset. Nevertheless, the hope is that, after the initial shock and requisite digestive period, this strategy may provide a more concrete view and a clearer, more specific theory as to the underlying function of emotions, what is so special about their role and operation, and how they all fit into the larger conceptual picture.

2

Emotions as a Relational Phenomenon: An Alternative View

Historical Precedents for the Relational Dimension of Emotions

It is easy to notice in our daily interactions that most of our emotions have to do with the way we relate to other people, objects, situations, and ideas, or with our relationships to the elements around us. For example, we often say that we love somebody, hate something, are angry at her, or are afraid of it. These are all relational propositions.

This critical idea that emotions are relational phenomena is based on the observation that most emotions are "about" something, a realization suggested rather early in the game and now widely accepted in the professional literature. Two millennia ago, Aristotle proposed that "...the anger of the angry person is necessarily always directed towards someone in particular..." (as quoted in Solomon 2003, 6). Hume wrote in the eighteenth century that emotions are always felt *about* or *toward* objects, and Brentano in the nineteenth century stated that "mental phenomena...are uniquely characterized by the fact that they have an object, upon which ...they are directed. Whoever thinks, thinks about something, whoever is angry is angry about something, and so on" (as quoted in Solomon 2003, 161). This he called "intentionality." Dewey continued along the same lines, saying that "emotions are experiences of the world—they are directed towards things in the environment that possess such emotional qualities" (as quoted in Solomon 2003, 88). Most contemporary studies tend to agree that emotions have intentional objects, they are about something, or directed towards something (Manstead, Frijda, and Fischer 2004). "Emotions, as intentional, are typically, if not necessarily, reactions to something that happens to us" (Solomon 2003, 225).

Surprisingly enough, though this dimension of emotions is well-established among the narrow group of experts who study emotions as a general phenomenon, it is not well-known among many psychologists, psychiatrists or the general public. Perhaps some of the resistance to a relational view has to do with the traditional understanding of emotions as personal subjective experiences, a view that fits Western philosophy's emphasis on individualism and personal autonomy. It also goes along with the idea that emotions are sensed within and can be altered conceptually, so they seem strictly private, internal, and cognitive. What we may not have appreciated enough, or at least studied sufficiently, is the critical importance of external relationships to our emotional constitution. We might recognize the importance of our relationships, but what we may not have realized, or paid enough attention to, is the idea that we have a multifaceted but somewhat consistent way of relating to our environment, and that we can actually sense and experience the way we relate.

A few key writers and researchers of emotions have picked up on similar clues and have recognized the close connection between emotions and relationships. For example, Arnold writes that "to arouse an emotion, the object must be appraised as affecting me in some way . . . . [This] means that I know it not only objectively, as it is apart from me, but also that I estimate its relations to me. . . (Arnold 1960, 171). Lazarus states that ". . . each emotion arises from a different plot or story about relationships between a person and the environment. . . " (Lazarus 1991, 125). Frijda notes that "...they [emotions] motivate behavior meant to maintain or modify a particular kind of relationship with the environment. They aim to change (or modify) the relationship, not the environment itself" (Frijda in Solomon 2003, 134). "Once de-essentialized, emotions can be viewed as a cultural and interpersonal process of naming, justifying, and persuading by people in relationship to each other" (Lutz in Solomon 2003, 144). "In a relationship, one mind revises another; one heart changes its partner" (Lewis, Amini, and Lannon 2000, 144). "Emotions have come to be regarded as the major social glue, with extensive empirical research supporting that view. . . . Emotional exchanges belong to the social fabric and regulate interpersonal relationships" (Manstead, Frijda, Manstead, Fischer 2004, 263). Smith and Kirby (2009) even call for a relational model of appraisal and emotion similar to previous attempts of Lazarus. Parkinson, Fischer, and Manstead (2005) emphasize that emotions are primarily not a personal experience but a social relational one. Even though Prinz emphasizes a more somatic approach, he nevertheless claims "...it is important to show that emotions are not merely perceptions of the body but also perceptions of our relations to the world" (Prinz 2004, 20).

Among all the various theories of emotions, appraisal and social theories currently present the most serious recognition of this relational dimension. Namely, they describe people's relationships with their environment as necessary for the rise of their emotions. However, this condition is still considered only an "aspect" or a "component" of emotions, together with cognitive appraisal, motivational elements (or goals), physiological changes, behavioral expressions, and action tendencies. In most cases, cognitive appraisal remains the main component and the focal point for these theories.

Although this essay will continue to emphasize that concentration on cognition and appraisals is very helpful to the study of emotional formation and therapy, this emphasis unfortunately misses or even obscures their main relational function or purpose. Cognition might help formulate emotions, but it is nevertheless not their function. Cognition is similar to other general concepts used to explain emotions, such as "human function," "subjective experience," "passions," or "feelings." These utterly generic descriptions are part of the reason emotions are still unclear to most people as well as to most psychologists and philosophers.

This lack of clarity makes it crucial for us to take the extra step or leap, and recognize the actual function or the unique responsibility of our emotions. We must realize that even if emotions are not solely defined by a relational aspect, this is nonetheless their primary role, purpose or job; that this is probably why they developed, what we use them for, and how we use them.

Even though we have found a few theorists who acknowledge this feature of emotions, the overall relational function of emotions is rarely mentioned, and when it is, it is viewed as a secondary by-product or aspect of emotions. Clearly, in most assessments, the relational dimension does not seem to be central to the way of looking at emotions, nor does it seem critical in explaining their overall place and function. Even Lazarus and the more contemporary appraisal scholars who recognize that emotions influence relationships still view them as a separate, more cognitive or mental phenomenon, experience or reaction. The same goes for Solomon, who does not sufficiently emphasize the relational importance of emotions and ends up pushing them more toward the realm of cognitive judgments. This is true for most psychologists as well. They recognize the importance of relationships in our emotional lives, and emphasize the importance of emotions to our relationships; nevertheless, they are still taught to view emotions as primarily personal cognitive constructs which can affect, or be affected, by relationships while yet being basically a separate phenomenon.

Since it is obvious from daily life that emotions play a central role in the way we relate to others (or to other things and situations), and because it is widely accepted in the literature that emotions are "about" something, perhaps there is more to the relational dimension of emotions and their role in our relationships. If an experience is mostly "about" things, does it not have something to do with the way we *relate* to things? If we typically hate somebody, or love someone, or are angry at a person, does it not mean that emotions constitute a unique role in the way we relate to our environment?

Emotions as a Relational Phenomenon

This essay proposes to take a step further and argue that to have an emotion about or toward something is actually to form a particular *way of relating* to this element, or to initiate a specific *type of relationship* with it. It is not just that emotions influence the way we relate, it is that our emotions *are*, or *can be seen as*, the way we relate to these elements, and that they are personally configured for these relationships.

As will be evident throughout this essay, this seemingly minor rephrasing is not just a semantic insistence on definitional precision. It aims at a fundamental conceptual change in our views of emotions and many other key, related concepts.

There are many ways to describe the meaning of this conceptual change, and none are perfect, because these kinds of relational categories are not common in our psychological or philosophical lexicon. To arrive at a good initial feeling for this view, it is best to leave exact terminology aside for now, and start with a presentation of some diverse, overlapping, and therefore occasionally repetitive terms and descriptions. Later it will be possible develop a more precise and complete picture of the phenomenon.

From the perspective this essay recommends, emotions are better seen as a particular relational configuration in which we orient and organize ourselves vis-a-vis other people, situations, ideas, institutions, and other elements of our world. This specific configuration of our whole body/mind system prepares, motivates, channels, and directs our energy in a very precise manner toward a selected element (ourselves included). As such, they don't only shape the flow of our thoughts, orientations, attention, motivations, and actions but also their nature, direction, content, and priorities.

In this sense, emotions can be said to be a unique relational method, technique, style, skill, or even a strategy (as Sartre described them).

They can also be viewed as a special form of relationship or interaction, or as a part or dimension of a relationship. As we will discuss later, emotions are probably not the only way we relate or the only type of relationships we have. They also do not include all that we typically mean by the term relationship. However, they are definitely one special style of relating that can result in a very distinct type of relationship.

So, we can think of emotions as types of orientation, attitudes, approaches, strategies, stands, and positions we take vis-à-vis other elements, as well as the way we organize or configure ourselves to deal with them. Accordingly, they can be viewed as a relational phenomenon, a relational policy, or a "mode of being" which combines a particular orientation to a specific element with special motivation and dynamics that support it.

The Functional, Developmental Point of View
From a developmental point of view, the emotional "function" could be said to enhance our relational skills. Emotions provide us with

a powerful, highly refined, specifically customized, sophisticated, forceful, and dynamic relational capability. Scherer (2009) states that they allow each individual to react flexibly and dynamically to environmental contingencies. All organisms relate to their environment. However, more complex, communal, and cognitive organisms needed, developed, and learned to perform more complex, specific, flexible ways of relating and committing. These were necessary for social organisms, and particularly for humans with a long and intricate care for offspring, complex and dynamic social systems, and highly diversified geographical environments. It was important for the emotional person (for example, the parent) as well as for the object of its emotion (the child) to enhance its sense of connection, commitment, security, affection, education, and so forth. These qualities were all probably necessary to improve our human connectivity, interactions, development, and thus adaptability.

Organisms with less cognitive development seem to relate to most elements generically, categorically, functionally, instinctively, and typically don't commit to individuals for prolonged periods of time. Even in the instances when they do form long-term attachments, they seem to be more instinctual and thus more functional and less flexible (for better or for worse). The emotional capacity enables emotional organisms to relate and connect to individuals and specific elements beyond merely relating to general categories with simple, reflexive instructions. Human beings, in particular, can also modify these ways of relating as needed, foresee and project long-term interdependencies and relationships, commit, bond, empathize, and "care" for prolonged periods, "disconnect," detach, interchange various ways of relating with the same element, change intensity, and much more. Accordingly, people can relate and commit in a unique manner to each of thousands of different elements, retain these relational patterns for long periods of time, or change these "orientations" quickly as needed. These particular ways of relating to these many specific elements are what we commonly call emotions.

A Foreign Policy Metaphor

A novel analogy with familiar concepts of the domestic and foreign policy of nations may help clarify this view of emotions as specialized modes of relationship. Countries and other organizations (for example, the U.S., UN, or multinational companies) constantly devise and set policies vis-à-vis other nations or communities, such as ethnic groups, terrorist organizations, their shareholders, employees, citizens or clientele. These policies can be said to be some formalized instructions, strategies, and practices regarding the manner in which we should and actually do relate, perceive, interact and organize ourselves vis-a-vis other elements. In addition to forming positions toward these constituencies, nations and organizations clearly also organize themselves accordingly. For example, if a country relates to another as an enemy, it prepares for a confrontation and adjusts its internal organization, resources, and relationships to deal with it.

Governments and managers don't only form orientations and reorganize in relation to other countries and organizations, but also toward objects (such as oil or money), issues (global warming), geographical locations (outer space), and concepts (profitability, democracy, capitalism, communism, human rights, environmental preservation).

Our emotions can be seen as analogous to these foreign policies, positions or orientations, and the accompanying reorganizations that come with them (for example, preparing for a war). From this perspective, emotions are a part of our position and stand in relation to people, objects or concepts, the way we relate to them, the relationships that evolve, and the kinds of preparations we undertake. In other words, emotions are an important part of our "domestic and foreign policy" vis-a-vis all that surrounds us, a critical part of the way we interface with the environment.

Continuing the same metaphor, an intense emotional event can be seen as a state of emergency in which alert levels go up as the organization sets up a new policy that relates to an urgent issue and prepares for it, such as a war, a business takeover or a bankruptcy. However, emotional processes are subconscious to a large degree, and we are often either not aware of significant parts of them or not clear what we are aware of (awareness doesn't guarantee clarity). This could be analogous to many of our government's secret military preparations and all other "less than transparent" operations. We are also typically very busy with all the commotion of preparing for and responding to these new, intense interactions. Thus, they frequently seem like puzzling domestic transformations, which is another reason why we have considered emotions to be primarily "internal," somewhat spontaneous, and purely cognitive for so long. However, the main motivation or orientation is still preparing for and dealing with all the specific situations or elements that matter to us.

Like all analogies, while the ones above help to illustrate the view of emotions presented here, they have their limits in terms of similarity. At this point, it is enough to apply these metaphors to entertain the association between emotions and ways of relating, relational methods with a particular configuration, or to see them as a type or part of relationships. The next few chapters will make this view clearer and more apparent.

Unique Characteristics of Emotional Ways of Relating

Part of what is unique about emotions is the special way we relate to elements with which we perceive a connection, a link or certain *interdependence* (for a minute or a lifetime). Because we perceive that an element has, does or will influence our lives (physically or mentally), it becomes *specific* and significant. Accordingly, we care about the future of this element and about our relationship with it. We may hope for the best or the worst for this element, depending on our orientation toward it. In other words, we are invested in its destiny. This investment tends to *motivate us in a specific direction*—either to get closer or to run away. When this investment is intense, it is accompanied by particular physical changes and *sensations* which we often describe as "feelings."

We can sense, feel, and experience the way we relate, the manner in which our body/mind "sets up" for this, the particular relationship which evolves, the motivational force which accompanies it, and the pain, pleasure or other repercussions associated with these particular ways of relating.

In the *Encyclopedia Britannica*'s description of emotions, Solomon expresses it well, stating: "Thus, feeling must include not only bodily feelings but the cognitively rich experiences of knowing, engaging, and caring." He notes that "the experiences of anger and love also include various thoughts and memories and intentions to act in certain ways" (Solomon 2016).

This perception of interdependency also explains why many poetic utterances emphasize the importance of "intertwined destiny" with the object of our emotions. Arnold, Lazarus, and Solomon all stress that emotions are about something that *happens to us*. This specific connection is what motivates us to *relate* (that is, to care) and it also distinguishes an emotional kind of relating from other generic, utilitarian, purely instrumental ways of relating, some of which will be explored below.

Adding a New Classification of Relationships According to Emotion

Though we recognize many types of relationships and distinguish between them in terms of the participants, strength, duration, and so forth, we typically do not pay enough attention to their surprising sophistication or to the unique types or subgroups they are composed of. On one hand, it is clear that, as complex social organisms with long and intricate parenting responsibilities, we have very diverse relational and engagement abilities that we might see as varied "domestic and foreign policies." On the other hand, we seem to have consistent ways of relating to certain elements or categories, such as offspring, people we do not know, pets, food or animals. We tend to relate similarly and have the same *types* of relationships with the various members of each group, and most people within a community will have similar styles or categories of relationships.

Our traditional method of classifying relationships, which commonly groups them according to the type of partnership, whether family, coworkers, strangers, and so forth, is helpful but limited. Traditional views may also look at relationships in terms of frequency of interaction, that is, how often we communicate; their emotional desirability, which is to say whether they are loving, peaceful, honest, dependable; and according to quantity. In this essay, we present an additional and very different view of relationships or ways of relating that gives more attention to its type, structure, and analysis. It pays particular attention to the special components that differentiate emotional from the non-emotional relationships. For instance, the degree and nature of interdependency perceived with the object of the emotion, whether this object is unique or exchangeable, and what motivation we have regarding this object and our relationship with it.

We do not have to adopt Eastern philosophy or relational ontology to realize that we are interconnected to many things, and especially to our environment. Even a mountain interacts with various elements such as rain, water, sun, vegetation, and other living organisms. This state of interconnection is more clearly obvious for living organisms, which have to exchange resources with their physical and living environments, and impact it. For human beings, it is even more apparent when you add their social connections and their complex manipulation of information, ideas, and concepts (including the idea of self). Thus, we can say that everything—or at least every living thing—relates to many elements of the surrounding environment.

Throughout our lives, then, we relate to very many phenomena (emotionally or otherwise) in endless ways, all the time. While certain scholars tend to categorize emotions in a basic, limited group (for example, Lazarus's [1991, 1994] fifteen basic emotions and Plutchik's [1980, 2002] eight basic emotions), in actuality, we seem to have an infinite number of emotions with many shades and variations that reflect the endless multiplicity of relationships that characterize human existence. People might have certain common emotional or relational patterns that display internal similarities, but in fact one person typically has numerous emotions "with" or "toward" endless people, items, and concepts. These will be slightly different from those of all other people, who have their own unique emotional matrix with their respective environments. Most importantly, this situation is ongoing and dynamic, so all these ways of relating and emotional relationships constantly change, resulting in an infinite and ever-changing variety of emotions. In this sense, humans can be seen as a nexus of relationships, whether we look through the lens of Western ontology or Eastern relational ontology (Hershock 2013).

Living organisms not only have different relationships with different elements, but they have different styles of relating and different types of relationships. Though each relationship or way of relating is unique (depending on the particular object and circumstances), some ways of relating have peculiar similarities, family resemblances, and certain common denominators. This apparent commonality makes it worthwhile to group some ways of relating under one name or category. From this perspective, we can see "emotions" as a category that describes one such group, as a name for a special style of relating to things and the particular type of relationships we establish with them.

In other words, "emotions" can be seen as a term describing a certain style or method of relating, with particular characteristics and dimensions. Different emotions such as love or anger are particular subgroups of this type of relating. While relationships are never identical, these types of relating have a common, typical "feel," and motivation, and reflect similar thoughts, orientations, and behavioral patterns between people or over time for the same person. For example, hate usually involves a strong aversion, dislike, and possibly the motivation to hurt the other party. Fear describes the way our body/mind reacts and relates to elements that threaten it, and it is accompanied by motivation to avoid or flee. Joy stands for an extreme positive reaction to the appearance of an element or situation.

It is not that we "have" an emotion, and then a relationship that matches this emotion. It is that we have a relationship characterized by certain attitudinal, configurative, and behavioral patterns which we then tend to name, for example, a "loving relationship," and assume that it is motivated by a "loving" manner of relating.

Viewing emotions as a relational phenomenon is not the same as seeing the mutual influence between emotions and relationships. As hinted above, the relational nature of emotions should not be confused with true but markedly different claims regarding the influence of certain relationships on emotional development or well-being. For instance, it is well-established that our relationships with our parents influence us emotionally, and that social relationships can help us emotionally, for example through group dynamics. These claims commonly have to do with the factors that affect our emotional development and formation, and less to do with what emotions are all about. They typically refer to the influence of our social relationships with parents, family, friends or coworkers on our emotional development, tendencies, patterns, and well-being. For example, whether we tend to be happy, depressed, angry, suspicious, or the way we relate to people such as ourselves, spouse, children or society as a whole.

The new propositions presented in this essay have more to do with the general way we view emotions, and are less focused on how particular relationships affect emotions. Fortunately, these two perspectives compliment and support each other instead of contradicting one another. They both emphasize the relational aspect of emotions and show how some significant ways of relating in critical times can affect the way *we relate* to many other elements in our lives.

Emotions are a type of relationship—not merely that which influences relationships or is influenced by them. A person can have a relationship that is not emotional, but can hardly have an emotion that is not relational. Emotions can be seen as a particular mode of relating that characterizes many of our relationships and clearly most of the significant ones. As noted above, it is not that we "have" parental love, then experience a motivation to get closer to our child, followed by a relationship with this child that is an outcome of our love. It is that we have a "loving relationship" with our child. Without the emotion of love, we would not have a relationship with our child, or it would be a very different one (such as the one we have with a bank teller we spoke to last Tuesday).

In the same manner, we do not hate our bosses and therefore relate to them badly. Hatred is in fact the way we relate to them, so that the emotion itself is *the way we relate*. We might behave badly toward them because of the way we "feel" about them, or we might behave nicely because we are also afraid to be fired, but the way we relate emotionally does not change. We might also hate our boss when we are calm (without agitated passion) and feel no especially intense experience. Namely, we can retain the basic emotion or way of relating to a familiar object even when our emotional intensity is low or, as we typically describe it, when we are "less emotional." The same goes for our love for our children, say, when we happen to think about them while going to sleep or driving in a car. We are simply aware of the way we relate to our children. If a car cuts in front of us on the highway, the emotion of anger does not come forth in response to our relationship with this driver, since we have no previous relationship. We simply respond by relating to this driver in anger. Anger is the way we relate to the driver, and this is the emotional relationship we have with him or her for these few moments. Whether or not this encounter develops into a full interaction, the initial way we related is not altered.

These fine-tuned articulations of the relations between emotions, various ways of relating, and relationships are crucial for the understanding and treatment of our emotions. No longer are emotions mysterious, vague, cognitive experiences which somehow influence and are influenced by other known elements, such as relationships. Instead, emotions are recognized as an obvious part of our known conceptual and practical universe, where they finally assume a much clearer and more easily understood role as relational modes or positions with the diverse elements of our environment.

The Distinction or Overlap between Emotions, Behavior, and Cognitive Processes

Because of the historical ambiguity in the understanding of emotions, their position is somewhat puzzling. It is particularly confusing when it comes to our common separation between mental or cognitive activity and actions or behavior.

It is obvious that human processes are rarely separated by distinct lines, and behavior typically flows out, or is influenced by, our cognitive constellations and emotions. However, emotions were traditionally seen more as internal, spiritual or cognitive constructs and therefore were separated from actions and behavior. For instance, love didn't include "chasing" your lover, and hate didn't include fighting your enemy. Accordingly, this essay has retrained this somewhat imposed separation to parallel the typical, everyday notion of emotions. For the same reason, emotions also end up looking different from our common, full notion of relationship, interaction; or they may even seem like one-sided treatments that typically do not include actions and physical interactions.

At the same time, this essay emphasizes that emotions should not be viewed as purely cerebral or cognitive, and that they are more than just orientations, perceptions, judgments, and attitudes. It is therefore not perfectly clear where emotions are situated, or what they include or exclude.

Though we have decided not to include actions in our view of emotions, they *do* include an element of force or motivation, and obvious sensations which exceed the common understanding of purely cognitive constructs (for example, "loving a spouse" is more than just "a perception of a lovable spouse" or "a loving orientation" or even "a loving attitude").

Emotions are more than just contemplation, opinion or perception of an object. They are already a definite position or a relational configuration we have adopted vis-à-vis specific elements. We have already passed beyond the initial cognitive contemplation, and have taken a definite stance and commitment in relation to the element in question. This particular stance expresses certain values and acts as an extension of them, and it includes also a motivation and a normative, biased position toward this element, its future, and our future mutual relationships. On top of it, like a Karate stance, this specific stance includes or generates various internal mental and bodily changes, preparations and other sensations necessary for such an emotional reconfiguration.

The problem is that emotions are relational phenomena which cross our common boundaries and distinctions. This is why they either tend to fall between the traditional chairs of values, drives, relationships, behavior, cognition, and other mental activities, or sit in more than one chair. Thus we have to carve a new relational category or place for them, which will probably slightly confuse our traditional categories and cover a number of them simultaneously (for instance our popular but hard-to-practice call for body/mind combination).

For now, it is enough to see emotions as special ways of relating that are more than pure cognitive constructs and include a special set of biases, commitment, intensity, sensations, and very particular force and motivation toward a specific element which typically lead to a corresponding action and behavior. These connections will become clearer later when we discuss how emotions express our drives and values and relate to cognition.

Other Traditional Outlooks and Definitions

Emotions, then, should not be limited to the "agitated passions" of popular definition, because they happen constantly with or without excitement or passion. They are also more than just "subjective experiences"—another popular definition; they are closer to "relational experiences" that lead away from the private toward the interactive. They also include more than simple "feelings" with relational implications, and should be seen more as "relational attitudes" accompanied by physical sensations. They are better not confined to instincts and drives which we happen to sense, but should rather be viewed as styles of relating which express some of our instincts, drives, and values. Accordingly, the function of emotion should be extended beyond the informational and motivational dimensions suggested by some traditional theories, to incorporate their obvious relational role. Nor should they be restricted to or equated with cognitive constructs or algorithms with some bodily side-effects. Instead, it is preferable to view them as a special type of approach, a mode of being, or a relational formation of the organism, that is initiated, "administered," and helped by cognitive processes. Even the ideas of Lazarus (1991, 1994, 2006) and other scholars, which see emotions as special reactions to cognitive or environmental stimuli, do not tell us enough about their role and how they are different from any other reaction or behavioral phenomena. Most importantly, as suggested before, emotions do not stand apart from our ways of relating or from our relationships in such a way that they can be said to influence our relationships, or be influenced by them. Emotions are better viewed as an integral critical part of our relationships and ways of relating.

Imaginary, Abstract, and Communal Elements
We can relate emotionally to imaginary, abstract, and communal elements. Emotions can be part of a relationship with a person, an animal, an object, or an idea (such as love for a movie star or response to a memory), a situation (being at a party or taking an ocean swim), an event (such as an earthquake), or even a concept. Because these "ways of relating" are not limited to persons or physical objects, they seem to be able to stretch to encompass attitudes toward abstract concepts, circumstances, and collective communal elements such as a family, an ethnic group, a nation, or even the social or

physical environment as a whole (for example, a global perspective or orientation). In this sense, they can further be defined to include the way we relate to ourselves as well, or to the image or concept of ourselves, depending on whether we are guided by a philosophy that endorses the "ego" and the "self" or not. We will discuss this aspect of emotions in more detail later.

Typically, relationships have the connotation of some form of interaction, connection, association, exchange or influence, in which something connects the parties and certain elements are being exchanged. In cases where both sides share the same emotions, as in a mutual love, and the relationship is physically active, it is easy to view love as a type of relationship. However, often enough an asymmetrical relationship exists with an element, so that the "feelings" of the concerned person, situation, institution, and so forth toward us are different from our feelings toward them, nonexistent, lacking a tangible dimension or without mutual interaction. For example, it is possible to love an object, a fictional character or a movie star; to miss a lost friend or a deceased spouse; to feel nostalgia for past times; to feel sad when hearing an old song. According to more traditional Western views, in these cases, our emotions actually refer to our internal attitudes or orientations toward an imaginary element and should not be seen as constituting a relationship. However, according to theories with more social, cultural or conceptual sensitivity (whether Western or Eastern), emotions can be seen as special *types* of relationship, even if they are unequal or intangible at times.

As mentioned before, this human tendency to relate emotionally to physical as well as abstract objects was recognized long ago and well-articulated by Brentano in 1874 (Solomon 2003). According to Brentano, emotions are always aimed at something (that is, they reflect "intentionality"), but it can be conceptual. "This something (*which need not necessarily exist*) is the object of the respective mental state" (Reisenzein 2006, 922). This view of emotions was also adopted by James in 1885 and other phenomenologists like Husserl in 1929 and Heidegger in 1927. It was emphasized again in psychology by the appraisal approaches, as well as in many other theories of emotions.

In these instances, emotions can be seen either as a part of or a necessary instigator in certain relationships we have not only with people, but also with concepts, ideas or theoretical notions (including our own self-image). In those cases, we can simply see emotion as a way of relating to a conceptual element or as a special dimension of a relationship—a relationship that may not completely materialize and that does not include a tangible connection.

Emotions as directed primarily toward persons or other elements instead of as purely internal experiences. The totality of emotional experience, as discussed above, our ability to relate emotionally to concepts, the "intentionality" of emotions, and their basic relational nature, can transform our understanding of the nature of emotions. As previously stated, the traditional view of emotions as personal, internal, "subjective experiences" is a natural extension of our individualistic, entity-based, Western philosophy. However, this view falls short of providing an accurate, comprehensive perspective, and must be revised to make way for a different image of how emotions function and the role they play.

To start with, as hinted above, emotions are proving to be much more of a social and cultural phenomenon than previously thought. It seems they are developed in a communal manner, help facilitate and communicate social ties, and appear less and less as an inner, autonomous, personal subjective formulation. (See excellent studies in the anthropology of emotions by Lutz and White 1986 and White 2008, among others.)

It is clear that the image of emotion as an "inner subjective" experience was reinforced by our common intuitive sense, and by the popular view that cognitive and sensory processes are strictly private, interior processes. This tendency is not surprising considering how personal and confusing emotions often "feel" and seem to most of us. (This is why we need therapists to interpret and clarify them for us.) When we are lying in bed worrying late at night, when we listen to old music or watch a touching movie, we feel wrapped up in our own individual world of thoughts, contemplations, and feelings. We seem to be enveloped in our own thoughts and emotions; nonetheless, most of those emotions prove to be, surprisingly enough, relational and aimed at our social, physical, and conceptual environment. (Parkinson, Fischer, and Manstead [2005, 2] make a very similar claim.) For example, on close analysis, most of our worries turn out to be primarily concerned with our children and how well they are doing, our spouse, our boss, our government, our body or our financial well-being.

External factors such as music and drugs can also trigger our sensations. Those seem to stimulate more diffused emotions and moods like happiness or sadness. However, even when we feel "emotional" about a piece of music, a good book or a movie, in most cases it is because we seem to relate to some fictional characters, the associations and memories which they arouse, or an overall state of affairs or imaginary atmosphere. All of these experiences are aspects of relating to everything and everybody that matters around us.

Viewing Emotions as a Way of Relating Instead of as a Finite Resource

A relational view of emotions can open new theoretical and practical opportunities and prevent old misconceptions and confusions. For example, it can lift the spell of the common but mistaken perception that emotions, and particularly love, are a finite internal resource or limited capability. When someone pays attention to more than one lover, one of the lovers often feels that they are loved less than the other or that they are being somehow short-changed. This dynamic is often apparent even on a wider scale, when it comes to questioning patriotism, ethnic or religious loyalty. These reactions arise from the common perception that love (or any other emotion) is some sort of a finite resource or capacity—something that we "have," rather than something we practice. However, we all know that a mother can love more than one child and can even love ten without running out of love. The same is unfortunately true for our ability to hate many people without much limitation.

The sense that our capacity to feel is quantitatively limited vanishes when we view emotions as relational phenomena. If love is a way of relating, and not a noun, an object, a resource, or a mysterious experience, it is not necessarily limited or finite. Thus, the idea that we can only love one person can be seen as a romantic myth. In fact, we can relate to one person or many in a similar manner (though not identical), and we can love an endless number of people without diminishing the strength of our love. Although we might love one person more than another, or switch our love from one person to another, this has to do with our emotional constellation, and not with an intrinsic condition in which love is limited.

What we probably experience in typical reactions of jealousy is diminishing attention, commitment or exclusivity; but this envy rises out of a more traditional territorial agreement and expectation rather than an inherent emotional limitation of love. This is not an argument for the reinstitution of polygamy, and in some situations exclusivity has benefits, especially when it is agreed upon by both sides and it is based on trust. It is not easy to love many people intensely, or for that matter, to have multiples of any other intense emotional relationships. Such relationships often increase our vulnerability and tend to have a high emotional and energy cost. However, it is definitely possible to have numerous loving relationships in the same manner that we manage to have plentiful hating ones.

What these examples intend to show is that a basic change in perspective about emotions can often resolve misconceptions as well as emotional and social conflicts. It also opens the road to the possibility of wider horizons of love and empathy (and not just hate) that are crucial not only in personal and family spheres, but also in broader international, national, religious, and ethnic circles.

The first step toward improving both theoretical and practical views of emotion may be to stop thinking of ourselves autonomously, as self-sufficient individuals. Instead we might reconsider ourselves as relational creatures with a multitude of relationships and relational methods. We would also realize that we are highly, personally affected by them, thus increasing our awareness and appreciation for these relationships, as well as our sense of accountability for our own well-being and that of others.

Emotions are Neither Strictly Cognitive Nor Strictly Sensory

As a true body/mind phenomenon, emotion is neither strictly cognitive nor strictly sensory. Some of the considerations that lead observers to describe emotions as internal subjective experiences have also guided scholars to view them as cognitive phenomena. While emotions were initially called "feelings," suggesting their origin in the sensory realm, cognition gained importance among theorists, and they later came to be considered primarily cognitive. As mentioned above, the fact that we are able to alter our emotions by changing our perceptions and beliefs reinforces the idea that they are cognitive constructs, and it is not necessarily wrong or illogical to associate emotion with cognition. When the complexity and relational function of emotion is not clear, the tendency is to define emotion according to whichever component seems most crucial to their operation, for example, sensation or cognition.

However, such classifications and categorizations tend to obscure much of the uniqueness, function, and complexity of emotion. They deemphasize or even exclude a major part of the body/mind process. Associating emotions with purely cognitive elements and processes, such as concepts and conceptualizing, thought and thinking, appraisals, evaluations, and judgments, misses for instance the aspect of emotional *intensity* that arises out of their close connection with drives and values, and their operation as "modes of being" or fully systemic body/mind interfaces. Most importantly, such categorizations overlook the relational role of emotions.

Although many of our bodily processes and life activities—sports are a good example—require cognitive participation and even leadership, it doesn't seem beneficial to view them as cognitive phenomena or to restrict them to cognition. (This will be discussed more fully in the section on Cognition.)

Restricting emotions to cognition is as partial as limiting them to feelings or sensations. Both approaches are a throwback to the body versus mind division of Descartes' philosophy or the earlier division proposed by Thomas Aquinas (2002), mentioned previously. Emotions are a relational phenomenon that requires a truly synergic, unified view of body and mind. To better understand the function and role of emotion, it is not enough to simply acknowledge that both body and mind are important aspects of the human condition. Rather, to follow the thread of this essay, readers must be receptive to a genuinely synergic body/mind view that will make it possible to step out of the historical body/mind dichotomy and continuum to enjoy a new understanding of emotions. The need for this departure will become more evident in the following discussions, as we consider a new terminology, model, and view of emotions, cognition, rationality, objectivity, and "Self."

The perspective proposed here doesn't seek necessarily to contradict established understandings of emotion as much as it intends to offer a more concrete, new, and helpful understanding that demonstrates how diverse theoretical pieces and descriptions fit together. In so doing, this view also provides better initial clues about the possible reason for the development of emotions, their special function, role, advantages (something we will explore further), and some of their unique qualities. It will become apparent that this new understanding of emotion also resolves much of the tension or misunderstanding regarding the relations between emotion and related concepts such as cognition, rationality, and values.

As a first step in reducing some of the vagueness, generality, and or confusion generated by traditional descriptions of emotions, we will now explore some of the unique dimensions that distinguish emotions from other ways of relating.

3

Unique Dimensions of Emotional Relationships

Emotions have special characteristics that are common to this subgroup of ways of relating. The combination of these shared properties or dimensions is unique to this category and distinguishes it from other relational modes.

Some of the more helpful theories of emotions, particularly the Appraisal theories, recognize at least partially the dimensions of emotions discussed below, such as interdependence, motivational force, and sensation. However, we have added the aspect of specificity, which is lacking from or underestimated in most of these approaches, yet seems critical in differentiating emotions from other methods of relating. We further expand existing ideas by looking at these special characteristics from a relational point of view and trying to understand why and how these characteristics differentiate emotional from non-emotional ways of relating.

Interdependence
The first unique and necessary dimension of emotional relationships is the sense of *interdependence* with the object of an emotion. Namely, we perceive that a change in a certain element to which we are related, in its actions, or in our relationship with it has in some way influenced us, will or should influence us, and vice versa. This

makes us *relate* to this entity and often leads to an emotional relationship with it. The experience of interdependence also gives this emotional element, or our relationship with it, a special significance and meaning.

Ekman emphasizes the same tendency, saying that, "The most common trigger [of emotions, is] when we sense something. . . that seriously affects our welfare. . . " (Manstead, Frijda, and Fischer 2004, 121). This is also recognized by Arnold (1960), Lazarus (1991), Solomon (1997, 2003), Ben-Zee (2000), and Plutchik (1980, 2002).

For example, love for a spouse, children, or friends consists of a sense of mutual dependency in which we feel that our futures are intertwined, and therefore we care for, empathize with, or are invested in their situation. Such matters as our spouse's or children's health, happiness, success, looks, and the relationship between us are all connected with our own concerns. The existence of love usually means that we perceive a positive correlation between their well-being and ours, and feel that we will be better off, or simply happier, if they do well. Hatred on the other hand, typically indicates the opposite type of interdependence, in which we perceive an inverse correlation between the well-being of an entity and our own well-being. The better off the other entity is, the worse off we are, and the worse off the other, the better off we are.

In most cases a person is born with, learns of, or develops certain categories of elements, based on predictable possible effects. Certain categories of entities tend toward certain interactions that may change depending on the particular situation. For example, some snakes can bring death when encountered closely on a trail, but not in a zoo. This understanding is somewhat similar to theories that claim that most organisms constantly identify and classify elements in their environment (Maslow 2013 and others). Elements in the environment are classified into such categories of interdependency as food, enemy, potential sexual partner or team member, and then treated accordingly. However, as human beings, we have a very high level of cognitive capacity for differentiations, distinctions, recognition, analysis, and predictions; and, as members of a very flexible and complex society, our perceptions of interdependence are vastly more elaborate and varied, and they are frequently adjusted. Thus, humans are able to go far beyond established categories to identify or perceive very specific, intricate interdependencies with very many *particular* elements, and we relate to them in endless different and unique ways, and change them as needed. It is our emotional skills that give us these exact, refined, multidimensional, and dynamic relational capabilities.

Seeing emotion as an important relational skill may be perceived as a self-centered, utilitarian approach. However, the mutual dependency involved with emotions does not end with utilitarian, materialistic concerns, but also extends to social, mental, and emotional interchanges, and it results in important contributions. Furthermore, mutual dependency does not imply that we are acting in a purely utilitarian, egotistical, selfish sense, concerned only with ourselves and how other people or objects can benefit us. Mutual dependency can give rise to benevolent, moral, and altruistic relations as well. For example, our love for our children results in the continuation of genes and heritage, reciprocal care (at a young age for the children and at old age for the parents), mutual help in growth and development, pride and joy for both sides, empathy, and so forth. A similar argument can be made for Mother Theresa's mercy for the needy or for love of art. In one form or another, all these relationships require and include a sense of "give and take" or mutual contribution, and the sense that the "other side" somehow enhances or expresses the values and goals of the people who have these emotions.

In actuality, this *mutual* dependency and connection seem essential to our ability to form emotional relationships and to our interest in forming them. In *A General Theory of Love* (among many other sources), Lewis, Amini, and Lannon (2000) argue that emotions and the recognition of interdependency were developed in mammals as part of the limbic brain to enhance care for offspring and to support interactions in social communities. They state clearly that "limbic regulation mandates interdependence for social mammals of all ages" (87). H. Harlow's (1958) experiment with baby monkeys in the 1950s further emphasizes the importance of emotion over the purely utilitarian satisfaction of meeting mammals' basic needs for food and safety.

It is also important to emphasize that we readily sacrifice self-interest in some situations of interdependence with certain entities, for example, with our children. Some even see self-sacrifice as going beyond mutual dependency to a state of selfless caring and empathy which they see as the base for morality (see Hume 1977 and Solomon 2003).

This is often associated with the notion of "care" which we will further explore below. It signifies the added commitment, connection, and a sense of involvement in the particular object of our emotion. This dimension makes interdependence markedly different than in general treatments that describe it as a purely utilitarian relationship, and it runs opposite to not caring or being indifferent. The state of being invested results in a preference about what happens to the object of our emotion. We care about what happens to them because we want to make sure that "they get what they deserve" or what we wish for them, whether good or bad.

The use of the term "interdependence" instead of "dependency," "influence" or "care" emphasizes that emotions are more about mutual connection rather than about a passive, one-way, causal interaction. It is not so much that we sit passively in the middle of the universe and everything affects us. Instead it is more as if we interact with many things in our environment and build scenarios as to how a change in one of us, a change in our relationship, or a change that one of the sides can bring about, can affect both sides. Emotion-based relationships involve the sense that our destinies are somehow intertwined—for a moment or for a lifetime, significantly or marginally, physically or mentally or both. Accordingly, we establish particular emotional relationships with specific elements that reflect our "interdependence scenarios." These kinds of scenarios we envision are heavily dependent on our particular belief system, perceptions, and values, which in turn vary according to our culture and our particular mental configuration. It seems that we tend to develop them more with individuals, situations, institutions with which we perceive a somewhat longer and specific interdependency; thus we are concerned with their future and the future of our relationship, and not just their immediate function or service (either wishing them the best or the worst). Lazarus writes that, "What makes the relationship personally significant, and hence worthy of an emotion, is that what happens is relevant to the well-being of one or both parties; in effect, each has personal goals at stake" (as quoted in Solomon 2003, 126).

Because emotional ways of relating seem relevant to the well-being of both parties, they typically include a goal and an active force or motivation to preserve or change the entity we are related to, ourselves or our mutual relationship. This is done in the hope of improving the situation and advancing goals and values that seem to represent an improvement.

A typical example of these "interdependence scenarios" is the kind of relationship we build at work with our boss, coworkers or employees. These scenarios include our perceptions (mostly subconscious) about how these people can affect us; for example, they may help our job, improve our condition, become our friends, or annoy and hurt us. If we see someone as a threat to our job (or our company), we might be angry at them, afraid of them, hate them, or a combination of these emotions.

The second aspect of interdependence scenarios has to do with our ideas about how we should react to these people and influence their effect on us. For example, if we are afraid of them, our goal or motivation might be to hurt, destroy or avoid them. If this is the case, we will strive to either change their position (fire them), our position (quitting) or limit our interaction (avoidance or confrontation), and thus change our relationships and their effect on us. Although such scenarios are more complex in real life, at base they all seem to exemplify a principle in which emotions constitute our position in relation to elements in our environment according to our perceived interdependence with them.

One might ask what is so special about the recognition of interdependence in our interactions, as this seems to be an obvious component of any relationship. If we have ongoing interaction with our children, spouse or an art form, it is only natural that we will be influenced by them, and vice-versa. However, the interdependence proposed here is not just a logical, intellectual, calculative, analytical, abstract or utilitarian interdependence, but an a priori one. It is not based on an "after the fact" analysis of a specific relationship, or relationships in general, such as we find in a philosophy book, in chaos theory or in a Buddhist teaching of the "interdependency of all things." This is rather the determination that a specific interdependence is perceived before or with every emotional relationship, and that this takes place in a rather subconscious, spontaneous manner. It is our fear of a specific person, animal or situation as we sense a particular threat in their presence, our love of a certain work of art which "speaks" to us instantly when we see it, or our affection for a friend who makes us feel good. It is not the logical conscious realization that art or friends are important, or the recognition that we are connected to them or to all mankind and thus influence each other. Rather, this sense of interdependence seems to be an integral part of our outlook on most things around us, and it is our immediate, intuitive mode of positioning of these things relative to our drives, values, and goals. This subconscious, impulsive notion of a mutual tie comes in different shapes, strengths, and intensities, depending on the particular context, the perception of significance, and the sense of connection with the elements at hand.

Unlike some philosophical notions of interdependence (including the Buddhist view), interdependence in this sense is not universal (that is, "with all things"), and definitely not necessarily moral. Instead, the type of interdependence described here is specific, with particular entities or groups, and not with all. While we may appreciate and love some of them, we may want to destroy others or eliminate our connection with them, as in cases of hatred, anger or fear; or we may simply not care about some—those with whom we do not find or foresee any significant interdependence. Thus, we might love our family and hate the neighbors, be proud of our ethnic group, despise some others, and care less about the rest.

In other words, the emotional perception of interdependence is not a purely cognitive intellectual or analytical one, it is not generic, and it is not necessarily positive.

In sum, the interdependence invoked here is a visceral sense of mutual connection that arises only in specific cases, toward selected elements and groups, and has a particular direction, form, intensity, and strength. It also generates clear preconceptions, biases, and preferences as to the future of these elements, the shape and desirability of our specific relationships with them, and the way we would like them to develop (if at all).

From an evolutionary, developmental point of view, emotions seem to express and facilitate some similar drives and motivations for different organisms. For instance, they serve to preserve genes, enhance our search for power and safety, and support a whole assortment of communal values. Organisms assess their interdependency with most of the elements they encounter and quickly determine whether these elements facilitate, block or are irrelevant to their drives, goals or values. Those organisms relate accordingly, and if some of the elements are relevant, significant or unique, they might relate to them emotionally (if they are cognitively developed). As we will further explore later, the assumption is that while the fish forms such connections by a hard-wired, instinctual mechanism, people have higher cognitive capabilities and additional or alternative relational methods which we call emotions. We consider them emotional, partially because they further process these interdependencies, goals, values, the way to achieve them, and the proper way to relate to the relevant elements. For more complex, social, and cognitive species, emotions probably provided a more suitable, flexible, and sophisticated way of relating, and thus facilitated drives and goals more successfully for human needs (at least they have so far).

By comparison, as we will shortly demonstrate, if we do not sense any mutual dependency with a specific element, or the potential for one, we will probably have only a generic reflective or utilitarian relationship with it.

While walking or driving on a street, or even when handling a list of anonymous people at work, we may encounter people whom we remember later; but since we experience little or no interdependence with them, we establish only a reflective relationship with them, one with no emotional connection. In a somewhat similar manner, we might have a purely utilitarian, generic relationship with tools, the beef we ate yesterday, a teller in the bank, or an employee in a large company. We might depend on them for a service or function, but we assume that we can get it elsewhere, or from somebody else, so we don't particularly care about what might happen to them or our relationship with them in the future. However, if we feel particularly dependent on these entities (for example, if they have to approve our loan), or if we are affected by these elements, or somehow might be or wish to be affected by them, we tend to develop an emotional relationship with them. For example, they may manage to anger, frighten or attract us. In other words, they lose their generic position, and gain instead qualities of uniqueness and specific interdependence.

We might wonder why then we are concerned with a killing in a far-away school, a war, or viral infection in a distant country. The hypothesis is that we are either afraid that it will affect us (for example, spread to our children's school), or we feel somehow connected to wider social circles that trigger our empathy. It is possible to feel connected to specific but communal concepts such as family, ethnic or religious group, country or even humankind, so that in certain situations we empathize with members of wider groups who represent those communities (according to their level of significance for us). Thus a war hero who has received a lot of publicity in the media can become a symbol for the country's struggle and evoke emotions connected with our interdependency with our nation.

We can also experience interdependence with a long-lost friend or a relative who has passed away. Because they have influenced us, their disappearance changes our life and leaves a void, and they have a lingering effect on our well-being.

The experience of interdependence thus can create a sense of emotional relationship with past, present, and future elements—not only to people, but to objects, ideas, communities, situations, and images.

Particularity and Specificity

Closely related to the perception of interdependence is the object-specific orientation of emotions. Emotional relationships seem to take place only with specific elements and groups, and not with general categories or generic ideas (perhaps because we can't perceive interdependence with them). In other words, the "target" of emotion is not a generic object, a non-specific person or a theoretical category, but a particular, unique element toward which we feel emotion. Because of our personal and particular relationship with this irreplaceable element (typically through a sense of interdependency and significance), we are concerned with its overall destiny. We don't care only about its function or utility, but also about its fate and our relationship with it. (See Heidegger's [1962] *Being in Time* for related ideas.)

For example, we love certain people and these people alone, we hate specific things, and we are afraid in specific situations and of particular elements. If one of the people we love leaves, we cannot be sure that we will feel the same toward another person (for example, toward a stepfather). Emotions are typically not aimed at roles, functions or categories of people and elements, but are rather person- or object-specific. We do not love wives in general, we love our specific wife, and we do not necessarily love people, but specific family members and friends.

Although emotions seem to express our ability to form endless and ever-changing relationships with numerous individual elements, they retain a quality of specificity. Beck (1979, 1997) and other scholars mention a notion of "specificity" as well, in which they emphasize the specific conditions and therapy for each case of emotion. However, their idea of specificity is mostly an intellectual understanding of the differences between various cases of emotion. Here, we are emphasizing an idea of particularity that is more an intuitive perception, in which the person feeling emotion experiences the object of his/her emotion as special and not easily exchangeable. Not only does the relationship seem unique, but the object of the emotion is seen as "one of a kind" and irreplaceable.

A careful look at Aristotle's discussion of anger reveals that it not only emphasizes the intentionality of emotion (it is always "about something"), but also the particularity of this emotion: ". . . the anger of the angry person is necessarily always directed toward someone in *particular*, (e.g. Cleon), but not toward all of humanity . . . " (as quoted in Solomon 2003, 6) . Martha Nussbaum pays close attention to this dimension, which she calls "localized emotion," saying: "I do not fear just any and every catastrophe anywhere in the world, nor (so it seems) any and every catastrophe that I know to be bad in important ways. What inspires fear is the thought of the impending damage that threatens *my* cherished relationships and projects. . . . The emotions are in this sense *localized*. . . rather than general distribution of light and darkness in the universe as a whole" (as quoted in Solomon 2003, 277). Like interdependency, the particularity of emotions endows them with a sense of meaning and significance.

The Element of Specificity as it Relates to Communities and Groups. One question that keeps arising concerns the ability and tendency to form emotional connections with communal elements and certain groups, but less with general categories and roles. When emotions are focused on a clear and specific object or person (such as our house or child), it is easy to separate this kind of relationship from obviously non-emotional, generic relationships (such as with a supermarket cashier). However, how is it that we seem to get emotional about communal elements (family, nation, ethnic group), events (earthquakes), groups (spiders), situations (party, law suite, vacation), and even ideas (human rights, natural environment)? Where is the dimension of specificity in our emotional relationships with communal elements?

One simple explanation has to do with the tendency to group certain communities (not categories), and even some events and situations, and view them as unified, specific elements. Two common ways of grouping are relevant here: a singular entity with numerous parts can be experienced as a group, and similar elements can be experienced as a group. The first type of grouping sees certain communities as whole, unified, special, irreplaceable entities—such as one's family, the nation, or one's body—rather than as just a random assortment of individuals or parts. In such cases the sum is more than just a collection of the parts and represents a unique connection or coordination among the parts and/or a particular cohesiveness. When groups are viewed as a particular whole, they can be treated emotionally. My spouse, myself, and our children are more than just a collection of individuals; rather we constitute a special unit—namely a particular family. The same goes for one's body, which is more than a collection of body parts, one's nation or even a hurricane, which is more than just a collection of winds and air particles (and so they are identified with particular names). In such instances, it is possible to relate emotionally to specific groups or communities and to treat members of those as representatives of a single whole.

In the second manner of grouping, various elements are categorized into a group because they seem similar to each other or share a common denominator, such as ethnic groups or bears. It is possible to relate emotionally to the group only if we assume it to be organized as a particular community, or if all the members are perceived as identical and/or perceived to have a similar effect on us that warrants the same emotional relationship. This second grouping can be helpful on occasions, for example by saving valuable time and analysis when facing a similar element to others we have experienced before (for example, another poisonous snake similar to others we have learned about). However, it frequently also leads to preconceived assumptions of similarity which is a nice way of describing prejudicial practices toward ethnic groups, gender categories, animals, and so forth.

Emotional relationships with groups of these two types are specific, because they are reserved solely for members of these particular groups, and they are different from our relationships with other groups and everybody else. We do not love families or countries, but a specific family or country. Likewise, fear of snakes does not extend to fear all of all animals or even to lizards, or to fear of snakes in a zoo, where they have no dangerous effect.

The same could be said of emotional reactions toward events or situations. A close look at our emotions toward most situations seems to indicate that they reflect our reaction to specific elements of a particular occasion. For example, if one is afraid of speaking in public, it is often due to fear of embarrassing oneself or being criticized; and if one loves a party, it is often because one likes specific people and/or anticipates having fun. In each case, we anticipate a specific interdependence with these particular situations and the elements or people involved in them. This particular emotional capability might also be the explanation for our ability to have more widespread emotions like moods or happiness which seem to express the way we relate to our overall situation at the time.

We don't have this type of anticipation when, for example, we walk into impersonal situations such as going into a bank, eating a routine lunch, or walking down the sidewalk (unless again it is especially cold, raining, crowded or in the midst of a festival of some sort).

Without perfectly realizing the reasoning behind this dimension, the dynamic of specificity that makes it possible to relate emotionally to a group beyond our immediate sphere is very familiar in the media, politics or advertising. It is often described as putting a "face to the issue" or making the issue personal. In addition to the national hero of the previous section, many more examples of this tactic appear in the media as reporters provide personal histories for soldiers at war, athletes in sport events or movie stars. The media attempts to increase viewer participation by establishing an emotional relationship between the viewers and the element viewed by making the story of a generic athlete or soldier "particular" with name recognition and personal, "relatable" stories, or by making it a symbol for a larger community. It is also a common tactic in hostage negotiations, political campaigns, political or ideological brain washing, and multiple other cases in which emotional connection is either necessary or undesirable.

This dimension of emotional relationships that makes it possible to extend a sense of connection to a group is clearly crucial for ongoing intimate, familial, friendly interactions, and empathy. It is also necessary for a commitment to "unselfish" relationships (as required for example in rearing offspring). It saves us from having deep, costly empathy to the whole universe, and at the same time prevents us from treating everybody around us in the same manner or in purely utilitarian terms as solely a means to an end. It also guarantees a specific, personal connection to and treatment of individuals and particular communities rather than limiting interactions to generic treatment of categories, such as treating all our children the same, treating all members of an ethnic group in the same manner, or treating all communities with no distinction. As noted earlier, Lewis, Fari, and Lannon (2000) argue that emotions developed and continue to function to help social animals care for their offspring and connect with the rest of the members in their community. Thus such relationships require very detailed, personal recognition of many particular individuals, objects, and concepts, and, at the same time, add a highly diversified treatment of specific individuals beyond the strictly categorical or communal. The emotional interactions of social animals are also much more flexible and dynamic connections in comparison to those of social insects, for instance.

This personal element differentiates emotional relationships from scientific ones (relationships that are supposedly "objective"—a matter we are going to discuss later), which are primarily generic and reflective (such as working with experimental mice). It also distinguishes emotional relationships from public, utilitarian connections, such as in business or politics (for example, the generic treatment of employees, clients, citizens, and members of other countries by large companies and governments).

Force and Direction

Another special dimension of emotions is an element of power that we are going to identify as a "directional force." In the literature, this force is often described as a "motivational force" or the "propensity for action," but it also appears in association with such diverse topics as preferences, biases, drives, desires, will power, intensity, volume, and energy.

Emotions either add this aspect to interactions or relationships, or articulate it. Alternatively, emotions can be viewed as the special manner of relating that includes or facilitates this dimension of directional force—in contrast to, say purely cognitive constructs or reflective relationships with elements we know but don't particularly care about. In fact, as we are going to discuss in more detail later, emotions can be seen as specific expressions or extensions of ongoing motivational forces that we often describe as drives or values.

A familiar description of love is as a connection and attraction, whereas hate and disgust are identified with rejection and repulsion. When we care about something, we want to get close to it and do something about it, even if only preserving it, or being closely informed about it. For example, if we are attracted to a person or love a person, we want to pay attention to him or her, know about, be with, take care or somehow interact with the person. We are said to be very "attached" to people or objects we care about, and describe a non-emotional tendency as "detachment." The motivation to flee in the case of fear is one of the most obvious examples of emotion as a directional force. We are "drawn" to things we love as to food when hungry, or run away from things that we hate or fear. Even if literal physical interaction is impossible, or blocked (by other values and other emotional or practical considerations), the desire for connection is still there when we love a person, even if the relation is one-sided, like love for a movie star or a lover who has died. The same dynamic is true for hatred, anger, fear, and most other emotions.

The use of directional terms in describing emotions seems to express a vector of force that we feel in the way we relate, or in the relationships between ourselves and the object of our emotion. Depending on the emotion at hand, this relational force can change its target (the "object" of our emotion), its internal bearing (pull, push), as well as its strength and intensity. For example, we can love somebody a little or very much, care more or less, and our empathy for another often weakens with distance and time. The intensity and strength of this motivational force vary according to the significance of the object. This in turn is affected by our perception of the extent of our interdependence with it (that is, how important it is), our emotional constitution at the time, and other factors. In contrast, we cannot **know** something very "strongly" or reflect "weakly." Purely cognitive constructs lack this dimension of intensity, volume, and strength.

Perhaps a metaphorical comparison with natural forces will be helpful here. Natural forces represent our assumptions about how and why different bodies have a relationship with each other, or in simple words, how they pull, push, attract or reject one another (like stars or magnets). In nature, we don't see the forces between objects, but we still believe, assume or conclude that they are there based on the way elements interact with each other. The same could be said about our relationships. We don't see love, but if we see or feel a strong attraction between two people (or a person and an object), we can say that there is a strong force between them. If for example, drive is analogous to gravity, emotion is the specific weight of different elements. Namely, as weight is the expression of gravity, attraction could be seen as the expression of sexual drive. In the same manner, fear could be seen as the expression of the desire to preserve life, and love of children the expression of perpetuating the species. Even the love of music can be viewed as an expression of artistic values, which take the shape of an enjoyment and appreciation for music and art. One can view this dimension of emotions as *a form of physical energy directed by mental constellations* (analogous to the physical energies we find in nature, only directed in this case by mental constellations).

It is important to keep in mind that this is only an analogy, and there is no attempt to equate emotional forces with physical ones. However, the metaphorical comparison with physical forces in nature is intended to help transform our view of emotions and emotional relationships—away from the recently popular cognitive reflective imagery, and toward a more connective, interactive, forceful relational model.

The idea of "forces" might sound strange at first, but as noted earlier, this concept has been presented occasionally under different names. For example, it was recognized indirectly by philosophers in discussions of "will power" and "intentionality" by Aquinas and Augustine (King in Goldie, ed., 2010, Schopenhauer 1969 and most of the German Romantics of the nineteenth century, as well as by Nietzsche 1997 and Heidegger 1962). It was discussed extensively in the psychology of basic needs, desires, drives, and motives (Maslow 1970, 2013) as well as described as a "motivational force" (Turski 1994, Sabini 1996). Last but not least, it appears in Eastern philosophies and religions, as well as in the work of some recent biologists and psychologists, as mental energy or "chi."

Nevertheless, most of the recent work in psychology explores directional force in relation to motivation. A number of theorists view emotions as preset responses (partially instinctual and partially learned) that help us react properly, and often quickly, to various stimuli for purposes of survival, socialization or otherwise. Different theories of emotions, and clearly the appraisal ones, recognize the motivational aspect as an integral part of emotions (Ben-Zeev 2000). Some see it as a secondary component, while others view it as the main function of emotions (Aquinas, King in Goldie, ed., 2010, McDougall 1960, Arnold 1960).

Western social philosophy, with its roots in Greek philosophy, has tended to concentrate on such issues as knowledge, rationality, intellect, truth and objective reality, thought, interpretations, language, and reflection. These concepts are typically more analytical and intellectually focused and less focused on issues of force and power, which have been left more for political science, the laws of nature, and the "hard" sciences.

This "directional force" is a very important and unique dimension of emotions, and has significant theoretical implications. Though the directional force is associated with emotional intensity and arousal and may vary in intensity or strength, it is present to one degree or another in most emotional relationships. Thus, this quality seems to distinguish emotions from typical cognitive elements such as thoughts and appraisals, and from other types of relationships (for example, reflective relationships, as we are going to discuss below). As noted above, we can't say that we had "a *strong* thought" or that "we *very* evaluated something." We might have thought a lot, or evaluated something very well, but these assessments refer to quantity and quality. When it comes to emotions, we can say for example that "we are *very* angry" or that we "hate somebody intensely."

Emotions seem to involve some commitment, and the emotional person feels vested in his or her position, and experiences a connection to the object of the emotions. As we hinted before, if you are angry, you have gone beyond your initial contemplation and the sorting of various options as judgments might imply. If you love your children, spouse or nation, you are in "for the long run," including a readiness to help, fight, and sacrifice (even your life). You have already taken a position and are invested in it, and you desire some action, direction, and consequence, which are what motivation is all about. Without this dimension, we might think more rationally, but the chances are that without emotional motivation, instead of behaving more rationally, we would hardly behave at all. Or else we might behave like bacteria, with only instinctual aversions and attractions. We might have only utilitarian relationships or behave like a computer with preprogrammed reactions to generic categories. Lack of emotions would probably lead to less motivation, connection, commitment, and less ability to form specific and flexible ways of relating. Lack of emotion would also probably result in automatic, generic relationships and a deficient sense of connectivity (part of what Heidegger has called "being in the world"). In this sense, *our emotions could be said to add the third dimension or topography to our otherwise flat instrumental universe.* Alternatively, they could be seen as *adding a dramatic sound track to a cold, functional silent documentary.*

It is important to note that the use of the term "directional force" was intended to expand the view that sees emotion as a motivational force—a psychological concept that is widespread but limited in scope. First, "emotional force" is not just a motivation for action. It can also include a motivation for non-action and other goals, such as in cases of preservation of a person or a situation. Second, it is not just the one-sided propensity implied by the term "motivation." It is an actual binding force that indicates connection and interdependence. The additional element of "direction" is of particular importance in understanding emotion, and it signifies a number of unique emotional components, including its aim at a person or an object (emotion is "about something," it has "intentionality"), and its "bearing" (it can pull, push or otherwise affect participants in ways that go beyond our analogy to physical forces). This emotional force can also be said to have a direction over time, in the sense that we often want it to change or develop over the life of a relationship. Furthermore, emotions can be seen as expressions of ongoing *directions* in life. Namely, emotions are the expression of drives or values that act as ongoing forces, giving our lives specific directions and goals.

Certain aspects of this complex connection will be discussed later in more detail, in the chapters dealing with emotional intensity and the connection between emotions and drives or values. In short, in this narrow sense, emotions can be seen as the way we relate to people, ideas or situations according to, or in order to facilitate, our ongoing needs, drives, and values. Put differently, these needs, drives, and values provide the unique and specific type of motivation which is expressed in emotional relationships.

By comparison, while utilitarian relationships might also present a source of motivation, say for receiving a service or a product such as sex or food, emotional relationships include a motivation that is tied to the object of emotion and our relationship with the object.

Sensations ("Feelings")

Sensations are the most obvious and most widely acknowledged dimension of emotions, which is why they are also called "feelings." Though these feelings or sensations are very apparent to all of us, their function or place in emotions is not so clear or agreed upon.

Feelings are often considered synonymous with emotions, and the terms are frequently used interchangeably. Some prominent thinkers, such as William James, saw them as one and the same, and some recent thinkers like Prinz (2004) and Goldie (2010) are trying to either revive this approach and/or improve on it. From Prinz's perspective, every dimension added to the physical or somatic sensations that constitute feelings should be viewed as a part of cognition, as the result of other human activities, or as an aspect of social norms. Though this model might have some theoretical validity, the general tendency among contemporary researchers is to emphasize the cognitive dimension of emotions, and diminish the role of feelings and sensations. What then is the role of sensation, if emotions are viewed as cognitive constructs or even, as proposed here, "relational phenomena"?

One possible explanation is the simple idea that, at times, no functional connection exists between emotions and feelings. It is possible to see sensations as by-products of emotions that do not contribute much to their operation. Feelings might be like the noise that our stomachs sometimes make while digesting food. We can hear it, but this does not mean it is necessarily functional.

In times of intense emotional experience, the body and mind go through major changes that might be seen as a form of "mass mobilization" in preparation for dealing with an urgent and consuming relationship, such as the appearance of a bear nearby. Such changes, like those caused by an adrenaline rush with all its effects on our brain, heart, muscles, might be sensed and become the basis for much of what we call "feelings." While some of these changes could be considered functional (such as a faster heart beat for a quick escape) others might be seen as by- products or side-effects. The distinction between functional changes and side-effects would depend on one's views of emotions and familiarity with our biological system.

Another explanation is that feelings are a form of communication between various body/mind subsystems and the cognitive subsystem. They "inform" the cognitive subsystem and create awareness of the process of establishing relationships and carrying them through. Since cognition is an active participant in establishing relationships, these sensations might be a type of feedback or information for the purpose of reevaluating the situation and one's positions vis-à-vis the environment, adjusting them, and dealing with possible repercussions. According to Meinong, "Emotions are feelings of pleasure and displeasure whose main function is informational; that is, they inform the experience about the value of objects and events" (as quoted in Reisenzein 2006, 931). Damasio writes ". . . feelings are the mental representation of the physiologic changes that occur during emotions," noting "that an emotion is a neurological process with accompanying feelings, the feeling of what is happening in our brains (Damasio in Manstead, ed., 2004, 52). (See Damasio's articles in the bibliography for excellent and detailed discussions of feelings).

Sensations related to emotions are also shaped by social norms, and in turn help communicate emotions, our internal situation, and our relationships to other members of society. Thus, if we are angry, our feelings together with our behavior send clear signals to the community around us to "watch out," while if we are happy, we feel and communicate very different signals[4].

Beyond communication, feelings, just like the experience of pleasure or pain, go beyond pure information to create incentives and disincentives, positive or negative somatic feedback for certain relationships and elements. This motivation can be viewed as part of our drives, needs, and values, or as a component of the emotions which express and facilitate these directives. Emotions attach or articulate motivational forces that correspond to the desirability of specific ways of relating. For example, fear, anxiety, and shame feel rather awful and act as forms of pain, while joy and happiness feel great and reward us positively.

These qualities, as well as the overall dramatic dimensions of emotions discussed above, make certain emotional experiences highly desirable. This is obvious from the enormous industries which simulate or stimulate desirable emotions through music, books, movies, substances, drugs, and sex.

Thus, we may have a special capacity to sense, be aware of, and be guided by the intensity, desirability, and direction of our relationships and our interdependence with the objects of our relationships. If we are in love, we can sense the reconfiguration of our body/mind and the repercussion of this emotion (for example, pain); we can also feel a force that pulls us with distinct strength toward a particular person or object and motivates us to act in a specific way.

Emotions are called "feelings" because people feel "touched" by them, in the tactile sense, yet lack specific descriptions for them of the sort used for other senses, such as bright light, loud sound, strong smell, good taste, and nice touch. It is clear today that people have many more than the five traditional familiar senses—and we could

4 See Lutz [1986] for a good, detailed discussion of the cultural context of emotions; for more on the subject see Manstead [2004].

probably add to the list sensitivity to weight, balance, and temperature, as well as pain, hunger, exhaustion, nausea, and so forth.

Typical sensations could be viewed as a body/mind sensitivity and reaction to stimuli or environmental variations and changes (including our body itself) in light, sound, smell, and so forth. Those could be seen to also include sensitivity and reactions to various conditions of our body/mind such as its balance, temperature, internal injuries or pressure on skin and organs, and level of sugar in the blood.

Looking at this diversified group of sensations, emotions might be seen to constitute a whole different sensory dimension or subcategory. In some sense, they could be viewed as sensitivity to relational stimuli or variations and changes in our relationships and interdependencies with our environment. Thus, in the same manner that we feel pain when our skin gets cut, we feel some sort of pain or strong discomfort and unpleasant sensation when one of our relationships is cut (for example, loss of a lover or a close friend). Pain can be seen to function as a form of communication, alarm, and disincentive, or as a strong incentive for change. The sensations associated with fear and anxiety might be fulfilling similar functions. They communicate, alarm, and discourage us from remaining in the same unfavorable circumstances and relationship with the object of our fear (for example, a bear, debt, sickness, family danger), and they encourage change.

Although emotions seem to communicate certain signals that raise awareness of changes, these signals defy clear verbal explanation and leave much room for speculation. Since we do not sense emotions in the same clear manner that we sense light and sound, and because we mostly sense subconscious processes and secondary sensations from our body, we are often perplexed as to how we should interpret them. As mentioned before, awareness does not guarantee clarity.

When emotions are intense, we are also so consumed and overpowered by sensations that we may believe sensations to represent all there is to emotions, so that sensation becomes synonymous with the entire phenomenon. (This was the experience of William James.) Intensity of sensation may also be the reason that emotions seem like solely internal experiences. Going back to our foreign policy analogy, we can imagine a child or a poorly informed person living in the U.S.A. before the Second World War. Such a person may not have been clear about the purpose of the country's changes and preparations for the war until the war actually started, and may have assumed that all these processes were solely internal practices and experiences. They would not have realized that these processes were all shaped by the way the U.S. was preparing for war and relating to Germany and Japan.

Clearly, feelings are correlated to and associated with the intensity of emotional relations or events, and are more apparent in situations characterized by imbalances and extremes. In such times, motivation is much more powerful, and internal configuration is more extensive. Attention is highly concentrated, which only intensifies awareness of the change and the "feeling" of it.

Calmer emotions on the other hand, may come with softer sensations, as is the case with "moods." It is typical to sense different types of general or diffused feelings throughout the day, and feel good, bad, stressed, energetic, depressed, happy or impatient. Many of these feelings are probably associated with different emotions, though we might not be aware of the connection, because many of these emotions may be subconscious, less powerful, diffused or escape close attention.

Reflective or utilitarian relationships do not seem to include these kinds of sensations, which is yet another justification for distinguishing them from emotional relationships.

In sum, we have raised a number of possible associations between "feelings" and emotions. First, feelings could simply be a by-product of emotions. Second, feelings might be the sensation of an emotional position or transformation. Third, sensations could be a form of communication between different body/mind subsystems, and particularly between various subsystems and the cognitive subsystem (which might be described as a type of awareness). Fourth, because they are partially shaped by social norms, sensations also help communicate emotions to the environment and guide social behavior. Fifth, sensations act as motivating factors (like pain and pleasure). It is important to keep in mind that these possibilities are not mutually exclusive and can be combined in various ways. Feelings are more apparent in times of intense emotions, but we should not limit our view of emotions to these instances just because they "feel" stronger or are most noticeable. As indicated previously, intensity doesn't always correlate with strength in emotional relationships, and we might have very strong emotions which remain surprisingly calm much of the time (for example, with our children, unless we are suddenly worried about them or mad at them).

Non-emotional Relationships

In the previous section, we discussed some of the special dimensions that characterize emotional ways of relating. While the particular combination and vigor of these aspects can change quite dramatically from one emotional relationship to another, these qualities can be found in most emotional relationships. The characteristics suggested here might be modified, added to, or amplified, but they represent a good start for capturing the key aspects of emotions as relational methods.

In explaining the emotional dimensions above, we partially introduced the possibility of a heuristic distinction between emotional styles of relating and non-emotional, "utilitarian" and "reflective" relationships. We will further discuss this distinction here in the hope that it will help explain what is unique about emotions and amplify the role of the special characteristics outlined earlier.

"Utilitarian" ways of relating refer to a purely instrumental relationship in which we receive goods or services from a person, an animal or an object that we care little about. Therefore, we could easily replace this anonymous object with another like it, or with a machine. For example, we might relate in a utilitarian manner to an ordinary hammer, a cashier in a gas station or a food animal.

"Reflective" ways of relating refer to the way we relate to people, objects, or ideas we know of, but have minor interaction with and care little about (unless combined with utilitarian or emotional aspects). This might include residents of remote locations and countries, geographical locations on earth and in outer space, general trivia, and random facts we have heard (for example, how far the moon is from earth). At times, it might include even people we have to deal with, or "process," with complete indifference, such as individuals in a survey or data bank. Thus, they are left as generic entities or bits of information with which we experience no significant interdependence. Accordingly, we could be said to be indifferent to them, to have little personal attachment or little interest in their future or our relationship with them.

These ways of relating typically do not include all the aspects that characterize the emotional dimension. For example, utilitarian relationships do not involve specificity and feelings. Reflective relationships by themselves do not include the force of motivation, interdependence, bodily sensations or the sense of significance characteristic of emotional relationships.

Utilitarian ways of relating could be seen as analogous to the way flowers and the bees interact for mutual benefit, or the way we use a live bank teller or an ATM machine interchangeably. These relationships have a *generic* quality and exist for the purpose of receiving a service or a product. In the case of a purely utilitarian relationship, we care little about the *specific* partner on the other side of the relationship or our future relationship with this entity. While it is possible to be very concerned about the *function* of a tool or the service of a person, we typically do not really care about the tool itself or the provider of service. These relationships could also be described as categorical ones, with objects whose identity is not essential. This is why we can exchange them rather easily if necessary (for example, a phone operator or a computer), as long as the function is carried out by other tools, people or means. Although we need the service, we don't feel too dependent on its provider.

The recognition of this way of relating is not new, but earlier instances do not clearly realize that this is one of the key differences that distinguishes emotional ways of relating. For example, Heidegger and many scholars thereafter criticize mankind's technology and purely instrumental treatment of the environment and other species such as food and utility animals (Heidegger 1993). This categorization of the global environment as generic, purely functional, and replaceable might be one of the key reasons why many dominant traditional cultures related to it in a utilitarian, almost indifferent manner. This is also why the recent change of attitude toward the environment, and its new perception as unique, irreplaceable, necessary, and beneficial resource or community, has led many of us to relate to it more emotionally and often develop more empathetic and loving relationships with it.

Should we become attached to a "generic" service provider (for example, raise a chicken and give it a name), get to know the service provider well (become familiar with a particular bank teller), or feel dependent on them (recognize the importance of a single difficult immigration officer at the airport), they suddenly become specific and unique. Accordingly, a perception of personal interdependency develops and we may then relate to them emotionally as well, beyond the general need for their service.

Reflective relationships can be compared to the *reflection* of light on a mirror. Even though cognitive theories of emotions question William James for equating emotions with feelings and sensations, a careful reading shows that he has nonetheless made some distinctions similar to the ones proposed here. He states: "If we take away the sensations, we are left with a cold and neutral state of intellectual perception" (James in Solomon 2003, 65). These perceptions sound very much like reflective ways of relating and make a good distinction between emotional ways of relating and other types of relationships.

It is not completely clear why, for example, we consider fear an emotion but not hunger, thirst or simple sexual desire. After all, these involve strong motivational forces, a powerful sense of interdependence, and a clear sensation. However, each of these lacks specificity, which has been identified as one of the critical dimensions of emotions. Namely, hunger comes as a desire to eat something edible, and we probably don't care which particular chicken we eat, making the relationship more generic and utilitarian. The same can happened with a simple sexual need that is satisfied by a visit to a prostitute. The situation becomes very different, however, if we have to consider eating our dog in Antarctica, as some hungry explorers have had to do, or if we start preferring one "commercial" sexual partner to others and caring about him or her. In these cases, we probably have developed an emotional relationship with them *as well* as a utilitarian one, and they have lost their generic position with us.

One way to approach these three types of relationships is to view them as different but equally important, and suggest that they simply fulfill distinct functions. For the purposes of this essay, it is sufficient to identify three categories (although one might slice our vast relational styles into many more different types, according to various theoretical goals). It is important to note that the view proposed here does not require the different types to be mutually exclusive. Namely, more than one type of relationship can be combined in one ongoing interaction. For example, the interaction between a husband and wife could combine all three, since they know each other (reflective), fulfill mutual functions (utilitarian), and have an emotional relationship.

Another way of viewing these types of relationships and their various combinations is to suggest some form of a hierarchical order. We can propose, for instance, that most relationships are first reflective, but under certain conditions they can grow to be utilitarian or even emotional. For example, we might know of a person or an object without ever interacting with or caring about them, which means that we have only a reflective relationship with them. However, if later we find that we need or can use their services, we might transform our relationship to a utilitarian one (by using their services to perform a job for example). If it happens that we get to know them personally and care about them, and not only about their function, it means that our relationships have expanded to the emotional dimension. Dating or marriage may have started with a reflective relationship in which people are introduced and come to know each other, then become a utilitarian one involving cooperation in school or at work, and then evolve to an emotional relationship involving affection and love. It is important to note that emotional relationships necessarily include mutual knowledge and *might* include a utilitarian exchange, but they must also involve the emotional dimensions mentioned before. Stated in reverse, if the elements of interdependence and specificity are added, reflective relationships can turn emotional, manifesting intensity, force, direction, and feelings. Thus, more complex relationships tend to include the simpler ones, but not necessarily the reverse. The hidden assumption is that emotional relationships are more elaborate and complex (not necessarily better), and more conditions are required for them to occur.

In this hierarchical view, emotional relationships are a subcategory of the reflective or utilitarian ones, with some special additional dimensions. In other words, emotional relationships are an expansion or an augmentation of the other relationships, in which a specific stance, position or way of relating develops toward a particular individual, institution or idea when we perceive or experience or foresee the possibility of personal and specific interdependence. We then develop a specific idea and position regarding how we want this element and our relationship with it to evolve; and we feel a particular force between us, with a specific direction and motivation.

Overall, it is important to realize that regardless of how we position these relating styles relative to each other, it is obvious that the division between them is not clear-cut, so that it is often more a question of combination and degree of participation rather than a sharp distinction. Nevertheless, as we hoped, this relational distinction and perspective does help sharpen some of the emotional unique dimensions and aspects.

Evolutionary Speculations: Organisms and Machines

Almost all organisms have ways of relating to their environment. One interesting question is how these ways have developed or diversified during the evolutionary process.

One hypothesis is that, in order to survive, most organisms begin with some simple form of recognition of elements in their environment, and some process that enables them to decide how to relate to them—whether to utilize, protect against, avoid or ignore their presence. Few of these earlier, more instinctual ways of relating could be said to resemble reflective and utilitarian modes. Alternatively, these more instinctual methods might be considered pre-emotional patterns of relating, since they seem like more rudimentary versions of human fear, parental care, and aggression. They might also include an element of social cohesiveness that could be described as duty, say, to offspring, and loyalty to community. It could be debated whether to view these earlier means of relating as utilitarian or as pre-emotional, but it is clear that they are different from our emotional ways of relating. They tend to be instinctive and, accordingly, they are applied categorically and inflexibly. They often lack the dimension of specificity, the complex process of appraising interdependencies, the capacity to customize modes of relating, the diversity, the dynamic nature, and so forth.

With the development of the brain in certain organisms, and the increased complexity of life and society, extra needs emerged, and techniques and skills developed to meet them. For example, higher levels of analysis, manipulation, information, consideration, and commitment in human behavior supplement these basic instincts, learned behaviors, and simple processes (conscious or not). Thus, over time, some simple ways of relating might have evolved to become what we now consider emotions in cognitive organisms. In some cases and contexts, simple ways of relating have been replaced altogether by emotional methods, but it seems that in most instances, emotions have been added or combined with more instinctual modes.

Emotional improvisation vs. complex neuro-chemical algorithms. Some of the biological, neurological descriptions of emotions view the evolution of emotions as a development of neuro-chemical "algorithms" (see Harari 2015). These algorithms are considered simply to get more complex along the evolutionary "ladder."

While we might agree with the increase in complexity, flexibility, and sophistication, the term "algorithms" suggests a mechanism that is too purely rational, pre-programmed, and pattern-like. This model deemphasizes humans' emotional flexibility, the intensity and force of human emotions, and their relational role. It also doesn't shed much light on the social, cultural, and conceptual processes that affect emotions, or on their unique function in the human body/mind, society, and evolution. Namely, it gives an impression of a mechanical evolutionary progression instead of the qualitative change which emotions seemed to have brought about.

Most importantly, whether or not we believe in free will or choose to accept this idea, the basic beauty of flexibility (and the cognition that enables it) lies with people's ability to cope with novel and unexpected situations and conditions, in unique, innovative, personal ways, beyond fixed categories. Thus, if we speculate about relational evolution, emotions could be said to also increase social diversity, and possibly creativity and adaptability. This might have been possible because human communities involved a less centralized, rigid system with many "highly-cognitive" brains (such as those of humans), instead of one, highly centralized or uniform community with many "less-cognitive" brains (such as those of social insects).

However, as people are compelled to join more overpowering and homogeneous institutions (such as work places, corporations, and large nations with strong centralized governments), and are increasingly guided and controlled by them, the difference between human populations and social insects may be shrinking rapidly. Human populations have also expanded in numbers and concentration to such a degree that we may survive increasingly like insects—by mutation and sheer numbers instead of through cognitive solutions and emotional flexibility.

Although biological neuro-chemical and algorithmic descriptions of emotions must be approached with caution, it is nonetheless important to emphasize that emotions do seem to have an instinctual evolutionary base and aspects that are found universally in most people (as Ekman 1994, 2007 and Plutchik 1980, 2002 might argue). Therefore, we have to avoid falling into the other extreme of cultural relativism (Mead 1999), which views emotions as purely cultural. The truth is most probably somewhere in the middle, with some combination of these factors.

More complex needs require more complex relational capacities. An evolutionary perspective suggests that the drives and needs of organisms formulate the way they relate to their environment. Maslow proposes a hierarchy of needs, and there are various related theories. If we accept the basic evolutionary model, we can imagine that the fish's protection of its offspring develops to the level of the bear caring for its cubs, and then to the love humans feel for their children.

The evolutionary outlook on emotions can be traced to Darwin himself (1872, in Solomon 2003), who saw emotions as helpful mechanisms for survival and adaptation. He emphasizes some basic similarities among all human beings as well as between humans and animals. Such similarities seemed to rise from some common instinctual behaviors and expressions. Some of his early claims are controversial today, but many have become the basis for more helpful and sophisticated theories developed by later scholars such as James (1922), Dewey (1958), McDougall (/1960), Ekman (1994, 2007), Plutchik (1980, 2002), Frijda (1986, 2007), Ackerman, Abe, and Izard (Mascolo and Griffin, eds., 1998), and Meyer, Riesenzein, and Schutzwohl (1997).

What portion of our emotional system is instinctual and universal, and what portion is cultural or personal, is a controversial topic and far beyond the scope of this essay. However, for the sake of the relating theory posed here, it is sufficient to assume that the new, intricate, social needs of mammals, and particularly of humankind, along with the increase in mental capacity, led to the development of more shades and types of relational styles. Thus, they have ended up with a large, diversified relational arsenal, a repertoire of relating capabilities, including a wider and more refined, dynamic emotional "tool box."

As we suggested before, not only does human cognitive capacity give us a better ability to analyze our interdependence, but we can also build intricate possible scenarios of mutual influence, existing or desired. We can maintain these scenarios over prolonged periods of time (past and future), and select (mostly in a subconscious manner) whether and how we want to relate (whether emotionally or not, and, if so, which emotion and how intensely). At the same time, we can, and often do change these perceived interdependent scenarios temporarily or permanently.

Most importantly, it is critical to emphasize that humans don't only experience more shades of relationships or more advanced relational skills, but also seem to have more modes, styles or methods of relating, which is what is manifested in the complexity of human emotions and other ways of relating.

The special requirements of social animals and mammals. Beyond this more gradual, incremental aspect of evolutionary human relational development, many researchers argue that emotions develop only, or mostly, in social animals and particularly mammals (Panksepp 2004).

These new emotional capabilities probably evolved not only because they serve the emotional beings, but also the objects of their emotions. Namely, offspring and other members of the family or social group also often require emotional glue: a contract, long-term commitment, empathy, affection, ongoing contact, and emotional communication. It seems necessary for their long-term development and education, safety, sense of security, cohesiveness, affection, and particular needs and treatment.

For example, Harry Harlow's experiment with baby monkeys in the 1950s and many studies thereafter showed clearly that most mammals need positive personal contact and affection to develop well. They need those extra emotional provisions, beyond the simple functional needs of food and safety provided by purely utilitarian methods of relating. (See various studies and hypotheses described in Harlow [1958] *The Nature of Love*; Lewis, Amini and Lannon [2000] *A General Theory of Love*; Solms and Turnbull [2002] *The Brain and the Inner World*; and Harari [2015] *The History of Tomorrow*.)

The cohesive communal role of our emotions. Another interesting evolutionary hypothesis raised by Harari (2015) has to do with people's tendency to believe in common myths that have enabled them to work and cooperate in large groups, and thus to dominate the world. We already mentioned that beyond the ability to relate emotionally to other members of their society (as do many other mammals), people can also relate emotionally to big communal elements, such as nations and other institutions, as well as to abstract notions like God and Humanity. Thus, even though humans can't exactly know all the members of a large community or necessarily empathize with them, they can relate emotionally and develop commitments to large communal notions that bind them all, such as God and Country (that is, patriotism). In other words, we can keep the cohesiveness and cooperation of our huge communities by developing and formalizing large social-relational structures, which are embedded with particular values, promote and enforce them, along with certain emotions and behavior. Most importantly, we can and often do develop emotional connections to these organizations and the ideas that they promote. We either develop certain emotions toward them, are brainwashed, are convinced to love, admire, and serve them with duty and loyalty, or are taught to fear them (say, by being reprimanded, fired or jailed). These types of emotional connections further facilitate the operation and longevity of institutions and ideas.

In discussing biological approaches, we noted that large institutions may contribute to a growing similarity between human communities and those of social insects. Due to the enormous size of our institutions, their concentration, their influence, and the populations that they command, our unique *communal* organizational, cognitive, and emotional tendencies become critically important to the understanding of our culture. They are particularly crucial for our future interactions, values, and emotional development, including our personal and communal well-being. As various institutions progressively overpower our personal values and emotions (causing us to think, for example, "I have to do this because of my job, regardless of my personal values and preferences"; "I only follow orders"; or "I do it for the larger good"), we may nevertheless have progressively more to learn from social insects, in addition to looking at other mammals.

The addition of awareness and language. Along with a more diversified relational and emotional toolkit, humans have developed high cognition, self-awareness, and language—capacities which enable humans to make more and finer distinctions, as well as to identify more shades and types of relationships (which is what this essay is doing). Thus, beyond the growing styles and the number of ways we relate, our awareness and language actually enable us to have more emotions as well as give us the impression that we have even more. The more developed our general knowledge and vocabulary to describe our life, the more refined are our distinctions and categorizations of elements in the environment and the emotions which are available for us to relate to them. Accordingly, we can relate to more elements (as we separate wider groups and categories into finer multiple smaller ones), as well as have more nuances or ways of relating to them. At the same time, because of linguistic proliferation in the discussion of emotions (larger and more diversified vocabulary in a familiar and explored area), the more emotions we think we have. In other words, the more we develop as human beings, as persons throughout life, and the more we "study" emotions (not necessarily in a scientific way), the more emotions we can practice, and the more names we have for them.

Greater evolutionary development isn't necessarily better or more moral. According to an evolutionary hypothesis, utilitarian relationships appear to be more basic and seem to reflect an earlier stage of evolution, while emotional ways of relating are assumed to have come later, along with the availability of more flexible cognitive "powers" and more complex social needs. It is important to emphasize that this view is not only an unproven hypothesis, but that it also should not be taken to imply that emotions are somehow a better means of relating. Just because emotions were developed later and are more complex doesn't mean that they necessarily lead to better moral practices or increased well-being. Some, like Hume, argue that emotions have made morality and empathy possible; however, it is also possible that higher cognitive and relational capacity lead to more hatred and wars, to more worries and anxiety, and to more emotional problems and pathology. As we all know, the more complex the system, the more can go wrong with it, which is what most of our psychologists are occupied with.

Unfortunately, purely utilitarian, non-emotional relationships can also be problematic and encourage exploitation, indifference, and other forms of sociopathic behavior. These can be horrifying, particularly when it comes to the treatment of individuals by large organizations such as corporations, governments, and opposing nations. The hope is that an improved understanding of relational dynamics and a better choice of values might enable our complex system to attain greater balance among the different types of relationships and lead to more desirable moral performance.

The possible lack of emotions in organisms and machines. Since we are already speculating about the evolution of emotions, we might as well hypothesize about the impact of a lack of emotions (a scenario we sometimes find in books and movies). The absence of emotions is often attributed to organisms that people consider "cold-blooded" (such as bacteria or fish), or to computers and futuristic machines.

If we discuss less cognitive organisms, we should first decide arbitrarily which forms of relating and relationships we include in the emotional category, and which we will consider instinctual or non-emotional reactions. For example, is a bird's care for its offspring an emotion? We must choose whether the answer to this question is a matter of complexity, some qualitative standard, or a heuristic preference.

The evolutionary hypothesis mentioned above distinguishes less cognitive organisms with purely utilitarian or pre-emotional ways of relating from more cognitive organisms with additional emotional capabilities. A similar distinction differentiates between hard-wired, automatic drives or reactions, and complex, cognitive responses supposedly based on free will. Yet we can differentiate organisms that relate only categorically to objects of relationship—offspring or mate—from organisms that can also relate to specific elements in a particular way and change each relationship momentarily. For human beings, it is clear that the element of self-awareness or conscious thought constitutes a major difference in terms of emotional behavior. However, it is hard to claim that self-awareness is an essential part of our emotions and that emotions are uniquely human. This is particularly obvious when your dog is so happy to see you coming, so disappointed if you don't take it on a walk, and so sad to see you leaving.

Overall it seems that human beings still combine most, if not all, of the various ways of relating—the basic and primitive as well as the complex and sophisticated. Thus, the dividing line among organisms is gray, unclear, and more a question of degree than of sharp separation. The evolutionary difference actually seems more like a spectrum, showing endless shades of complexity and skills, and indicating different combinations of methods and styles of relating that befit the varying needs of different organisms.

Likewise, if we delve into a more current discussion and examine the question of emotions and machines, computers, and artificial intelligence, we may also face a difficult task. For example, we need to wonder about the machines' values, drives, and particular preferences, which their emotions are supposed to express and enhance. We also have to speculate about their ability to form and change endless specific ways of relating to a multitude of elements according to scenarios of interdependence (instead of on the basis of pre-programmed relational categories). Similar questions will arise regarding their commitment to various relationships, motivation for actions, and specific behavior, or their use of rationality to sort through endless options.

Another typical association with the lack of emotions is a pathological absence of empathy observed among some psychopaths, sociopaths, machines, certain institutions or in other such pathological cases. However, a closer look may reveal that some of these entities show an emotional pathology, but not a complete absence of emotions. For example, a sociopath who appears to lack empathy may demonstrate other emotions such as love for their dog or certain forms of happiness and depression. Unfortunately, many people or organizations seem capable of killing or directly order the killing of millions despite the presence of emotions (for example, Hitler loved his dog).

One common view assumes that a lack of emotions will lead to calm, rational cognitive processing and thus to more peaceful behavior and a more peaceful life as a whole (this was the view of the Stoics). However, this view may confuse a reduction in the intensity of emotions with their possible disappearance.

At the risk of being highly speculative, a supposed lack of emotions will not only make people or other entities emotional calmer and more rational; it will void them of most of their key relational capabilities and skills. If we eliminate the higher, more cognitive emotional skills, and reduce humans to social insects, say, we might be left with a categorical, generic, instinctual relational map in which everybody and everything is viewed as a utility or instrumental element to be used, consumed, avoided, or mated with, for purely functional purposes. This would eliminate the personal, customized relational ability that gives us the capacity to relate in unique ways to numerous elements and change them quickly as needed.

It will not leave us with much empathy, compassion or love, and thus will eliminate much of our morality and ethics, as well as our ability to form other long-term social commitments and sacrifices. However, it might also eliminate our massive hatred and our race toward the global nuclear destruction of all life.

More likely though, if emotions are viewed as an evolutionary continuation of more basic relational capabilities and skills, it could be speculated that their full elimination would lead quickly to the elimination of the forms of life that depend upon them. For instance, people and other organisms would lose all their relational skills, including fear and love, and thus not run from danger or raise offspring upon which survival depends.

As indicated earlier in this essay, emotions and other relational methods and choices express, manifest, and serve the promotion of our values. Unless programmed, machines do not have values and thus also don't have specific preferences and biases, which are then served by the appropriate relationships to their environment. If for instance we endow or program machines with certain "life-like" values, such as survival and reproduction, we then need to program them to relate to everything in such a manner that these relationships will serve and promote these values. We will also have to ensure that any variations and changes in these relationships will affect these machines themselves (physically but also internally/sensationally). One can go on speculating about the lack of emotions, but it would clearly result in more dramatic changes than just calmer, more rational behavior, as the Stoics assumed.

Though fascinatingly interesting, these questions are clearly beyond the scope of this essay and, should be discussed more comprehensively in future studies. (See a very good treatment of these issues in Harari's [2015].)

Considering the limited knowledge this essay brings to question of evolutionary development and emotional development, the goal here is simply to apply the new relational approach to formulate some questions and possible hypotheses, in the hope that better-informed and -equipped research efforts will come along to tackle these issues in more depth.

Different Dynamics: Adding a Chemical Image to the Neurological Model

We have shown thus far some of the special dimensions that distinguish emotional relationships from other phenomena or styles of relating. However, it seems that emotions not only differ in their conceptual characteristics, but they may also diverge in the way they operate, or in their internal logic and dynamics.

One of these operational differences may be approached through biological studies of emotions (Panksepp 1982, Sousa 1990). These often point toward a possible distinction between the neurological system, which is described as a "fast" system, and the chemical hormonal system, which is described as a "slower" system (Lewis, Haviland and Barrett 2008, 163). "Emotions are *bioregulatory reactions . . . .* They are constituted by a *patterned collection of chemical and neural responses* that the brain produces when it detects the presence of an emotionally competent stimulus" (Damasio in Manstead, ed., 2004, 50). These two systems are shown to be highly connected and to work closely together, but at the same time each seems to have some important, unique properties, and they can, to a degree, carry on independently of each other.

According to this model, the neurological subsystem processes stimuli by moving and sending signals in complex neurological circuits, but the basic channel or process is a quick, electrical/chemical motion along nerve cells. By comparison, the chemical, hormonal subsystem works by spreading specific chemicals (for example, adrenalin) in the body and brain, and these influence the function of different subsystems, including the neurological ones. For example, they affect the chemical transmission between nerve cells, increase excitation of neurological circuits and specific organs, inhibit them or bias their functioning in various directions.

If we view emotional process as also having chemical/hormonal characteristics, we can also imagine that emotional configurations act more like the diffusion of a drop of paint on a piece of fabric. Namely, they diffuse in all directions, permeate other subsystems, do not only run along specific lines, and do not have a precise "on/

off" switching (unlike electricity running along electrical lines, or stimulus along nerves). If emotional internal configuration and preparations also spread like dye, the principle of their working, or their "inner logic" and dynamics, could be different. Namely, they might differ from familiar, reflective, symbolic or logical thought processes, which run more along nerve channels and circuits, even when associations are concerned. This is perhaps why hydraulic analogies for emotions are common in most cultures, why in India their distribution is analogous to the diffusion of dye (Solomon 1995), and why in English we say that emotions "color" our perceptions. Solomon discusses this analogy in his writings about emotions (Solomon 1995, 196). He gives the example of the common use of this metaphor in Buddhism, in which emotions, and particularly calmness, are equated with calm water or ocean (*Citta*). This same understanding could be extended to chakra centers of energy and the whole philosophy of "chi." In the West we find it in the traditional images of the humors and the flowing passions. These depictions were adopted by early psychologists like Freud, as well as by more recent ones, as well-exemplified in the notion of "flow" (Csikszentmihalyi 1990).

The analogy of the hormonal/chemical subsystem makes it is easier to explain how emotions might "mass mobilize" most of our body/mind subsystems, change our overall mode of interaction (that is, our overall disposition), and alter our relations with elements in our environment. It could also be easier to see why, as we said above, we feel certain emotions even after the logical reason for them is gone (for example, fear after avoiding an accident, or anger that lingers after a conflict has been resolved). The chemicals might spread quickly after the initial cognitive analysis, but perhaps take longer to clear out of the system. Pure logical thought by comparison, while it may turn off quickly, might also be more limited in its scope, linear, and restricted to specific connections and actions.

This dimension of emotions also helps explain why emotions are not only evoked and affected by perceptual changes. They also seem to rise and be influenced by drugs and substances as well as by other external stimulus like music, smells, exercise, health conditions, and so forth. These factors can change perceptual processes and the general way we relate. They can affect diffused emotions and moods, as well as trigger associations and encourage us to relate to specific elements in particular ways (consider focused emotions like hate).

This neurological versus hormonal/chemical comparison has some similarity to Epstein's (1999) CEST model or to Kahneman's (2011) distinction between fast and slow reactions or thinking processes (also see Solomon 2016). Similar to Kahneman's view, this comparison demonstrates interesting variations and differences in the patterns of our psychological workings.

For the purposes of this essay, it is not important to determine whether, and how exactly, the hormonal subsystem is tied to our emotional relationships, or which specific biochemical substances influence specific emotions. This is not an empirical biological essay and the hormonal subsystem is mentioned here primarily to provide a heuristic model for considering emotional behavior. In general, the tendency to make dualistic distinctions often limits comprehension of our much more complex, multivariable, multidimensional, interwoven, non-linear systems. However, here we hope to exemplify how the actual human biological subsystem might work according to another logic that is very different from computer-based paradigms of neurological, cognitive, reflective processes that are currently popular. Given this possibility, the hormonal subsystem may offer a good alternative, an additional model or metaphor, for viewing emotional behavior (Lakoff and Johnson 1980, 1999). At the same time, it is important to bear in mind that all metaphors have limits, and to avoid getting too stuck on any particular, currently popular one. Unfortunately, models tend to become quickly outdated, as have those based on the clock, electrical machines, computers, AI, or even on rationality.

In sum, the inner working proposed here implies that emotional relationships may differ not only in their characteristics, but also in their operating principles, logic, and dynamics.

Part B: Applying the New View to Selected Emotional Questions

4

Emotions as a Diversified Category

Though it is obvious when we think about it, many seem to forget, or never completely realize, the fundamental difference between terminology or the explanatory models and the "real life" phenomena we are trying to describe. In the case of emotions, it is particularly important to remind ourselves again and again that real life processes and patterns are much less distinct in scope and time than the typical terminology and language used to describe them.

Relationships, interactions, actions, behavior, processes or events are complex, multifaceted, blurry, interconnected systems, internally and externally. They are also intricate, continuous, connected, infinitely diversified, and ever-changing. Therefore, our cognitive, linguistic/verbal choices for dissecting, categorizing, defining, distinguishing, and analyzing real-life phenomena like relationships are bound to be somewhat arbitrary and simplified. Considering our limited knowledge of the brain, they are also necessarily based partially on guess-work and many assumptions. On top of it all, our terminology and descriptions are also dependent on, and limited by, past models, culture (Lutz 1986, Russell 1991, Nussbaum 2001, Mesquita and Markus in Manstead, ed., 2004), analytical intentions (that is, what we want to prove), and pre-existing vocabulary. The relationship between a husband and a wife after 50 years is a multitude of interconnected emotions, memories, actions, opinions, considerations, obligations, expectations, and much more. This comes on top of being connected through other relationships such as those with children and friends. In this sense, life perhaps is better described as a "soup" rather than as a "box of chocolates" with various distinct portions. Namely, our ability to discern the components (ingredients) and the interactions among them is highly limited and arbitrary. In the "real world soup of life," there are no pure emotions like love or anger, or pure thoughts or actions. These are only categories and names chosen to artificially distinguish and parse partial segments of live phenomena. In any case, it is not clear whether we completely understand or even fully comprehend many of our complex psychological, philosophical systems. No matter how much we perfect our categorizations and models, they will always remain drastically simplified reductions of real life. Once this is accepted and kept in mind, we must continue to try to improve the sophistication of our models in the confined world of words (with the occasional help of music and images). Unfortunately, we do not yet have many better alternative methods to explain, depict, communicate, and discuss such phenomena.

All in all, people have a multitude of emotions, different people have different ones, and they all change over time, presenting an infinite and ever-changing matrix, which may explain scholars' observations regarding the extreme diversity of emotions (Barrett 2007, 2016, Barrett and Russell 2015, and many more). Each emotion is different as each relationship is different, while each person has different interpretations or analyses of what they feel or observe in others, and how others observe them. Thus, when we name two relationships as loving ones, it is obvious that these are almost certainly slightly different types of love or even markedly divergent. They might also not be considered love at all by another person or in another culture (depending on their understanding and definition of love). These determinations might even be different for the same loving persons as their moods or views change.

When it comes to nonspecific, diffuse emotions such as happiness, depression or moods, it is still harder to decipher the emotion involved or to agree on its characteristics unless it is highly intense. This is true in part because these emotions tend to depend on general assessments and evaluations, and it is hard to understand what they are "about." They are also triggered more easily by external stimuli like music, exercise, and drugs, or by the domination of intense events and emotions, which we will describe below as a "spillover" effect.

When considering diffuse emotions, we are not only dealing with different emotions, but probably with different subgroups within the category that may share some of the typical emotional characteristics but differ in others. It is possible, for instance, that focused emotions are more clearly relational, while diffused emotions constitute a less relational subcategory. Alternatively, this diffused group may involve a different assessment process and relational method. Diffused emotions may represent a particular way of relating to overall situations, circumstances, periods, and "states of affairs." Thus they tend to combine or express various assessments of multiple variables and their overall dynamic interactions and/or equilibrium. This might be part of our complex route to happiness and other moods (see Hade's forthcoming monograph on Happiness).

The view of emotions as numerous, diversified, ongoing ways of relating that constitute relationships raises many new questions. The best classifications and terminology for describing the way emotions operate, are grouped or maintain consistency over time, despite their ongoing change, are not so clear. Besides the question of nonspecific emotions and moods, people often wonder what to consider emotional, since events are typically considered "emotional" only if their intensity is high. Similar questions arise regarding our ability to practice multiple emotions simultaneously and carry them over prolonged periods of time.

The following discussion attempts to consider some of these questions with the help of our new relational view. This effort will hopefully reconcile some seemingly conflicting aspects of emotions as well as propose some initial typology, categorization, and terminology. Though this preliminary discussion is simplified and incomplete, the hope is that these initial attempts will provide examples and an incentive for further study and discussion of these issues.

Short-Term Emotional Events

Traditionally, emotions have been seen as high-intensity, out-of-control events, and the higher the arousal level, the more "emotional" those experiences seem to be. When we see people having an intense reaction, we describe them as being "very emotional." This is why many theorists include only brief, intense experiences in the emotional category, and consider the rest a form of evaluation, judgment, orientation, opinions or beliefs (Sorrentino and Higgins 1996).

Emotional multitasking, alternating emotions, and multifaceted emotions. All of us experience some form of emotional connection with a range of elements in our environment, such as family members, friends, different objects, and ideas. In addition, most of us experience intense emotional events daily or weekly—some form of attraction, anger, frustration, anxiety, fear, guilt or joy.

One option for viewing these various experiences is to consider that people are capable of carrying out relationships with numerous elements, simultaneously or in close proximity, and that many of these relationships include (or express) emotional dimensions. Typically, when we are calm, we are able to juggle many relationships with many elements at once or to alternate quickly between them, and thus it is possible to experience many different emotions closely together. For example, at a party it is possible to talk to many people and to relate emotionally to each one in a different way. We can talk to one person we love, to another we have always been attracted to, and to yet another we secretly hate. In this type of situation, it could be said that we are in a state of *"emotional multitasking,"* and we seem capable of maintaining several emotional relationships of variable low intensities.

Beyond having multiple emotional relationships with various elements in our environment, it seems rather obvious that people can also experience multiple emotions toward one element *over time.* For example, we might love our children or spouse and still be angry at them occasionally. These relationships are characterized by *"alternating emotions."* We will develop this idea further in the discussion of long-term emotions below.

However, it is possible to feel confused or conflicted by the experience of having multiple emotions toward an individual, situation or another element *at the same time.* For example, we might appreciate our boss, respect and admire him or her, but at the same time feel fear of this person, experience jealousy or resentment, and so forth. We can describe such an experience as *"emotional multiplicity"* or as a *"multifaceted emotion."*

As noted earlier, much emotional relating is determined by unconscious mental processes, and though we may be somewhat aware of these processes, the unconscious element can create a sense of obscurity and confusion. Furthermore, relationships are not necessarily confined to socially accepted categories that are readily verbalized, such as love or fear. Clearly, they are not always limited to a single emotional tag. If the relationship and interactions are complex and multifaceted, they may frequently combine components of different emotions, giving us the impression of multiple emotions or multifaceted emotions toward the same object at that same time. If we continue to consider emotions as methods or ways of relating, it might be more helpful and appropriate to describe complex relationships as multifaceted rather than as composed by a multiplicity of emotions.

This type of relationship exemplifies yet again the existence of a very complex, dynamic, diversified emotional ability which might not be fully captured by verbal explanations, but which illustrates well the view proposed here: namely, that humans possess highly sophisticated, flexible relational skills that support multiple and intricate ways of relating, and different types of relationships.

Emotional concentration and emotional biases. The dimension of force, which has been introduced as a characteristic of emotion, can vary considerably in intensity, depending partially on the changing significance of the object of emotion and the general arousal level. The level of significance and arousal are in turn influenced by fluctuating perceptions of the extent of interdependence with this object (another of the characteristics attributed to emotion).

In some instances (usually for a short time), it may seem that one of our emotional relationships becomes so significant and consuming that it takes most of our attention and dominates our overall orientation and behavior. Typically, this intensity is triggered by the appearance of a sudden, urgent, and significant new element (for example, the appearance of a shark), or by a marked change in an existing relation (such as a sudden nasty and impolite remark by our boss). This intense emotional reaction can bring about a high level of arousal and influence most of our body/mind subsystems. It may even result in a total transformation of our whole body/mind system (that is, its configuration), in an attempt to deal with this situation in a specialized way. This configuration could be viewed as a state of *"emotional concentration"* that typically competes with the capacity for emotional multitasking described above.

This emotional intensity goes beyond the typical concentration of attention and activity demanded by a specific task or a job, such as sports or work. The more intense this convergence, the more it also biases our thinking and our motivation in a very specific, predetermined, subconscious way (*Handbook of Emotions* 1993). Namely, it not only changes what we think about, but how we think and feel about it. It can also alter our behavior and the way we relate to other seemingly unrelated elements. For example, if we find ourselves suddenly in a panic over a certain condition, not only do we think about it all the time, but the fear tends to grow and distort all other possible scenarios and possibilities. It also changes the significance of all other issues in our life and the way we relate to everybody and everything else, even if they are supposedly unrelated to this particular fear. The same could be said for intense love or infatuation, an extreme fit of anger or other such intense emotional occasions.

We will demonstrate later how cognition and rationality do not necessarily disappear or diminish in times of intense emotions as is commonly believed, but rather seem to change in order to accommodate this specific emotional or relational mode and need. "When we feel a strong emotion, our thinking is organized to serve that emotion . . ." (Ekman as quoted in Manstead 2004, 127).

We can revisit our military analogy, with its alert levels and emergency states. In calm times, the military has routine patterns and behaviors that involve functioning in a multitasking state. It deals, on an ongoing basis and in a regular manner, with various tensions and conflicts around the world. However, as a particular situation becomes more demanding and moves up the alert status, the military reorganizes and moves more and more of its resources and attention in a specific direction (for example, toward crisis in the Middle East or North Korea). It performs with a higher level of concentration and mobilization. Just as a state of high alert is typically brief, intense emotions tend to be of short duration; and since they are temporary, they do not create fixed marks on our long-term network of meaning.

However, as history has demonstrated many times before, "temporary" modes of high alert can often last a long time, and can in some cases even become permanent, a consideration that will be discussed in relation to long-term emotions (for example, cases of prolonged anxiety, or frequent rage). It is easy to assume that certain people in certain periods tend to "run up" the alert levels quicker than others and experience intense emotional episodes more frequently. Depending on one's view of the necessity of these reactions to a particular set of circumstances, some of these might be viewed as *too* intense and *too* frequent, particularly if they cause serious emotional difficulty or even a pathology which require therapy.

Thus, in times of intense emotions, most of our physical and mental subsystems seem to be completely ***biased, aimed, and "mass-mobilized"*** in a specific direction, and they are more ***committed to a desired outcome***. "We evaluate what is happening in a way that is consistent with the emotion we are feeling, thus justifying and maintaining the emotion. . . . Our attention is focused and narrowed in a way that serves the emotion we are feeling" (Ekman 2004). This is why, in situations of emotional intensity, we seem to have a "one-track mind" and to be less open to contemplating alternative tasks, alternative views or general theorizing about the situation. All of these alternatives or secondary considerations may be perceived as a distraction from the narrow task at hand. "Once they begin, emotions change how we see the world and how we evaluate the actions of others" (Ekman 2004, Frijda 2000, Lazarus 1991).

Lack of control. In addition to the prevailing tendency to contrast intense emotions with cognition and rationality, there is also an emphasis on the sense of helplessness that accompanies emotion or on the lack of control in these instances (for example, one can't help "this 'crazy' love" or outraged anger).

When a person is madly in love, the person may realize the need to act slightly "cool" and uninterested, yet can't help acting anxious and highly interested. The same can be observed in the behavior of an amorous couple, such as Romeo and Juliet.

The idea of what constitutes personal emotional control varies dramatically across cultures and philosophies. However, in most cases it tends to be associated with conscious behavior in line with social norms, and with the capacity to be guided by a "logical/rational" calculation of risk and benefit. For most of us, it also presumes a match between our perception of our real feelings and actions, and how we think we should feel and behave. However, intense emotions tend to express strong subconscious drives and motivations that can overpower more conscious, typical social norms. We therefore often perceive in these instances a strong discrepancy—a gap—between our feelings and behavior, and what is deemed socially or commonly "appropriate." Much of this sense of having no control may be the result of this perception of discrepancy and our limited ability to control our subconscious drives and the emotions that express them. This will be further explained later when discussing the interactions between emotions and values or rationality[5].

---

5 More about such "gaps" can be found in Multiple Discrepancies Theories of Well-Being [Michalos 1985], as well as in theories of arousal and motivation [Sorrentino 1996] and other such studies. See also Solomon 2003, Hade forthcoming monograph on Happiness.

Spill-over effect and the idea of diffuse emotions, moods, and "global disposition." We noted above that the greater the emotional bias of our cognition, the more it affects the way we filter incoming information, the way we make connections between elements in our environment, the "reality models" we build of past and present, and the future scenarios we construct (for a more detailed empirical study see Hoffman 1986). For example, if we are angry (say, if we just lost a job), we mostly see things that correspond to this emotion, or see them in a way that confirms the emotion. Thus, intense emotional episodes seem to have a **"spill-over"** effect that is often described as a "coloring" of overall perception or mood.

Our earlier hypothesis suggested that, besides emotional relationships with specific elements, we also have what might be described as overarching emotional relationships with the environment as a whole, with life in general, or with our overall position or progress in it (either at that moment or over time). These relationships might be described as a global disposition marked by general, non-specific, diffused emotions (such as happiness or depression) or moods. These moods change frequently even in times of calm emotions, but they are obviously further affected by intense ones.

Since these moods mobilize, influence, and bias overall orientation, they often transfer or spill over, so that they manifest in unexpected channels and occasions that seem to affect *other* relationships and emotions as well. For example, you end up fighting with your son, boyfriend or spouse over a ridiculous, benign subject, only to realize that you were actually simply hungry and tired at the time, or upset about work that had little, or nothing, to do with the arguments at home. Thus, strongly dominating emotions such as fear or anger, as well as physiological conditions such as stress, exhaustion, hunger, pain, or the influence of substances or drugs such as alcohol can alter seemingly unrelated interactions. In a sense, it is similar to our previous example of the military in a state of emergency. Such situations can lead to higher levels of suspicion and overly exaggerated reactions to otherwise harmless situations.

In some ways, the spill-over effect seems to contradict the dimension of specificity as a characteristic of emotions, which we proposed are mostly aimed at specific elements. However, these dominating emotions do typically start with particular items and not with general categories or generic, interchangeable elements. They seem to affect an individual's global disposition or mood, which again is related to a specific situation at the time. Last but not least, diffuse emotions don't so much spread beyond the general categories assigned to emotions as they blur across certain periods or contexts. For example, diffuse emotions retain the element of specificity, and do not lose their specificity to become non-emotional relationships or utilitarian relationships; but they do stretch to extend to seemingly unrelated objects, just because of their proximity in time or their context, so that an individual who just happens to be around, or a situation that occurs soon after a significant emotional trigger, may become implicated.

As human beings, we are able to perform parallel processing better than most computers. However, it is important to realize that, at times, our processes may be simultaneous, but not necessarily as independent of each other as parallel processing might imply.

Notions of emotional states or modes. At the time of an intense emotional episode, many body/mind subsystems seem to be affected or mobilized so that an individual behaves in a particular manner. For a lack of a better term, we can view these overall configurations as different "modes" or "states." In such instances, everything about us changes and is reconfigured to deal in a very specific way with the relationship at hand (for example, fear when we are running away from a bear). Our previous analogy of military states of emergency or responses to high alert levels remains relevant here.

It also seems that in such contexts (particularly urgent ones), a quick, predetermined, overall "packaged preparation" helps us get ready for a specific task and situation as quickly and fully as possible. For instance, such situations can be a sudden, critical threat, an unanticipated physical or emotional loss or gain of importance, a sexual encounter, a fierce hunger, a forceful rage or a greatly embarrassing event. The mobilization that occurs at these times is a way of putting the overall organism in a special state or *modus operandi*. "In brief, even in this oversimplified description, an emotion is a complicated matter: a collection of preparatory body changes and ensuing behaviors that is accompanied by a particular style of mental operation. . . . As an emotional **state** gets established, a number of thoughts congruent with the emotion are also evoked" (Damasio 2004, Manstead, ed., 2004). Prinz also indicates that emotions are "perceptions of the body's preparation for action" (Prinz 2004, 228). Many other experts view emotions as a state of readiness for action or a change of readiness (Frijda 1986, 19-20, Oatley 1992).

In this view, powerful emotional episodes could initiate preset patterns of change or prearranged configurations that are partially instinctive and partially learned, but once triggered, come as a whole "package deal" to affect our body/mind. Different emotions induce different modes.

In some narrow sense, emotional modes, and particularly intense ones, are somewhat similar to other whole body/mind modes such as sleep, exhaustion, hypnosis, and the influence of drugs. Those also affect our whole body/mind operation, our overall global disposition, and our cognitive processes.

The division of various types of emotions into "states" and the depiction of "modes" is useful because its heuristic clarity supports ease of discussion; but this model is obviously another simplification. Body/mind emotional configurations change more along a *spectrum* of intensity (instead of occurring dichotomously or at distinct levels), and they could probably be better described in terms of degrees, rather than as separate floors in a building (see Graham 2014 for a similar "continuum of intensity"). The stronger the significance and urgency of the leading relationship, the deeper and narrower the concentration (mind and resources), the more intense the emotional reaction (even momentarily), and the more extreme or total the transformation. Body/mind subsystems also change constantly and don't freeze in one state or mode for too long a time. They are dynamic, not static, as the term "state" might imply.

Nevertheless, these images emphasize a more holistic view of our interactions and relationships, and acknowledge an inclusive physical and mental change that is closer to the notion proposed here, that emotions are a complete, whole, body/mind arrangement that involves thought, physiological preparation or response, feeling, motivation, reconfiguration of the mind, and so forth. Thus, it takes us beyond both a more "componential view" and purely cognitive, psychological explanations and metaphors.

In sum, some of the more apparent characteristics of intense emotional events are an increase in our mental concentration, a rise in the focus and direction of our energy and other bodily systems, highly specific cognitive biases, elevated motivation for a particular behavior, and an extended effect on other relationships. Sensations make us consciously aware of these internal changes and the state of heightened motivation, and specific emotional behavior informs our environment of this transition.

As we will further discuss below, most of what has been proposed above seems relevant to all emotional relationships, including the calmer ones, though these characteristics may only be apparent when emotions are more extreme and arousal is high. Though they are often considered less emotional, calmer emotional relationships still share most of the basic and unique dimensions of emotions proposed here. Therefore, they remain distinct from cognitive, reflective, utilitarian ways of relating, and can best be understood as part of the emotional category.

Long-Term Emotional Relationships

Thus far we have looked at both calm emotional states and intense, short-term emotional events from a relational view and considered some of the cognitive and behavioral configurations typical in such circumstances. But how does the relational approach bear on the controversial topic of long-term emotions?

When describing the length of emotions and relationships, we must distinguish between the immediate duration of emotions and their overall lifespan. Duration refers to the extent (minutes or hours) of a particular, continuous emotional event. However, an emotional relationship that spans over a long time (months or years), is better described by the word "term."

Long-term emotional relationships, such as those that constitute a life-long love or years of animosity, differ from relationships defined by transitory emotions in more ways than just the extent of time. Long-term emotions seem more cognitive and more dependent on judgments and evaluations, they are often interrupted or discontinuous, and in many cases they lack the high level of excitement and the physical sensations so evident in more intense emotions of shorter duration.

Cognitive evaluations and judgments. When people talk about a long-term emotion, they often engage in an *evaluation* of a relationship or a person's life. Frequently, if we say that someone is generally "a happy person" or "had a happy life," we are in fact evaluating the person's life as "good," based on some impression of frequency of this emotion or "ease" of practice. This is how a couple can conclude, for example, that they are in love even though they fight and are angry at each other most of the time. When considering long-term emotions, we assess an emotional history or an overall quality and determine the most dominant or pervasive emotion for this person or interaction. This difference is reflected in the recent U.N. distinction between long-term happiness (more evaluative) and short-term happiness (a more experiential sense of joy). These kinds of assessments are based on cognitive processes such as judgments and evaluations. They could be said to define intellectual constructs rather than immediate emotional experiences or relationships of the kind we have discussed thus far, which have been characterized as including force, sensations, and so forth.

Because long-term emotions involve such evaluations, they are often left outside the category of emotions by scholars (for example, William James would not include them because they lack sensations), and they are frequently viewed alongside more cognitive phenomena such as evaluations, judgments, assessments, orientations, and attitudes.

However, it seems that some long-term emotions are not merely evaluative, logical constructs. Some actually share common elements with short-term emotions and demonstrate most of the characteristics ascribed to emotions. For example, characteristics like force, intensity, and sensation are very familiar in the long-term love for children, spouse, pets, or in other situations that involve long-term emotional relationships.

The more cognitive, evaluative quality ascribed to long-term emotions derives in part from the difficulty of identifying, classifying, and constructing a historical emotional pattern. Like any other long-term historical process or pattern, it is a delicate, often controversial, sorting out and reenactment of many past experiences. It is not necessarily the case that the actual emotional experiences were less experiential and more evaluative (as in the love of a lover) so much as it is that after-the-fact figuring and labeling may be somewhat like describing a dream after we wake up. (See Epstein 1999 and Kahneman 2011 for more about this distinction.)

The problem of characterizing emotion might be less common in emotions of short duration, but it is not really rare. For example, it is not uncommon for passionate lovers (especially those who are young and inexperienced) to be initially confused by their own emotions and in conflict with the opinions of all those who surround them. However, intense emotions of short duration display more obvious "symptoms," dominate attention, and are continuous—characteristics that make them easier to read or agree on. Long-term emotions, on the other hand, are often less clear (characterized by fewer physical sensations), less dominating, and are always interrupted and mixed with other emotions (for example, anger with a much-loved child). Thus, long-term emotions leave more room for complex or contrasting summation, interpretations, identification, and labeling. These activities are more cognitive and add a more cognitive dimension to long-term emotions.

Nonetheless, this does not mean that long-term emotional relationships are less emotional than short-term emotional relationships. On the contrary, as we are going to show later, in many other ways some long-term emotions stand even further from conscious cognitive processes than short-term emotions and display even more characteristics that might be considered uniquely emotional.

Continuity, patterns, and multifaceted relationships. What provides continuity (even if an interrupted one) for long-term emotions is their close connection with meaning and significance, a characteristic shared by all emotions and a defining factor in the way we relate to particular individuals and situations. Clearly, persons or objects with high significance and a special meaning persist in our memory over time. (This is described in psychology as bearing an "affective tag," in Fiske and Pavelchak 1986, 167-203.) It is possible to describe these emotions as a type of pattern defined by many short-duration but consistent emotional incidents over time. From this perspective, we can perhaps view them as "recurrent emotions" or "patterns of emotional relationship." Thus, people could be described as afraid of flying if they experience fear most times they fly, or they may be assumed to love their children if they feel this way most of the time when they interact with them, even if this feeling is periodically mixed with other emotions and not continuous (Manstead 2004). Even mixed feelings can be still viewed as part of an ongoing, consistent pattern, in the same way a journey, cultural development or motion, is made up of smaller segments and can be occasionally interrupted.

Kahneman's idea of the "narrative self," which is also discussed at length in Harari's (2015) book, seems pertinent. He describes the tendency or ability of the "narrative self" to add an ongoing story and a sense of continuity for a life that would otherwise seem like a series of disconnected experiences and events undergone by the "experiential self."

Once we establish a way of relating to a specific person or element, every time we think of or interact with them, the same type of position, configuration or attitude comes back as our prevailing emotion with regard to this individual or situation. Clearly, over time, our emotion toward a particular person or circumstance can change. For example, we might fall out of love. However, emotions can be fairly consistent over a long period of time and have all the dimensions of short-term emotions. In other words, long-term emotions can still be a subconscious way of relating that manifests force and direction, a sense of interdependence, specificity, and even physical sensations. The love of one's children demonstrates this, every time we are worried about them or proud of them.

Thus, some of our long-term emotions are more than just a cognitive formulation or an accidental accumulation of emotional incidents; they include subconscious patterns that are internally cohesive, consistent, and often persistent into perpetuity. Long-term as well as short-term emotions fit with the view that emotions are a special way of relating which, once established, can be triggered each time we encounter a person or situation, particularly if the situation or person behaves in familiar ways.

Combining Long-Term Relationships with Other Relationships and Other Emotions

Because we are required to relate to many elements over time, we cannot be occupied with one relationship continuously, lest the relationship become a pathological obsession. Thus long-term emotions must inevitably allow for interruptions, and give time and space for other relationships and emotions with the same and other elements and situations over time.

Long-term interaction also combines characteristics of various emotions, and these emotions can fluctuate in their relative dominance, and sometimes appear to alternate. For example, love and fear may alternate in a strongly dominating relationship or one that involves abuse. Thus it is possible to love and fear a spouse at the same time, and the relative weight of these emotions can change depending on the particular occasion and context.

Beyond the possibility of simultaneously combining multiple emotions in one relationship, a change in the situation can prompt a different sort of short-term emotion toward a person. For example, it's possible to be very angry at an otherwise loved child for coming home late at night without calling. Over years of interaction with a person, we practice a wide array of emotions, each with a different frequency or pattern. Some of these will be rather common, while others are intermittent, and still others may occur rarely or irregularly.

In addition to such temporary changes, more permanent and long-term changes can affect long-term ways of relating. It is possible to experience something as extreme as a complete alteration, such as hating an ex-spouse, or something as subtle as a mild drift in the frequency, intensity, and strength of various emotional orientations and events, such as fewer occasions of a loving attitude and more cases of anger and resentment.

It could be speculated that our ability to relate to many elements over time, combine different emotional orientations in one relationship, and even vary our way of relating to a particular person or situation when necessary, provides for the necessity for some continuity, while allowing for flexibility. This flexibility is essential for responding to changing circumstances and enacting momentary improvisations required to interact with a complex and dynamic world. Thus not only are we capable of different emotions towards various elements in our environment (a sort of emotional multitasking), but we often experience diverse and even conflicting emotions toward the same element in a long, ongoing interaction or relationship. This ability can be described as a "multifaceted emotional capacity." Such a concept allows for an appropriately complex model of human emotional skills and capabilities, which prove vastly adaptable and limber.

The lack of continuity proposed as a characteristic of long-term emotions may frustrate readers who wish for more definitive determinations, hoping to see some sort of prevailing emotion, a pattern, or even the determination that long-term emotions are in fact simply a collection of *individual* short-term emotions. However, the work of this essay is not to offer conclusive definitions. Such definitions can too easily lead to precisely the reductionist, analytical view that we are trying to avoid—say of viewing emotions as a combination of feelings and cognition (and so forth). Instead, this essay emphasizes a systemic view of emotions in which the sum equals more than its parts. From this perspective, long-term emotions are clearly more than a collection of short-term emotional events, and it is crucial to recognize their unique dimensions beyond their components.

Here we are viewing emotions in the context of relationships, and in this context long-term emotions are not required be continuous, defined by their smallest components, or even to move as a typical process. Describing long-term emotions in terms of patterns might be actually more helpful than attempting to define them through notions of entities or processes. Such entities and processes seem to imply cohesiveness, but in fact, they too lack a smooth continuity, and might also be seen as fluctuating patterns similar to those of long-term emotions. For example, concepts like the human body, growth, drives, values, and light may seem to imply consistent phenomena, but in fact all are composed of smaller parts and empty spaces. Philosophers such as Bergson (1889, 1907), Margaret Mead (1999), and various Buddhist philosophers, emphasize the temporary and ever-changing nature of all things, and we can apply this view to emotions that persist over time as well.

Lower-intensity and physical sensations. In distinguishing long-term emotions from emotions of short duration, we noted that they are calmer. They are often more mellow, and lack some of the bodily sensations or "feelings" associated with intense, immediate emotions. Even if we have loved our spouse for the last fifty years, it is unlikely that "our blood is boiling" every time we meet, or that we feel the same excitement we might have felt during our first night or year together. This feeling might rekindle periodically after a long separation, in times of crisis, or on an especially romantic night; but most of time we are likely to feel what could be described as peaceful affection, appreciation, mutual need or ordinary routine, without strong signs of emotional tingle or intensity.

It might be hypothesized that long-term emotions tend to be calmer because it is difficult, inefficient, and even dangerous for any system to maintain a high level of arousal and an intense focus for a prolonged period of time. These states tend to demand high resources and provide lower flexibility, as do high levels of alert or wars, to return to our military analogy. Neurological studies show the same phenomenon, all the way from the behavior of a single nerve cell to the conduct of the nervous system as a whole. A number of psychological studies show the same trajectory in intense emotional events: the tendency of excitation and arousal, or intensity, is to rise to a temporary peak and drop off thereafter (see Lewis, Haviland-Jones, and Barrett 2008, *Handbook of Emotions*). In some cases, recurrent emotional episodes of depression or euphoria, for example, can sustain a rather high level of intensity for a long period of time, but these states are usually seen as undesirable or even pathological.

As we mentioned and are going to discuss again, a lower level of emotional excitation or arousal does not necessarily mean less emotional strength. Although long-term emotions may be calmer than intense, short-term emotions, they are not necessarily weaker.

When looking at differences among the members of any category, questions may arise about whether it is still theoretically worthwhile to keep them together, or whether they should in fact be separated. For the purposes of this essay, it seems beneficial to emphasize what long-term emotions *do* have in common with their short-duration siblings. Commonalities demonstrate how their shared characteristics distinguish them from other ways of relating and other categories of experience. The category of "emotions" is not presented as a homogeneous one, and categories in general are not required to consist of identical items; it is sufficient if their constituents share some common denominators. For now, we are committed to keeping the notion of long-term emotions; for, as the saying goes, "we need to believe that love can last . . . ."

Emotional Intensity vs. Emotional Strength
The issue of intensity is not only important to the distinction between short- and long- term emotions, but it is also central to the way we view emotions in general.

It is common to define emotions through a basic comparison between intensely emotional times and calmer times. Based on observation of behavior and thought processes during intense episodes as compared to those of calm periods, it is easy to conclude that being *intensely* emotional also means being *very* emotional, *more* emotional, or having *stronger* emotions.

The hidden implication of this assumption is that the special symptoms of intensely emotional events must somehow exemplify the fundamental nature of emotions, capture their characteristics and influences. Since the effects of intense emotional episodes are often considered contradictory to sound, cognitive, rational, objective thought and behavior, emotions have typically been contrasted with those capacities.

The bottom line is that emotions have been mostly observed, judged, and studied along a continuum of intensity. Thus, their existence has also been associated with intense events and their absence associated with composed, logical periods or states of mind. Put simply, the emotional spectrum has been construed to be identical to the spectrum of arousal.

Thus if one is assumed to be less emotional in calm times, it means that during these periods we either have no emotions, fewer emotions or weaker ones. However, if this is assumed to be the case, what happens in calmer times to persistent emotions, such as our incredible fear of death, our strong love for our children, our immense hatred for our enemies, our profound empathy for our sick friends, and a host of other deep, strong, persistent emotions. Do they all disappear in calm times? Do they just temporarily hide from view? Or are they simply neglected for a short period?

It seems quite obvious that they don't simply vanish, since any small change can trigger them to a dramatic level, say, when our children have a sudden problem. We could suppose that these abiding emotions are for a time weaker, forgotten or temporarily out of the focus of our attention. However, the lives of our children are not necessarily less important to us when we are calm. This emotion of love for our children remains central in our considerations, calculations, and priorities, and we constantly and consistently operate and act as if it is continuously significant. This example and others we might construct imply that our basic emotional dimensions, characteristics, and influences are present, no matter how low their intensity seem. Even without somatic, physical sensation or focused obsessive attention, we still typically maintain our sense of interdependence with multiple aspects of our environment; their significance, specificity, the force that connects us, the motivation, the care, and the commitments continue to be a pervasive factor in our lives. This means that we maintain this cognizance of connection along with its related biases even in calm times.

We might still choose to understand emotions as somehow disappearing or being unattended in calm times, leaving only their "cognitive constructs" behind. But, alternatively, we might view long-term emotions as patterns or ways of relating that are with us most of the time, even if we don't focus our attention on them. We can assume that our attention changes according to the intensity of the emotion, together with a number of other variables in our body/mind, such as somatic sensations and the extent of urgency attending a particular emotion.

Since, according to the view proposed here, emotions are people's essential method of relating to the majority of the significant things around them, and because these significant aspects of an individual's environment continue to be central to their considerations and behavior even in calm times, we might be better off supposing that people's emotions persist during peaceful periods. In general, as noted earlier, actual life processes and phenomena are mostly interconnected and continuous. Therefore, it might be more helpful for the understanding of emotions to view them as a continuous phenomenon, regardless of intensity.

Instead of, or in addition to, talking about being less emotional or more emotional in relation to a spectrum of intensity, we might talk for example about emotionality by comparing emotional and non-emotional relationships. Then the emotional dimension can be seen as a continuum of certain qualities including significance, meaning, strength (a matter of degree), or as a "yes/no" condition. In any event, it might be better not to assess the existence or non-existence of emotion according to intensity criteria. The existence of emotion and intensity clearly overlap at times and are closely interconnected, but they are not necessarily identical.

If we take water as a metaphor, emotional intensity can be compared to the temperature of the water, while the existence of emotion can be seen as the basic composition of water. The temperature of water can change, and as it changes the appearance of water changes with it (ice, liquid, boiling, vapor), but the basic constitution of water does not change. The quality of water for a chemist could be considered its molecular combination, and it can be measured against other liquids or chemicals regardless of its temperature and its form.

A calm ocean and a stormy ocean provide yet another metaphor, as does the volume of a song or the sound of an orchestra. Levels of military alert offer a more socially oriented example. Namely, intensity and arousal can be compared to many other volume spectrums. Although alterations in volume do change certain aspects and qualities of the system, these variations typically modify a system in a predictable and reversible manner, and do not always change the actual basic, central characteristics or components of the phenomenon.

Even in calm times, our long-term emotions can express a high level of interdependence with definite specific elements that are hard to replace or exchange. These emotional relationships are "deeply emotional" if they are very forceful, strong, significant, and meaningful to both sides, and they can include a profound and wide-ranging body/mind configuration when triggered. Such emotions are based on an extensive measure of investment and care about the intertwined destiny and relationship of both parties. In this case, being "more emotional" might mean relating to more aspects in one's environment emotionally, as opposed to relating instrumentally or reflectively, or being more invested in these relationships and more committed to them.

It may help to describe intense emotions as "passions," as they have traditionally been described, thus better capturing their intense tendencies. Accordingly, we can differentiate between intense or powerful passions and meaningful, strong, long-term emotions[6].

---

6 This distinction is somewhat similar to one proposed by Carse [2012] between power and strength when differentiating between finite and infinite games.

Calm times can be emotionally biased—only differently so. The following issues will be discussed again when we look at the association between emotions and rationality. However, it seems useful to first touch on them here since they are also closely tied to notions of emotional intensity and the question of long-term emotions.

It is important to note that emotional biases are not unique to intense events, as has been commonly supposed and traditionally emphasized. It is possible to be just as emotionally biased in calm times, only differently so.

While this is not an empirical study, it seems reasonable to hypothesize that we might have multiple types or sets of biases, including those related to arousal and intensity and those that affect calmer states. Future studies will be better able to tell whether the biases of intensity are in addition to, or simply different from, the more tranquil ones.

It seems that emotional intensity comes into play, or is triggered, when there are sudden changes or when changes are anticipated. In these instances, our universe becomes more contorted around fewer relationships, and thus becomes more focused, less flexible, more rushed, urgent and extreme, develops stronger physical configurations, and so forth.

However, even in calm times, we still perceive a biased and "contorted" universe. We simply navigate according to some wider combination of our emotional ways of relating and their individual characteristics. Namely, it appears that "calm biases" are more influenced by a *larger* number of *longer-term* values, norms, and emotions. Thus, when we consider biases, it seems that calm periods are not necessarily "less" emotional, but rather are shaped by another manifestation and format of this quality. Peaceful periods might be less intense, but on the other hand combine and balance *more* emotional relationships and consider them *more* carefully.

One of the key realizations to come from this formulation is that people *cannot* think or act in the absence of all emotions, without them or disregarding them, which is very different from much of the mainstream of Western philosophy from the Stoics to the Rationalists. Nonetheless, this essay is proposing that whatever emotional relationships people have, when they think or act, they include these relationships or emotions as part of their considerations and goals (even if subconsciously). In a sense, they should not even be considered "biases" as much as personal and individual constellations and preferences. In other words, people operate in the presence of their overall emotional constellations constantly and continuously, and live in a universe that is permanently and personally shaped by them. For example, our emotions, or the way we relate and "feel" about ourselves and our survival, our spouse, our children, particular other people, certain objects, ideas, and all other elements in our environment, express our values and mold our preferences. They shape what we see and pay attention to in the world around us, how important or negligible elements are in it, and how we act toward them.

One can argue that the shaping of our universe is an outcome of our beliefs, values, and perceptions. This is true, but since emotions are viewed here as the way we actually relate to elements as expressions and manifestations of these beliefs and values, it is one and the same. Whether we attribute this "shaping" to emotions or to values is already a question of definitional preference and the focus of one's study. In our view, since emotions emphasize and express the relational dimension of our perceptual universe, it is preferable to see them as expressing our biases and preferences toward various elements, and thus as the shape of our perceptual universe. The implication is that we must accept the idea that we have strong emotional biases or formations even in the absence of intense, emotional events. This is why a person's rationality operates within this world and not instead of it, in its absence or outside of it. It is similar to accepting and getting used to gravity. Here on earth we don't try to avoid gravity, ignore it or pretend that we can operate without it or beyond it. We simply deal with it and function within it and in consideration of its implications and impositions.

The idea of personal biases is not new. However, the realization that our emotions can contribute to these even in calm times is not common. While we typically think of our beliefs and values as shaping our world in terms of certain principles of conduct and priorities, our emotions seem to bias our universe, or express our biases, in terms of our relationships with our environment and the many people and situations that matter. They could be said to shape the topography or the curvature of our space and the way we view, relate to, are pulled towards, pushed away from, and interact with multiple elements (ourselves included). A similar version of this analogy is the image of navigating in space where an array of planets, stars, and black holes of different sizes and significance pull and push us according to their gravitational qualities and strength (or the curvature of space/time if we want to be more current with physical theories).

Distinguishing between emotional intensity and the presence of emotions is not merely a matter of fine verbal distinction for the sake of linguistic precision. Improved clarity about the association between emotions and intensity, together with some of the key terms involved, seems crucial to a new understanding of our emotional dynamics. It is also critical to the conceptual understanding of emotions in relation to other important concepts like cognition and rationality, as will be demonstrated below.

Part C: Repositioning Emotions Vis-A-Vis Closely Related Concepts

5

Emotions and Drives, Values, and Motivations

As part of the transition to a relational view of emotions, we must further explore the association between emotions and other related concepts. We have suggested numerous times that, as an interactive phenomenon with a powerful motivational vector, emotions are connected to drives and values.

Emotions and Subconscious Values

Emotions are affected by subconscious, practiced values more than by conscious, stated values. In determining what influences emotions, we will begin by accepting the widely-held idea that, in most cases, emotions seem to articulate subconscious, well-established preconceptions. These include long-term patterns of meaning and significance that express and guide long-term motivations. Emotions seem to be less affected by short-term, conscious thoughts and formulations. For some reason, while this is known to most psychologists, it still comes as surprise to many people. A M. Donaldson writes that emotions are "value feelings," that is, "[they] . . . mark importance. We experience emotions only in regard to that which matters" (Donaldson 1992, 12). In other words, emotions seem to manifest more our entrenched beliefs, values, life needs, drives, actual commitments, and long-term goals, and less of what we want to feel, or think we should feel.

In discussing what has more influence on emotions, it is common to note the dividing line between subconscious beliefs and motivations and more conscious thoughts. Some theories, like those of Beck and the Cognitive Behavioral Therapists (CBT), approach this distinction by differentiating among core beliefs, schemas, underlying "assumptions and rules" (intermediate beliefs), automatic thoughts, and voluntary ones.

Another useful but simple and practical way to make this distinction could be to distinguish between the values which we ***actually practice*** and are motivated by, and the ones we only ***say*** we practice. We might call the first group "practiced values" and the second "stated values." It seems that emotions express, and are largely evoked by "practiced values" and less by "stated ones." That is, they are less influenced by our image of ourselves, what we would like to believe in, and the values we say we have (but actually only wish we had). This is important to recognize since we find ourselves again and again in situations in which we think we should have one emotion, but in fact have another. For example, we think we should be calm, but are actually worried or nervous. The problem is that saying "be calm" is not enough; to be calm, we actually have to completely believe that there is no danger around, that the situation is peaceful and safe. The same goes for many other emotions such as anger, envy, and happiness that result in a major discrepancy between what we say or even think we should feel, and what we are actually feeling. As John Lennon sings "life is what happens to you while you are making other plans."

It is not that we are not conscious of our feelings, or even of some of the processes that initiate or influence them. It is more that we seem to be conscious of only some parts of these triggers and processes, and definitely have a hard time modifying emotions with simple analytical and wishful thoughts.

Because of this tendency, values, goals, and judgments that we select consciously, and that we may assume we hold, usually have to be with us for a while and become an integral part of our established and practiced belief system, before they actually manifest themselves in emotional experiences. In other words, as we repeatedly suggest, emotions tend to represent more *what we want and believe in* than *what we want to believe in*.

Emotions are Influenced by Values and Express Them

The influence of preconceived beliefs and various convictions on emotions is well-established and has been studied extensively in psychology. What is less clear and of more interest here is the role played in emotional composition by the various forces and motivations that shape one's life. Humans are born with various motivations and develop others; these arise out of a host of drives, necessities, desires, commitments, values, and goals that direct our lives. Thus, for the sake of this brief discussion we will bundle these forces together simply as "directives," as informed by Maslow's "Hierarchy of Needs" (Maslow 1970), which offers a more detailed discussion of basic drives, needs, and motivations, and by the many expansions of Maslow's ideas and responses since then (for example, Sorrentino 1996).

It may be assumed that we relate to different elements in our environment according to how they serve our needs, fulfill our desires and goals, and satisfy our motivations and values. If emotions are one of the important ways we relate to various individuals and situations, it is clear that emotions are also shaped by these directives. Namely, whether we relate to an element emotionally, functionally or not at all, what emotions we have and how intense they are, will be determined to a large degree by our directives. For example, the love for children and concern for their safety could be viewed as an aspect of the drive for genetic preservation, since children promote this goal. The same could be said of fear of a bear in the forest, which could be seen as an expression of the survival instinct, or of anger at someone who destroys the environment, if we are committed to its preservation.

The association between directives and emotions is also evident in the peculiar intensity and force proposed here as characteristic of emotion. Intensity and force also differentiate emotional ways of relating from other ways; these qualities are absent, for example, in reflective relationships. Emotions are not only the result of directives, but they also express directives as well as provide an element of motivation themselves, by being pleasant or unpleasant, by causing pleasure or pain.

In sum, it is logical to assume that directive and motivational forces are manifested in emotions, as well as reinforced by them. It is important to recognize that emotions are not merely *influenced* by life directives, but rather can be viewed as the actual expression of these directives, insofar as they are the way we relate to elements in our environment to preserve, protect, promote, facilitate, and/or execute our directives. (This perspective has also been argued by other scholars of emotions, including Aquinas, Darwin, McDougall, Arnold, Lazarus, Nussbaum, and more. See bibliography for details).

Beyond Utility
Emotional motivation goes beyond utility and includes the object of our emotion and our relationship with that object. As noted previously, utilitarian relationships are based on some functional motive. For example, we require service from a cashier, a bank teller or a generic tool, and we are determined to get it. If a relationship with

a person, such as a spouse, includes a combination of emotional and utilitarian relationships, we might expect some services from them as well (help with income, work in the house, and care of the children). However, in an emotional relationship, we are not only motivated by the need for a service or a product, but are also motivated by the object of emotion and our relationship with the object. In other words, it is not only that we demand a service and, once receiving it, could care less what happens to the provider. It is that we are invested in and somewhat committed to the destiny of this emotional element and our relationship with it. Namely, we are motivated to help it, destroy it, change it, get closer or run away, preserve or change our relationship with it somehow.

Interestingly enough, as suggested earlier in reference to the pain and pleasure of emotions, it could be said that emotions add yet another layer of motivation to reinforce the motivations they service and facilitate. As we said, fear for example is unpleasant, and we try hard to avoid it and whatever drives it. Joy and happiness, on the other hand, feel great and push us to seek more and promote the directives that seem to enhance them.

Some prominent thinkers actually view motivation as the main function of emotion. According to Meinong, "emotions are feelings of pleasure and displeasure whose main function is *informational*; that is, they inform the experience about the value of objects and events" (Meinong, 1894 in Reisenzein 2006). By contrast, Arnold suggests that emotions are "felt tendencies to approach or withdraw from objects appraised as good versus bad, and that their function is, correspondingly, primarily *motivational*" (Reisenzein 2006). Reisenzein claims that her ideas reflect the views of Thomas Aquinas (cf. Cornelius, Lyons, 1980) and William McDougall (1960), who see emotions as a motivating force. It is hard to accept that emotions are our sole source of motivation, as some of these scholars argue.

It is clear for example, that non-emotional organisms have strong motivations as well, and hunger and sex can motivate organisms to an amazing extent without being considered emotional.

There is much to debate about whether emotions express and facilitate existing motivations, add to them, or both; but in any event, it is clear that emotions are closely associated with our directives and with the beliefs and values that shape them.

Different Directives and Values Result in Different Emotions

The association between emotions and directives, beliefs, and values implies that variations in emotional nature may originate with differences in those areas and be explained by them. Not only do people's beliefs and values vary, but they prioritize and practice them differently.

For example, many people hold values of loyalty and honesty to friends and family. However, they may differ drastically in how important loyalty to another person is if it competes with the person's need for survival. Or the value of honesty may vary when competing and in the grips of the drive for success.

We differ radically with regard to the scope of specific values, as well. People may include or exclude a personal selection of individuals from certain values. Who is considered a part of one's family or community, who is loved and who is not, who can be taken advantage of in business and who is considered inviolable can vary.

In addition, people vary in the extent or gradient of their values. Not only do they include and exclude different elements from the scope of particular values, but the strength with which values are applied can also diminish or intensify depending on the extent to which these values "stretch." For example, if we are honest with ourselves, we can see that we have much less empathy for some far-away individual as compared to our child or friend. All these variations result in corresponding emotional differences.

Lofty values can shape our emotions, as well; and, despite their interdependence, emotions should not be reduced to drives and desires. It is important to emphasize that the intention here is not to depict emotions as a basic, somewhat primitive outcome of "primeval," "selfish" desires, drives, and instincts, or to equate them with some deterministic, unchangeable force. This essay does not propose the view that emotions are instinctual, innate drives or unconscious desires. It is also not the goal to reduce them to feelings based on predisposed habits and instincts, as William James has claimed, and as some continue to argue today.

This is why we added *values* to our list of forces that influence emotions over the long term. Cultural, spiritual, intentional, carefully selected, highly complex cognitive beliefs and commitments can and do play an important role in emotional life. They can be as strong and intense as basic sexual drive and the instinct for survival. For example, a person can experience strong emotions about the natural environment, human rights, a nation or a specific form of art. As said before, some of our most cherished and lofty values, such as morality and commitment to social contribution are closely tied to emotions such as empathy and love. Philosophers even argue that our capacity for complex emotions is the basis for morality. "Having emotions in itself has moral impact, which is presumably one of their functions" (Frijda, Manstead, Fischer 2004, 463)[7].

The possibility of morality may depend on our ability to relate emotionally, and particularly with love and empathy. However, the depth of our morality, the extent of our empathy, and the specific elements encompassed by it are actually determined by our directives and values. Namely, they guide which particular animals, people,

---

7   See also the writings of David Hume 1977, Solomon 2003, and Max Scheler 2008 for discussions of the critical role of emotions in morality.

and ethnicities we are empathetic to, choose to love, hate or care little about, and the degree of our feelings for them.

Long-term, deep, motivational forces and values thus tend to underline much of our emotional, relational configuration and seem to influence how we relate to those around us, and what emotions we have toward them. Our system of practiced directives might guide us to ignore or not care about some elements of a situation, to view some as purely instrumental, to see others as threats, or to love and empathize with particular elements which we view as an extension of ourselves or within the scope of our responsibility (children, for example).

Emotions Make Us Indirectly Aware of our Directives

Scholars sometimes talk about human drives so definitely as to suggest that they can actually observe them, and most people talk about their values with such certainty that it seems they have hard evidence for them. However, in actuality, we can't really see our drives or be directly aware of values, in part because they are often subconscious. Survival might seem a rather obvious instinct, but even the presumed drive for the perpetuation of genes is actually speculative and based on a theory. The intangible nature of values is even more evident with regard to lofty values, such as commitment to family, nation, environment, art, loyalty or honesty. If we think about life directives more carefully, it becomes apparent that much of what we assume about them comes from observation of behavior and emotions. For example, we observe human beings and other organisms protecting their offspring and fearing for them, and conclude about parental love. The same is true for our conclusion of our subconscious survival value which is manifested so clearly as fear and the impulse to escape in the presence of danger.

In general, actions seem to provide obvious indicators of values. However, at times, these values are obscured by reasons or excuses for why we must or can't do things. For example, we say we can't help poor people since we have to help our family. In comparison to this kind of rationalization, careful and honest attention to emotions can give a clearer and more immediate indication of the actual relative significance of various directives and values. Inferring the value placed on survival from a fear of sharks is rather direct. However, assessing values regarding ideas and elements such as environment, nation, and equality is much more difficult.

Amazingly enough, what emotions tell us about the genuine significance and hierarchical ranking of even our more abstract values can still be surprising, unpleasant, and difficult to accept. If we hardly care or are only mildly displeased about a massive killing in a faraway country, such as genocide in Cambodia, Africa or Syria, it suggests that the significance of these values is low in the configuration of our directives, no matter what we say or think our values are. If we are not convinced, we only need to compare our reactions to these situations with emotions about our own kids, our pets, the way we felt about getting stuck in a bad traffic jam last month or the outrageous tax bill we had to pay this year.

As suggested above, the strength of values is somewhat analogous to the pull of physical forces. We can't see gravity or electro/magnetic force, or even know they are there, unless we feel the pull of the earth, see the effect of magnetic force on our watch, or experience the lack of gravity in outer space. Similarly, we have to be attentive to our emotions to see how and how much different elements actually pull and push us.

In sum, the way we relate to or feel about specific people and situations, literally expresses drives and values and makes us aware of their presence and their particular forces. Unfortunately, they are often not perfectly clear and leave much room for speculation, pretentious declaration, wishful thinking, and if necessary—therapy.

Directives shape and can explain much of our emotional composition. Since causality is often a two-way street, at the same time emotions inform us about values, values can tell us a lot about our emotions.

Psychologists sometimes appeal to this assumption when they try to understand and heal certain pathologies. However, many psychologists suppose that our deep emotional problems result from something "going wrong," whether in the subconscious mind or in one's behavioral conditioning or rational belief system (Ellis 1994, Beck 1979, and Alford and Beck 1997). In other words, they believe that conflicting drives and erroneous beliefs are the reason for unwelcome or disagreeable emotions. This may be true in the extreme, pathological, and dysfunctional cases that psychologists are likely to treat.

However, it is often the case that "problematic" emotions have more to do with "problematic" values or goals. For example, if we see a lot of hatred in our world, it may be because we cultivate values that are manifested in these kinds of emotions. These are not mental constellations that have gone wrong, but values that have been purposely nourished. This might sound like a moral or religious argument. However, the intention is to recognize in a general way the overall association between values and emotions, regardless of whether they are "bad," "good," "moral" or "immoral".

For example, the extreme emphasis on the value of competition often leads to much hatred. It is one thing to compete for basic resources and survival, but many of our historical wars and mass killings had more to do with competitive battles over prestige, luxuries, a high style of living, and ethnic cleansing. This is not just ancient history: many of these values and the associated hatred were promoted to extremes by sophisticated ideologies such as Social Darwinism and Fascism in the last century. Even in recent society, we have cultivated an extreme, zero-sum, Darwinistic capitalism marked by severe competition (that is, in a view that resources and wealth are finite and we all have to fight over it for survival). In this environment, people and companies are encouraged to view every other person, company or nation as a threat, and to imagine that every other successful entity benefits at their expense. This type of world view and these values might promote efficiency and economic development, but they also increase suspicion, jealousy, resentment, and hatred. A milder version of capitalism (for example, modified by a welfare state), or a more cooperative one, might initially cost more and might slightly slow economic progress in the short run, but it might also result in more emotions of cooperation, compassion, empathy, and even love. Many argue that these changes will not only improve emotional well-being but could, in the long run, even prove more economically beneficial. For instance, they could reduce wars, terrorism, and defense budgets, lower unnecessary duplication, increase transfer of ideas, encourage widespread development and worldwide consumption, improve division of labor, decrease irreversible damage to the environment, and so forth.

This is not the place to debate personal and national goals and values, but only to mention that they have direct bearing on our emotions, which express these goals and values. For that reason, the call for more love, empathy, and compassion—the idea that "all we need is sympathy my friend"—tends to be rather ineffective. It might be more productive to call for a change of values, goals, and behavior, a change that would hopefully bring about the desired emotional change.

Attempts to promote and cultivate values that improve morality and relationships have taken place in the past and are taking place now. Examples can be seen in the teachings of Jesus in the past, in the teaching of the Dalai Lama recently, and in different progressive spiritual, educational, and social programs around the world. What they have in common is the emphasis on tolerance, cooperation, and forgiveness. This emphasis has been promoted as a step toward moral improvement, and this is a very important reason in its own right. However, if people realize that they might also benefit personally and emotionally from these value changes (in addition to helping others), such recommendations might have a much more powerful, convincing edge. For example, we can argue quite convincingly that certain values, attitudes, and actions can dramatically improve how people feel and bring more of the elusive happiness they so desperately seek (Mattheiu Ricard, "The Habits of Happiness" on TED Talks Nov. 2007, YouTube Apr. 15, 2008; Hade forthcoming monograph).

If we revisit our ongoing foreign policy analogy, we will find that in many cases, if nations (like individuals) relate to other countries, ethnic groups, and religions with hatred and animosity, it is because of national or government values. These are often based on competition, self-serving interests, territorialism, a sense of superiority, the benefit of uniting people by common hatred and distracting them, and the choice of relating to everyone else in a more utilitarian, less empathetic way. In the same vein, positive foreign policy (personal or national) is more often than not based on different beliefs and values such as interdependence, cooperation, social responsibility, and empathy.

The expression, manifestation, and facilitation of our directives through emotional relations to various elements in the environment can shed a light on other emotional phenomena as well. For example, we typically combine and try to fulfill various directives simultaneously, but they often compete or even overpower each other: for instance, the tension between heroic action and the risk of life; or between work, family, and free time. Thus, behavior most likely represents the combined outcome of conflicting vectors. This might be another explanation for the sense of mixed or conflicting emotions at times. As psychologists realize, if emotions express values and are supposed to facilitate their direction and goals, a confusing, competing or contradictory set of values will obviously result in a perplexing set of emotions.

It is difficult but not impossible to modify emotions with a change of directives. We have emphasized that emotions mostly express long-term patterns and directives, and so are difficult to modify in the short term. However, they can be changed over time by conscious decisions, significant events, or proper guidance (such as therapy or spiritual leadership). These transforming factors can advance certain conscious thoughts and commitments and lead to a particular change of beliefs, goals, values, mental configuration, and behavior. This is part of psychotherapy in general and an important aspect of therapies like Cognitive Behavioral Therapy (CBT). It is also the basis for many spiritual and religious practices. Typically, these schools realize that altering one's conscious, stated thoughts is not enough to guarantee a deep, lasting, emotional change. Rather, to bring a more long-term, fundamental, emotional alteration, people have to undergo a more profound transformation and modify their actual belief system, values, and behavior. As noted above, it is not enough to be told that the railing on a balcony is safe if you have a fear of heights—or even to say it or think it. To decrease or avoid fear, one must actually believe, deep inside, that there is little or no danger, or accept the risk and the danger. Some changes of beliefs are easy, such as decreasing fear by convincing a person that a shark can't follow them out of the water. However, other cognitive and behavioral changes are harder and require longer and deeper modifications, such as giving up money, power, and prestige for the sake of happiness. (See bibliography and other literature by Beck, Ellis, and other CBT experts regarding the change of "mistaken" beliefs in order to improve emotional well-being.)

Obviously, one study can't solve overnight the million-dollar question of how exactly to bring about desired emotional changes. Nevertheless, what becomes more apparent in this essay is that an emotional change is not a solely private, internal, cognitive experience, as much as a modification in our values and the way we relate and interact with the world and various elements in it (including ourselves). This does not contradict what many therapists and spiritual leaders already advocate so much as it gives a better explanation and theory for what and why it works.

The discussion so far exemplifies how seemingly slight but critical changes in the perception of emotions can change our understanding of how emotions interact with other key concepts and thus fundamentally shift and reconfigure our conceptual universe.

In the next few sections, we will take a fresh look at the interactions between emotions and other closely related conscious processes such as cognition, rationality, objectivity, relationships, and our idea of the Self.

6

Emotions and Cognition

The interaction between emotions and cognition is multifaceted. We discussed earlier how cognition helps formulate emotions and participates in them. Cognition also changes and adapts to various relationships, diverse emotions, emotional instances, and different emotional modes (for example, high intensity). Cognition has a vital role in triggering and shaping emotions as well. Acting through experience and culture, cognition helps to develop our emotional repertoire, emotional expressions, and indicates what emotional behavior is required or acceptable in different social contexts[8].

Emotions have been considered an expression of long-term drives and values, which can be seen as another type of mental configuration. It has been proposed that emotions articulate the directives implicit in drives and values through the specific ways we relate, and that emotions are motivated by these directives to act toward various individuals and circumstances in the environment. Here again, multiple cognitive processes are responsible for generating appropriate "action plans" toward these elements and coordinating their execution.

---

8 See Lutz and White 1986, White 2008, and additional anthropological and social constructionist literature. See also literature about emotional intelligence [Salovey and Mayer 1990, Goleman 2005, and others].

As the previous paragraphs make clear, the mutual interactions between emotions and cognition or mental activity are reciprocal, extensive, and complex. This complexity is compounded by a long tradition of alleged "tension" between the two realms, and by the continuous puzzlement regarding the place of emotions in our conceptual matrix. Although it challenges the limited scope of this essay, and though we do not presume here to speak comprehensively or definitively about cognition or mental activities, to understand emotions better and enable their conceptual change, it is important to discuss their relative position to concepts such as these. Therefore, after a short introduction to the term "cognition," we will offer several options for viewing the association between emotions, cognition, and other related mental and bodily processes.

Short Introduction and History of the Term "Cognition"

Cognition comes from the Latin word *cognito*, to get to know or to learn. For most of Western history, it was primarily used to refer to the faculties and processes of knowledge, as they were understood at various periods in history. It was adopted to distinguish, for example, empirical knowledge from rhetoric or beliefs; cerebral logical mental processes from emotional ones (Aquinas 1962, 1999, 2002); human mental capacity from that of animals; mind from body (as in Descartes' dualism [1964]); mental activities from physical processes; and higher/complex mental functions from lower/basic ones (such as breathing) (see *Encyclopedia Britannica* 1997, and Kazdin's (2000) *Encyclopedia of Psychology*). William James (1950) in his *Principles of Psychology* refers to cognition simply as "knowing," and Ernest R. Hilgard (1980) sees cognition as the "general term used to designate all processes involved in knowing" (12).

After the radical shift from behaviorism to "cognitivism," the term "cognition" took central stage in psychology, a position that, to a large degree, it still occupies today. With the expansion of the research and application of this category, and in response to attempts to soften the traditional boundaries between mind and body, cognition became a term so broad that its meaning expanded beyond "knowing" to incorporate the more general idea of most, or even all that is "mental." For example, many psychologists tend to adopt an older claim by Ulric Neisser (1967, 1976) that "cognition refers to all the processes by which the sensory input is transformed, reduced, stored, recovered, and used" and that "it is apparent that cognition is involved in everything a human being might possibly do; that every psychological phenomenon is a cognitive phenomenon." (See also Lakoff and Johnson 1999.)

In our introductory notes, we showed the same broad approach in contemporary descriptions of cognition: "It encompasses processes such as knowledge, attention, memory and working memory, judgment, and evaluation, reasoning and "computation," problem solving and decision making, comprehension and production of language, etc. Human cognition is conscious and unconscious, concrete or abstract as well as intuitive and conceptual. Cognitive processes use existing knowledge and generate new knowledge" (Wikipedia 2016).

For our purposes, we selected a rather common but slightly more restrictive definition which represents the traditional orientation to the topic but allows for broad interpretations: "The mental action or process of acquiring knowledge and understanding through thought, experience, and the senses" (*Oxford Dictionary* 2016). It is important for our discussion of emotions that the definition of cognition, as broad as this term is, remain limited to a certain portion of our overall mental activities. However, our understanding includes the common cognitive processes or constructs that are typically either contrasted with emotions or attributed to them, for instance, thought, appraisals, evaluations, judgments, rationality, objectivity, orientations, concepts, conceptions, knowledge, and pure information.

Since emotions are one of the main topics for psychology, they too have been investigated by cognitive theories and seen as an aspect of cognition, or considered heavily dependent on cognition. In other words, cognitive processes have now come to be viewed as an inherent, indispensable component of emotional events, or else emotional activity is seen as an integral part of the cognitive process.

This trend has had implications for modern philosophy as well, and particularly for areas closer to psychology, such as the philosophy of mind and the philosophy of emotions. Discussions of emotions are still not very common in modern philosophy, but most of the leading ones seem rather cognitive in nature, or at least they lean heavily in this direction (see Solomon 2003, de Sousa 2013 "emotion" in Stanford Encyclopedia of Philosophy).

One of the goals of these theories has been to improve understanding of emotions by using the most current theoretical models and concepts available. In addition, these approaches legitimized emotions by presenting them as "cognitive" and often "rational." Granting emotions membership in these kinds of categories was considered the key for wider scientific and social recognition and approval. This conceptual move aimed to shift emotions from their traditional position of opposition to cognition and reason, and to help them join the "in crowd" of cognitive processes, along with judgments, perceptions, and motivations. Most importantly, the assumption that emotions are somehow "rational" seems to make them more socially acceptable and functional, since they follow a rational, cognitive process.

Cognitive studies have made very important contributions to our understanding of how emotions function; to therapy; and, indirectly, to the acceptance of emotions in psychology, philosophy, and society as a whole. For example, it is now much more acceptable to argue that emotions are as important as cognition, and that they therefore should not be suppressed indiscriminately. On the contrary, more open expression of emotions is often encouraged and they are allowed to guide our behavior, on top of, or instead of, cognitive rational evaluations.

Though these theories have made an important contribution to the discussion of emotions, it seems that if the conversation does not move forward, emotions could end up in a theoretical bind as problematic and socially dangerous as the one they are being rescued from.

Because of the history and long tradition of the concept, cognition cannot so easily shed the heavy connotation of "knowledge" and all the epistemological background and traditional categories that come with it. Many philosophers and psychologists have abandoned the obvious "mind versus body," dualistic connotations of this concept. In addition, the models applied to cognition have changed over history—from a watch, to a machine, to a computer, to a sophisticated system of artificial intelligence. Nevertheless, the dominant tendency to view cognition as a mental information processing system still persists. Cognition is seen to work with facts or bits of information in an analytical, calculative, impartial, and preferably rational and logical manner. This understanding renders cognition somewhat foreign to emotions and inhibits any profound change in our understanding of emotions. The approach to the study of how the mind works takes an *information processing analysis* viewpoint described in detail in *Cognitive Psychology and Information Processing* by Lachman, Lachman, and Butterfield (1979) and in Kazdin's (2000) *Encyclopedia of Psychology*. Another more recent example is Harari's (2015) association of cognition and emotions with sophisticated algorithms, an equation that he feels will persist and intensify in the future.

In addition, knowledge, and therefore cognition, has been closely associated or even equated with reason, rationality, and objectivity; and these have been defined to a large degree by their opposition to emotions (see the next two sections). Accordingly, focusing on cognition in the treatment of emotions implicitly brings along these multiple, traditional dualistic notions. We still say, for example, "his actions were very emotional and far from rational."

Typical strategies for dealing with the traditional tension between emotions and cognition end up either reinforcing the dichotomy, suggesting the need to choose sides, or incorporating one side into the other (that is, emotions become an element of cognition, or vice versa). They rarely encourage any fundamentally novel understanding of the association between cognition and emotion—an understanding that seems to be needed.

Tension Between Cognition and Emotions-Some Alternative Views

The question is, how can we avoid the traditional dualism between cognition and emotions and relate them in a manner that preserves their respective uniqueness as well recognizes their interdependence? The discussion that follows outlines several different ways of positioning these two elements relative to each other.

One element dominates the other. Most Western philosophical traditions since the Greek era have been inclined to accept the conflict between cognition and emotions, and have mainly argued for the benefits of one over the other. The Stoic tradition, and later, Rationalism, for example, made extreme calls for the advantages of rationality, and therefore of cognition and knowledge, over emotionally-driven behavior. Romanticism, on the other hand, argued to increase the relative weight of the emotional component. However, even strong advocates of the emotional element, like the Romantics, accepted the dualism between the two, and even recognized the need for the dominance of cognition and rationality in many human endeavors such as business, science, law, and so forth.

This dualism is still apparent today in many areas of life, and it is often portrayed as two different perspectives or modes of operation. Roughly put, one mode tends to emphasize efficiency, productivity, objectivity, Darwinistic competition, logical/rational thought, numerical analysis, quantitative progress, and "finite game" interactions (competitive with one winner) (Carse 2012). The other mode tends more to emphasize imagination, artistic appreciation, subjectivity, excellence as a goal, quality as a measure for progress, mutual appreciation and cooperation, and "infinite games" that replace competition (collaboration and mutual contribution).

For example, the dominance of cognition with the emphasis on practicality, efficiency, rationality, and logic is supposedly more common in business, court, military, government, and conservative parties. On the other hand, perspectives that support the dominance of emotional, cultural factors are more typical in the arts, social and cultural projects, liberal thought, and some religious/spiritual approaches.

We can witness a similar division between professions like engineering, economics, and finance along with the hard sciences, and more artistic, cultural or spiritual professions guided by softer approaches. The third divide is typical to our common separation between the workplace, where cognition theoretically dominates, and the home environment, which tends to favor more emotional considerations. For example, we adopt a more emotional perspective to personal and social relationships, and favor an emotional approach when creating or experiencing art or entertainment. When it comes to art for example, we are more concerned with quality, the ingenuity it took to produce it, and the emotional insight it confers as opposed to assessing it according to a scale of rational, quantitative efficiency in making money or advancing our GDP.

Some of the more sophisticated versions of this approach, which will be discussed in the material that follows, accept the tension and/ or recommend a hierarchy between the two. They agree that cognition "should" dominate some world views, professions, and environments, while emotional considerations ought to have a higher priority in others. They claim that the wisdom is not to fight this tension, but to know how, when, and where to combine the two or give preference to one over the other.

Changing the view of emotions to fit cognition better. Some theories that are intent on resolving and dissolving dualism suggest incorporating one side of the duality *into* the other. In the case of emotions and cognition, the first step is to change the image of emotions so they fit better in the realm of cognition, a strategy argued by a number of cognitive studies. For example, they claim that emotions are an aspect of cognition or perform as good cognitive functions should—namely they are rational and factual (see again Ellis, Beck, and much of the CBT literature). These studies also show how cognitive processes such as judgments, appraisals, and beliefs, or even motivations, explain and determine emotions. The agenda is to demonstrate that emotions accommodate the necessary requirements and models of cognition.

As different as it may sound, claiming that emotions are part of cognition, or that they should be rational, is a sophisticated way of assuming the dominance of cognition and rationality. This view can be seen as a modern version of rationalism, with rather similar theoretical and practical implications.

As Solomon (1998) argues, reducing emotions to other mental processes such as motives and beliefs (Sabini and Silver 1997) is another form of reductionism. Perhaps it helps us understand one portion of emotions better (especially their cognitive component), but at the same time, it eliminates some of their most important differences and unique characteristics (de Sousa 1987, Turski 1994a, and others).

Changing the meaning of cognition to include emotions more easily. A similar but opposite effort to the conceptual strategy described above is to change the meaning of cognition, thus making it more amenable to the incorporation of emotions. Such approaches argue that cognition should allow and give equal importance to a wider range of mental procedures and thought patterns. Accordingly, cognition will then supposedly be able to accommodate the emotional, spiritual, and rhetorical, and avoid the automatic dominance of pure traditional logic and rationality. This approach promotes adding non-quantitative, non-calculative, and specifically contextual variables and ways of manipulating them. This augmentation is proposed instead of, or in addition to, the standard symbols and logical rules that dominate most Western contemporary systems (particularly the scientific, legal, and political ones) and are idealized by them.

The intention of these more inclusive, "softer" views of cognition is not to suggest or promote an anarchic array of irrational principles in which there is no law, in which "emotions go wild" and religious extremes reign, as during the Inquisition or in some parts of the Middle East. The hope of these theorists is rather to emphasize the view that rationality, universal rules, and generic symbols are not the *only* way our mind (or social system) operates. Accordingly, these models argue against viewing cognition as a pure information system or as any attempt to mimic one. Namely, this view argues that our systems of thought and ideas about cognition can be and should be more open and attentive to alternative modes of operation. Cognition can then be expanded to include emotional goals and well-being, as well as spiritual, particular, contextual, unexpected, and exceptional variables.

Some studies of emotions have already attempted to take the first step in this direction (Solomon 1993 and Lazarus 1997 in particular). For example, they emphasize the growing relative importance of subconscious processes in our cognition, and the importance of nonquantitative variables and processes such as metaphors. At the same time, they argue for the reduction in the status of universal rules, objectivity, and rationality (for example, deconstructionist philosophy). Some of these ideas started long ago and were also developed by Freud (in Solomon 2003) and Jung (1989). Recently, they are gaining popularity in some philosophical and psychological studies, as evident in contemporary writings such as Lakoff and Johnson's (1999) *Philosophy in the Flesh*, Kahneman and Tversky (1979), and a few others.

Nevertheless, most of the attempts of cognitive studies, Western philosophy, and psychology, to change the idea of cognition to accommodate emotions thus far seem insufficient. At times, they even seem to also indirectly reestablish the traditional dominance of cognitive logic and rationality. An example is the recent assertion that cognition and economics are not purely rational (Beck 1979, Alford and Beck 1997, Tversky and Kahneman 1992). These studies show imperfections in cognitive or rational processing and point to the occasional, problematic dominance of emotional considerations. However, rationality persists as the ideal way of thinking or behaving. Most importantly, they don't shed much light on what is special about emotions and how they differ from many other cognitive constructs or processes.

Up to this point we have presented various attempts to ease the dichotomy between cognition and emotion through a strategy that endorses one side of the polarity at the expense of the other, or that incorporates one into the other. Since these efforts have thus far had only limited success in resolving the problem or explaining emotions, we might consider other avenues in which the two elements work side by side.

Cognition and emotions as equally important but distinct mental activities. As hinted above, another way to avoid dualism and the tension it implies is to see cognition and emotions as different activities or subsystems within our mental field that fulfill different functions of equal importance.

This view can be supported by updating and renewing the distinction between cognition and mental activity generally. Mental activity will once again become a general term that covers all the brain's activities and tasks. At the same time, the scope of cognition will shrink to cover mostly our higher thought processes and manipulation of signals, knowledge or theoretical concepts.

This view suggests that the association between cognition and emotions is more analogous to the connection between siblings than to the connection between a child and a parent (somewhat similar to the popular division between our right and left brain). It parallels the idea that different brain centers have different responsibilities, such as linguistic, hormonal, and visual functions.

Cognition from this perspective becomes only a part of a much wider and more diversified mental system, and the rationality it confers becomes only one, specialized way of relating to ideas and people. Thus, we don't need to change the traditional view of cognition radically, but rather need to limit it to certain capabilities of overall mental capacity (which is the impression we get from Beck's writings, for example). Cognition will then work *along with other* types of activities, duties, and ways of processing or dealing with the world.

The emotional subsystem then stands as another, equal component in the mind/body system—one that facilitates and is responsible for other types of relationships and circumstances. In some sense, it could be argued that this approach is simply a more sophisticated version of the theories described earlier, minus the aspect of competition between emotions and cognition. This view doesn't assert the dominance of one function over the other; rather, while maintaining a distinction between them, it proposes a division of labor, a basic similarity, and a complementary synergetic connection, with tight cooperation and mutual influence. For example, as we explained briefly before, Solomon or de Sousa argue that emotions can provide a framework for cognition, and cognition can initiate, eliminate or direct emotional activity (as CBT claims). A somewhat similar distinction is implied in Epstein's (1999) Cognitive-Experiential Self-Theory (CEST) model, which distinguishes between slow analytical rational systems and fast intuitive-experiential ones, and perhaps even in Kahneman's later (2011) *Thinking, Fast and Slow*.

If cognition is associated with information and knowledge, it is then characterized by its internal manipulation of generic symbols according to some rules of logic (even if it is not "the" scientific formal logic). On the other hand, emotional relationships, we have contended, require additional, unique dimensions such as force, interdependence, specificity, and feelings, and are characterized by the treatment of specific individuals, situations, and other elements in a particular manner.

Cleary the two subsystems overlap and interact closely, but describing them in this manner is a useful heuristic device that makes it possible to understand each function more accurately. This outlook helps to explain, for example, why certain organizations, professions, and environments prefer the dominance of one system over the other. Each function operates differently, and each has some advantages and disadvantages that make it a better fit for different needs and moral preferences. Some organizations or institutions may require impersonal efficiency more than a "personal touch" (businesses, for example). Others call for a more personal, qualitative, and emotional approach, even if this approach is slightly less productive or efficient (say, working with a child).

In this view, both cognition and emotion express and facilitate human needs, goals, and values (directives), but in different ways. Both are at least partially mental processes, as well, and require mental activity to facilitate their operations. They affect and help each other, but their aims and ways of operation are very different, not unlike many other different functions of the overall body/mind system. Besides mental processing, both also affect, and are affected by, other bodily processes and systems such as muscular, hormonal, and digestive processes.

All in all, this approach, which posits that emotions and cognition are equal but distinct, works well with the new view of emotions proposed here. It allows for the close interaction and interdependence of these functions, while diminishing the tension between them. Nevertheless, it might be worthwhile to take yet another theoretical step forward to an improved view. In it, the two elements maintain their mutual interdependence, but completely lose the potential for rivalry, thus eliminating the need to choose between them, either theoretically or practically.

Cognition and Emotions as Interconnected but Non-parallel Categories

In this essay, we are proposing fundamentally new positions for emotions and cognition. In light of the discussion so far, a more innovative and beneficial option is to realize that cognition and emotions are not only distinct activities, but completely different categories, or different dimensions of categorization that cannot be compared, contrasted or included in each other. They should not be viewed as two, somewhat equal but different parts of the mental system or as alternative styles of treating the world. Instead, it might be better to see them as two interdependent but very different subsystems or functions of our whole body/mind, fulfilling utterly non-comparable duties—one mental and one relational.

No longer would we compare cognition and emotions to a parent and child or to two siblings, but rather to parenting, on the one hand, and the family's orientations toward the outside world, on the other. A clearer example comes from the recurrent analogy of "foreign policy." Cognition could be compared to the process of analysis and decision making that takes place in the government and other relevant organizations. Emotions on the other hand, could be equated with actual foreign policies and the way a country relates to other countries and various other elements. Thus these are interconnected functions or categories that are mutually conditioning but don't compete.

Emotions should not be included in cognition. To start with, as we will continue to emphasize, it is better not to restrict emotions to typical, purely cognitive processes or constructs. Unlike cognition, they are not limited to the mind, brain or mental activities, and they do not specialize in analyzing, supervising, and manipulating signals, symbols, concepts or information. They may utilize or include these, but this is not their main function and they are not restricted to these functions. For instance, purely cognitive processes such as thoughts, concepts, judgments, appraisals, evaluations, recognitions, comparisons, and projections lack the unique sensations, full-body configuration, force, and intensity that characterize emotions.

Emotions can also be initiated by non-cognitive processes (such as chemical reactions in the body). For example, low blood sugar caused by hunger or pain can trigger anxiety and fear, exercise is known to be closely associated with happiness, and prolonged exhaustion often leads to a depressive state.

If every human function that requires a mental activity is considered "a cognitive function" or a "mental activity," most of our activities will become cognitive or mental. Thus, we end up with a useless category that is all-inclusive. Eating, having sexual intercourse or playing sports all include cognitive or mental processes, and yet they aren't considered cognitive activities.

The fact that cognition and emotion facilitate and influence each other doesn't necessarily imply that they are the same type of phenomena or even two extreme opposites of the same experience.

Emotions should also not be positioned as a parallel mental subsystem. It is not only unhelpful to include emotions in cognition or merge the two concepts, it is also problematic to place them as two comparable, somewhat competing mental subsystems or ways of viewing or handling the world.

First, though we might debate the details, we are somewhat clearer about the overall function of cognition as an analytical processing system for the manipulation of knowledge, information, sensations, and so forth. Placing emotions as a parallel subsystem of the brain might give us a supposed location, but not a clear and unique function. Viewing emotions simply as "softer," less rational, more personal and qualitative mental activities leads to one of these miscellaneous categories defined by negation that becomes a receptacle for everything that we don't seem to understand or only because it doesn't fit elsewhere.

It is not that we need emotions as an alternative mental subsystem to deal with the "softer," less objective, more personal qualitative and artistic issues. Cognition deals with these as well, only differently. It would be very hard to claim that artists, romantics, and psychologists are less cognitive than engineers, physicists, and military personal. It is also not true that we don't use cognitive processes at home or when watching a movie or reading a book. In the same manner, military or militant people are not necessarily more rational or less emotional than peace-loving people. They simply are often full of love for their countries, hate for others or simply obeying orders. The same is true for various occupations like business and so forth. As we will soon explain, we should be careful not to confuse being emotional with being emotionally aroused, or being rational with being non-emotional. We constantly use our cognition and are emotional most of the time. We only change the manner in which we use our cognition in different contexts, and have different ways of relating (emotional or not) and different emotions towards the various elements in those contexts.

Emotions are not another form of cognition or cognitive constructs, nor are they "softer," less rational appraisals or thoughts. They are neither irrational cognition nor non-objective personal judgments (as we will soon discuss). So, what do we need emotions for?

Emotions as a new and different whole body/mind relational category or function. Instead of viewing emotions as a cognitive phenomenon or as a parallel mental subsystem which competes with or complements cognition, we suggest viewing emotions from a new perspective, as a new whole body/mind relational phenomena or function.

To better understand this function, we have shown the need to form a new relational category which will intersect with many of our traditional categories. This relational category is not just another mental subsystem or center, but a whole different body/mind category or distinction. We pointed to some similarities between emotions (though not identity with) and various other body/mind states such as sleep, exhaustion, sex, physical activity or being under the influence of drugs. Like emotions, these other functions are not purely cognitive or mental; they cross typical mind/body categories, and include a number of them. Similar to the manner that sport or sleep affect our mind, body, and our interactions with the world around us, emotions channel all mental activity, energy, and behavior in a very particular way toward various individuals, situations, institutions, ideas, and other elements of the environment. Like emotions, cognition participates and changes to fit various states or modes of being. Nevertheless, it would not seem helpful to view sex, physical activity, and other such states as alternative cognitive activities or mental subsystems. Just as exhaustion, sleep, or various states of activity affect cognition, intense emotions tend to modify rationality and objectivity. Nevertheless, just as sleep is helpful and desirable, despite its influence on rationality and objectivity, so emotions are essential, helpful, and desirable. They fulfill a relational function that, though different from the cognitive function, is not less critical.

Again, the intention here is not to achieve some biological precision with regard to various mental and physical states or to find an exact identity between various biological/mental modes. It is obvious that all these analogies, examples of various states and particularly of emotions are very different from each other. Rather, the hope is to be able to see the possibility that emotions, as a relational function, cut across our traditional cognitive and physical distinctions and dimensions, and don't have to either merge or compete with them.

We can still think of these two phenomena as highly co-dependent, mutually influential, and thus as affecting each other's performance, without merging them or opposing them. It is important to note that all attempts to adopt a terminological framework that forces the domination of one of these phenomena over the other, preserving their competition, collapsing one into the other or mutually incorporating them, have historically resulted in a theoretical and practical loss.

Therefore, instead of retaining the traditional "conflicting" view of cognition and emotion, and/or a reviving a new version of their mutual tension, this essay is proposing a new more harmonizing, synergic, complimentary view.

Cognition remains a mental activity. Thus, according to the "foreign policy" analogy above, cognition could be seen as a theoretical, delineated subsystem, or an explanatory model, set around the human performance of a specific type of mental activity (depending on how broadly we define it). In either form, it still surrounds a specific human subsystem, a particular type of activity, capacity or even an organ (for example, the brain or part of the brain). We could argue endlessly whether to narrow the understanding of cognition to a specific type of mental activity (such as knowledge), or to widen it to include some or all mental activities. It might participate in many or all of our other activities, be defined broadly or narrowly. Nevertheless, due to its original, historical, and even contemporary connotations and applications, it is still primary associated with some kind of activity or capacity of the mind, to be distinguished from lower more basic mental activities, or bodily, physical or social ones.

As far as emotions go, as important as cognition might be, it would be better to view cognition as only one of the body/mind subsystems guiding, participating, and changing during emotional relationships, together with many other mind and body subsystems, such as the digestive, muscular, and sensory ones.

Emotions as a Relational Category and Cognition a Mental Category

All in all, this new outlook proposes that we view cognition more narrowly, as it has been viewed in the past, and see it as part of the more general category of "mental activity." Emotions will utilize cognition and probably other mental capacities, but will no longer be strictly limited to the category of mental activity. Here we are recognizing emotion as an aspect, function or state of our whole body/mind (not strictly mental) organization, position, process, and orientation, facilitating our relational interface with the environment.

Unlike earlier models, this view does not divide our spheres of operation so that we must choose to operate in either a "cognitive" manner or an "emotional" way (rational versus emotional). We don't, in fact, behave emotionally as opposed to rationally. The spectrum is no longer between cognition and emotionality. Instead, as we said, we use cognitive operations continuously, and relate emotionally most of the time. Nevertheless, we are calmer and socially rational in some instances, and in other instances more excited, prone to intense emotions, and less or differently rational.

In other words, we could be said to be dealing with two different spectrums or categories. The "mental" one includes cognition, together with other mental activities, and the "relational" one contains emotions along various other ways of relating (such as utilitarian). Following our political analogy, the cognitive category would include different types of governmental bodies and decision-making processes, whereas the relational category would pertain to different types of policies or examples of policies and other ways in which we relate to different countries (such as trade practices and policies).

Our governmental bodies operate continuously and constantly to analyze and formalize foreign and domestic policies, and these policies are an ongoing stance and a basis for positions we take vis-a-vis other nations and issues (even if these frequently change). These governmental bodies not only change the content of these policies (loving or hating a nation), but they modify their manner of operation, actual techniques, and emphasis in response to different times. For instance, the decision-making process during a time of peace is rather different from the same process during wartime or other emergencies.

In a similar manner, cognition could be said to change our "policies" and/or our ways of relating to various elements, as well as its own operational techniques, principles, and emphasis. At times, cognition may operate in a more common-sensical, methodical, logical, rational or objective way, emphasizing efficiency and quantitative progress (for example, when doing business). On other occasions, it can function in a more associative, flexible, improvisational manner, emphasizing alternative values such as quality, personalization, aesthetics, and morality (for example, when creating art or listening to music). On yet other occasions it can operate in a very normative, biased, "subjective," dedicated, and uncompromising way (as in the case of passionate love or anger). With our highly complex, sophisticated, and flexible mental and cognitive skills, many other possible combinations of the above principles are probably possible.

What is important and hard to get used to is the idea that what we have traditionally called an "emotional" way of acting is simply another cognitive way of thinking. This type of cognition is typically associated with more intense emotions or more intense expressions and/or public demonstrations of emotional behavior. It includes highly biased thought and behavior that is frequently also less normative and socially accepted. It often means that we pay less attention and put a lower emphasis on rational, objective, utilitarian principles, and/or social norms. It might also emphasize less quantitative, less harsh, more qualitative, intuitive, and, if intense, also more biased and focused principles that are closely associated with highly intense emotional behavior. Nevertheless, it is still our cognition operating, though in a slightly different manner, to help formalize emotions that keep on shaping the way we relate to and interface with the world around us.

It is obviously very hard to adjust and change our age-old way of viewing and talking about emotions and cognition. Changing our conceptions together with the associated language and manner of speaking is a difficult and lengthy process. In the meantime, we can simply be more precise and say that at times we think and act in a more *emotionally intense* manner while at other times we act in a more *emotionally calm* and tranquil style.

More important than proper and precise language or terminology is the conceptual change required. Whether one eventually chooses to accept this new constellation of cognition and emotions or reject it, it seems useful to understand it. It is one of the few feasible configurations that retains the close association and mutual influence between cognition and emotion while resolving the puzzling, mysterious, age-old tension supposed to exist between them.

Profoundly different from the traditional idea of an "emotional" manner of acting or thinking, according to the distinctions offered here, an emotional way of relating has less to do with intensity and level of arousal. It has more to do with relational issues, such as concerns for the object of our emotion, our relationships with it, our interdependencies with it, and so forth. It is distinguished from the more utilitarian functional manner of relating in which we are primarily, or only, interested in the function of some exchangeable objects and care little about their future, destiny, and our personal relationships with them.

Therefore, according to the categorization of ways of relating offered in this essay, an emotional way of relating is typically more common and appropriate in the home, in an art studio or in a spiritual place—not because we don't have to use our cognition or be rational, but because less quantitative, more personal, individual, specific caring relationships are required, and more personal biases and preferences are acceptable. At the same time, in areas of endeavor that require or allow a more detached, objective, efficient, and less personal method of relating to certain elements, it is often better to relate in a non-emotional, utilitarian manner, or at least with lower emotional intensity and fewer personal preferences and biases, for instance, at work when dealing with remote clients or masses of people we don't know or much care about, in military operations, or when performing experiments with lab animals.

All in all, including, comparing or contrasting emotions with cognition is not only unhelpful but actually misleading. Asking whether they are identical, part of each other (as in value judgments), included in each other or negate one another brings us back into the old dualism and conflict between emotions and cognition. It also gives the false impression that we are locked into this dualism, and thus actually confuses and blocks the conversation instead of opening it up and dispensing with the dichotomy all together. Instead of concentrating on contradictions, competition or dominance, it is probably more beneficial to study the mutual contributions and cooperation of our various human subsystems, how they trigger and shape each other, and how they change to accommodate one another.

To Summarize:

- Cognition can be seen as one aspect of our mental activities.
- Though certain cognitive processes, such as judgments, appraisals, evaluations, and cognitive constructs like beliefs, motivations, and values have a critical role in facilitating our

emotions, emotions should not be confined to these process-es or constructs, or compared to them. Any such attempt be-comes a form of reduction that misses the unique additional dimensions of emotions, such as intensity, particularity, and sensations, and fails to come to terms with their distinctly relational role.

- Emotions are better viewed as *whole* body/mind relational methods, configurations, and modes of operation which also affect and are affected by physiological conditions.
- We use cognitive abilities continuously, and we relate emo-tionally most of the time.
- Cognition changes often to accommodate different tasks. It changes noticeably with the intensity of emotions, in a state that is commonly viewed as "being emotional." When inten-sity rises, part of our cognitive modification includes an al-teration of our rationality and objectivity, as we are going to discuss below.
- Cognition and emotions can best be seen as two non-com-peting, interconnected phenomena that nevertheless do not fully overlap and should not be submerged in each other.

Given the highly controversial, loaded, intricate realm of cognition and mental activity and the limited empirical knowledge about it, it is obviously not possible to resolve their relative scopes of operation here or to propose final definitions. To reposition the role and place of emotions relative to such complex and ambiguous concepts is not an easy or clear-cut task.

On top of it, as mentioned above, the pervasive terminology, our long-standing metaphors, and accepted definitions have been set ac-cording to longstanding views of emotions in which they are seen to negate or compete with cognition and rationality. These deeply embedded ways of seeing make explaining or understanding a new view of the relations between emotions and cognition a difficult struggle. Therefore, it will be necessary in the future to continue breaking away from the traditional terms and relations and adopt new, perhaps somewhat strange, terminology and metaphors—a task we have begun here.

We must furthermore keep reminding ourselves that all of our categories for body and mind (and others as well) are theoretical distinctions between connected, continuous, but slightly different human phenomena put forward for heuristic purposes.

However, even if such theories and definitions are heuristic, the distinctions and relations proposed here between cognition and emotions have more than just linguistic, etymological consequences. They actually have important theoretical as well as practical implications for therapy, society, and politics. For example, the new view suggested here frees us to view emotions with very different models, for example, thinking of them as relational, and not as irrational, subjective, non-calculative, "softer" cognition. We can then better study and understand our relationships with other people, the environment, and various concepts, and find alternative ways to improve them. This in turn can change the place of emotions--not only for the purpose of therapy, but also to suggest far-reaching consequences in social and political discourse that could facilitate the pursuit of happiness and reduce hatred and wars, as we will discuss further in our concluding remarks.

7

Emotions and Rationality

The previous discussion of cognition has already shed some light on the connection between emotions and rationality; however, since the concept of rationality is so central to the understanding of cognition, emotions, and the relations between them, it justifies a closer look on its own. Although there has been an attempt to widen the concept of cognition and incorporate emotions into it, rationality has nonetheless been contrasted to emotions and left to dominate science, society, and, in many profound ways, Western philosophy. Thus, if the Western traditional tendency has been to contrast emotions to rationality or make them subject to it, recent strategies seek a solution in making emotions rational.

In this section, we will start by discussing briefly some of the meanings of rationality. We will continue by presenting some of the usual reasons offered for the traditional tension between emotion and rationality. And we will then turn to see how the alternative views presented in this essay might possibly reshape our understanding of the relations between emotions and rationality.

What Do We Mean by "Rationality"?

Like cognition, rationality is a heavily loaded term that carries with it important aspects of the Western tradition. The history of this term can be traced all the way to Greek philosophy and associations with mathematics (ratio), logical reasoning, and analysis. Much of it is encompassed in the scientific tradition and in Western behavioral ideals, which favor rational control over emotion and are familiar in different forms to most members of this culture. As with cognition, it is not possible to thoroughly cover the subject of rationality and its tension with emotions. Therefore, we will confine our exploration to two of the more common understandings of this concept, and show how they can be related to a new understanding of emotions. We will also mention a third common use of the term "rationality," but develop it only when discussing "objectivity" in the next section[9].

Instrumental rationality. This concept centers upon the idea of instrumentality or functionality: an element is rational if we can find its use and understand its function in a specific context. Thoughts and actions are rational when they seem to serve an end goal well, and people are rational when they choose the most efficient means for achieving their end goals. This understanding of rationality pertains to an effective, useful, efficient matching of means to an end.

Procedural or logical rationality. The second common meaning for rationality incorporates many of the traits associated with systematic cognition or behavior. It refers to a process which emphasizes logical, consistent, coherent, calm, reflective, objective, and often analytical principles, and which is methodically built and performed. This meaning seems to imply a dispassionate (non-emotional) thought process in which we select the best means and match methods to ends, and/or select the best route to these objectives. It also implies the ability to think or act efficiently or properly by selecting the most suitable and effective steps for achieving one's goals.

---

9 Numerous sources are available for a deeper and wider investigation of rationality, but for good examinations of the relation between rationality and emotions, see Solomon (1992, 1977, 2003), de Sousa (1979, 1990), Turski (1994) and others.

Solomon describes the idea of "procedural rationality" as the one ascribed to people who "practice a certain kind of thinking, follow certain procedures or methods of argumentation" (1992, 604), or with his eighteenth definition of rationality: "18. Rationality is a technique, a particular way of thinking, of entertaining possibilities . . . " (Solomon 1992, 607).

Objective rationality. The third common understanding of rationality is closely related to procedural rationality, but it is mostly used to describe the supposed ability to read reality "objectively" and thus "correctly." Therefore, we will discuss this idea of rationality in the next section, together with the idea of objectivity.

Traditional Reasons for Contrasting Emotions and Rationality

The same tension that exists between cognition and emotions is extended to common ideas about the conflict between rationality and emotions.

In "emotional" times, people are thought to deviate from their usual behavior or abandon social norms, engage in illogical decision-making processes or undertake unfit, inefficient actions to reach their goals, possibly demonstrating "temporary insanity." These three types of behaviors indicate to observers a reduction in "rationality."

The first and most common reason for attaching the label of "irrationality" to emotional people or their methods is the perception of a large gap between the behavior demonstrated during emotional events and an individual's usual behavior, or between actions undertaken in the grips of emotion and what *observers* consider to be the accepted social standard in these particular contexts. For example, when two people fall madly in love, they might appear to act irrationally since their behavior is far from usual or departs from the accepted social norms and doesn't seem (to observers) to serve well their *previous* conventional goals. For example, such people may act foolishly in public, give up promising careers, wealth or even life itself.

A second explanation often put forward for the conflict between emotion and rationality is that a reduction in procedural rationality seems often to lead also to a reduction in instrumental rationality (see definitions above). Commonly, thought processes are considered more rational if a number of alternative courses of action are considered, alternatives are compared with a degree of openness, options are studied in a calmer, slower, and more systematic manner, and long-term consequences are considered. For instance, people in a panic or rage are considered less rational since they tend to jump to conclusions, consider very few courses of action, and fail to take into account the consequences of their actions. On top of this procedural judgment, an instrumental evaluation by an outsider may examine the correspondence between the actions of emotional people with their values and goals, as perceived by the observer. Emotional people are usually found to be inefficient and ineffective and, therefore, irrational: they select the wrong escape from a fearful situation, choose an ineffective way to pursue a financial goal or opt for a futile attempt to get closer to a loved person.

Options for Bridging the Conflict Between Emotions and Rationality

For clarity and precision, we will try to separate the discussion into two main questions: First, how do emotions influence rationality (particularly intense emotions)? Second, are emotions somehow rational, or not? And, is it really helpful or beneficial to judge emotions for rationality, or is it just a confusion of mixed traits, like asking if being tall is rational?

How Emotions Affect Rationality

Unconventional behavior during intense emotional episodes, when evaluated by highly biased external judgments, often leads to branding emotions irrational. As noted in previous discussions, while Western philosophical traditions have often taken rationality to be universal and transcendent, most anthropologists and modern philosophers acknowledge that rationality is cultural and contextual. Many of them object to the idea that there is some sort of universal rational framework within which we can judge emotions. Instead, they argue very convincingly that rationality is highly ethnocentric and strongly influenced by Western views and values (White 2008).

It seems that rationality is most commonly judged on the basis of some external, but specific, personally or culturally loaded standard set by an observing judge. Namely, when a person or a society evaluates the rationality of a certain behavior, they *assume* that certain goals are inevitable, and thus view the actions of the emotional person according to their own standards. In other words, external assessment assumes that all people, at all times, should strive for what the judges consider to be acceptable social goals. The behavior is usually not evaluated by the emotional participants themselves, because they are considered "unfit" to judge, due to their emotional state.

Intense emotions, as we said before, can be viewed as modes of interaction in which one relationship or a few relationships dominate most of the person's attention, consideration, and behavior. The increased focus on these elements is often expressed in the establishment of new immediate motivations, priorities, and goals. Emotional events direct our attention and energy toward more urgent targets (for example, attraction, escape, attack), often at the expense of more typical practices, social norms, and long-term objectives, such as career or social reputation. They might also seem to take place at the expense of the object of these emotions, a situation that seems even less rational or logical. People in intense times are typically more motivated and rushed, so they often tend to push their agenda and act with less consideration for the *overall* well-being of the object of their emotion. For example, a desperate lover or parent might hold a lover or a child against their will, just because they are so locked into their position. In some situations, these actions might be justified, say if the lover or child wants to harm themselves, while in other instances it might be harmful to all involved.

Nevertheless, on the whole, the actions of people in highly aroused situations might be considered rational if they were judged according to the actor's *own* new goals. For instance, running naked to the street, if your house is on fire, could be seen as a rational action, as could compromising your safety for a friend at war, sacrificing your life for honor as a Samurai in traditional Japan, giving up everything to save a child, or giving up all your wealth for a lover. Judging by the danger of fire, the naked escaper could argue his or her action to be very rational. Judging by the values and goals of the Samurai himself, it was probably very rational to sacrifice one's life. The same goes for a loving person who finds their lover so valuable that giving up wealth is in fact the most logical course of action.

The gaps between emotional goals or values and conventional, social ones are more evident in intense emotional events. Nevertheless, as we demonstrated previously, long-term emotions share some characteristics with intense emotional events of shorter duration, and this disjunction with conventional values manifests in almost all emotions of all intensities. Emotions express personal biases, values, beliefs, relationships, and context, and these rarely conform perfectly to outside public norms that dictate efficiency and, on that basis, define appropriate, rational action or thought processes.

Long-term emotions may, however, appear to adhere to more "rational," socially approved norms. We noted previously that in emotionally intense periods we have higher concentration on fewer and more immediate relationships, whereas in calmer times we tend to consider a wider array of relationships and typically also longer-term ones. On top of it, since we are less intensely emotionally focused in longer-term situations, we typically can also relate in a non-emotional manner that is utilitarian and reflective, and this seems even more rational. Longer-term emotions commonly conform more to the acceptable social norms of the society we live in with regard to survival, career, mores, and so forth. Thus, it may not be so much the case that longer-term emotions are *actually* more rational, as it is that they deviate less from acceptable social patterns[10].

Thus it may be safer and more beneficial to talk about how emotional changes modify cognitive, behavioral, and motivational goals and values rather than tagging them as irrational. For instance, instead of claiming that highly emotional people or events are less rational, we can say that in extreme emotional states, people change their typical considerations and behavior. They conform less to social norms, but this alone doesn't make people less rational. "Though we may correctly speak of emotions being irrational, emotions need not distort thinking. Rather, it may be the specificity of goals invoked by an emotion that creates problems" (Oatley 1992, 176).

It must be noted that this essay mostly considers normal-range functionality and does not cover pathological cases. We argue here that intense emotional events probably developed extreme and unusual characteristics for a reason—for example, reactions in urgent situations that provide the strength for a quick escape. However, as with all human phenomena, extremes in which a person *over*-reacts

---

10 See relevant views in anthropological studies of emotions by Lutz 1986, White 2008, and others.

frequently and unnecessarily can become a pathological problem that negatively affects rational functioning.

Although intense emotions don't necessarily make emotions irrational, they may reduce the quality of decision making. The second influence of emotions on rationality has more to do with procedural rationality. At times of intense emotion, people seem to rush into decisions, be less flexible, entertain fewer options, and be more biased and less systematic. Thus, they tend to be less thorough and efficient in selecting the best path toward long-term goals and determining the best methods to reach them. However, this impaired procedural rationality often has more to do with the rushed or highly determined nature of the process.

It is obvious that many thought processes, and decision-making processes in particular, could be carried out more effectively if more time were available. Priorities, time management, and the availability of time become a question in various situations. Sufficient time to make a better decision might not be possible, or even beneficial: pilots in the air, stock brokers in a quickly changing market, lawyers in court, and surgeons performing operations must all make quick decisions while remaining emotionally calm and rational. Thus, emotional intensity is less a question of "having" rationality, and more a question of how well one performs it. Running away from a bear probably will not leave enough time to consider all options thoroughly. However, rushing is most likely preferable to staying by the bear while performing a fully rational appraisal of the situation. Thus, in a very emotional state, we are not only motivated by less conventional goals and considerations, but we often have less time and interest to apply to the *quality* of our rationality.

Procedural rationality and the capacity for theoretical thought also diminish when a person is tired, hungry, rushed or disturbed by noise. Emotions, too, affect individuals all the time in varying degrees, and we seem to remain rational through most of them. Although emotions influence rationality at certain times, they don't necessarily imply irrationality. "Emotions are not irrational, people are irrational," writes Solomon (2003, 235).

It seems that while in calm emotional periods, we can choose whether to be rational or not, in intense emotional times, our ability or our will to practice rational thinking diminishes.

Rather than distinguishing between non-emotional rational states and emotional irrational states, as thinkers have done in the past, this essay proposes to separate the issue. On one hand, it is possible to distinguish between calm and intense emotional periods. On the other hand, we can differentiate between rational and non-rational—or even irrational—thought processes, and among different qualities of rational processes. The two distinctions can overlap at times but they don't have to, and such an overlap cannot be automatically assumed.

Are Emotions Rational?

After discussing the effects of emotions on rationality, we can consider whether it is worthwhile to view emotions as irrational, rational or altogether outside the realm of such distinctions. In the following discussions, we will assess some ways emotions have been linked to rationality.

Emotions are rational because they are functional and instrumental. Many of the recent claims for the rationality of emotions are based on what we have referred to as their "instrumental rationality." Namely, emotions can be considered rational since they are instrumental and efficient in achieving specific goals. For example, paternal care is driven by love, the need for survival is sometimes supported by fear and anger, and emotions generally create social relationships and cohesiveness, and thus enable empathy and morality. This understanding attempts to find a rational explanation for the existence of emotions and to reestablish their validity in the process.

The views presented so far in this essay leave no room for doubt about the importance of emotions and their validity, and they hopefully show that the function of emotions goes even further than what has commonly been believed. In this sense, emotions are a very rational component of life.

However, this general instrumentality could be attributed to almost any category of life as long as we presume to understand its function. On top of it, this argument for the general instrumentality of emotion does not explain the rationality of specific emotional instances, such as the love of a particular person or a piece of music.

To say that love is more rational than hatred, or that a specific person should love his neighbors rather than hate them, is a very different claim. It implies a value judgment. No matter how important or moral such value judgments may be, they cannot be said to be rational or not, unless they are seen in light of a specific goal. Evaluating them as rational or irrational presupposes some external, universal, rational criteria by which to judge all human drives, values, and goals.

Accordingly, it could be said that emotions, as well as many other mind/body elements, are useful in the overall scheme of evolution. However, it seems more beneficial, helpful, and safer to describe them as instrumental or functional rather than as "rational"—a term that might have many other misleading connotations as we will see below.

Emotions are rational since they include rational elements and are processed rationally. Another approach to making emotions rational is putting an emphasis on the idea that they include logical/rational cognitive processes such as judgments, evaluations, and beliefs. In such studies emotions are often described as the outcome of a rational, logical process of thought, and therefore they are taken to be rational (particularly if you are assumed to have EQ on top of IQ, and practice CBT). According to these approaches, like all other cognitive processes and products, emotions can be rational at some times and irrational at others, depending on a person's personality, choices, and circumstances. However, as we will see below, this view doesn't hold if emotions are not considered as an aspect of cognition. This perspective is particularly problematic if emotions are viewed as a way of relating, a type of relationship which expresses or is an extension of drives and motivations.

Emotions are rational when cognition, behavior, and relationships are rational. A similar recent approach to reconciling emotions and rationality is to assess the rationality of emotions according to what might be called "emotional rationality." The different versions and interpretations of this outlook, which are interesting and important, can unfortunately be discussed only briefly here. Some of the better-known avenues to this perspective, as touched on above, evolved with behaviorism, with Ellis's Rational Emotive Behavioral Therapy (REBT) (1994), Beck's Cognitive Behavioral Therapy (CBT) (1979, Alford and Beck1997), and more recently around the preoccupation with "Emotional Intelligence" (EQ) (Salovey and Mayer 1990, Goleman 1995, 2005, in addition to Aristotle 1987). Related ideas from the philosophy of emotions even contend that "emotions constitute the framework (or frameworks) of rationality itself" (Solomon 1992, 611). (Also see de Sousa 1987, 2013).

One interesting example of this tack appears in theories of economics. Standard theories assume that most people act rationally most of the time in order to maximize utility, unless they are very emotional. Some more recent theories shift the responsibility to "faulty" irrational processes in these areas (Kahneman 2011). While these theories don't necessarily contest the tension between emotion and rationality, they tend to move some of the blame to cognitive processes, seeing them as flawed regardless of emotions.

As hinted above, Cognitive Behavioral Therapy argues that being cognitively rational typically leads to more functional, healthier, and less unhappy lives. In somewhat of a complementary manner, studies of EQ essentially understand emotional rationality as having the right emotions at the right time, of appropriate intensity, and suitable for the context, as well as being an emotionally engaged person who is connected to society and others. In functional terms, it means being emotionally developed and appropriate—or instrumental and efficient (terms used above to describe rational qualities) in achieving life and social goals.

The ideas and practices of Cognitive-Experiential Self-Theory (CEST) for instance, Cognitive Behavioral Theory (CBT), and Emotional Intelligence theories (EQ) have many benefits and bring much-needed attention to emotional development and forms of therapy that are useful in helping with emotional problems. However, when trying to understand the relationship between emotion and rationality, some of their terminology can be confusing. For example, CBT labels certain beliefs and cognitive constructs as erroneous and irrational, thus placing value judgments on viewpoints that may be hard to judge precisely (for example, the level of potential danger from traveling to a developing country). However, and most importantly, we have to be careful not to project these judgments onto emotions. While beliefs may perhaps be judged for their rationality or, more precisely, for their functionality (when closely associated with particular knowledge), emotions related to beliefs are not necessarily limited to cognitive processes, and they express values that cannot be easily judged for rationality. For instance, a parent's belief that their child behaves nicely and/or is very academically successful could be judged to be wrong and irrational on occasion, according to some external social norms (school performance); however, the parent's love for the child is based on a value judgment which is rarely up to anybody's judgment for rationality, as will be further clarified below.

A similar problem of relative values exists with EQ, which judges emotional behavior and/or actions as a means to an end—in other words assesses whether it is the right emotion at the right time for the right purpose. It assumes that in the same manner that we judge general intelligence for guiding analytical thought processes, we can judge Emotional Intelligence as a mechanism for sorting out the best emotional behavior. This approach might be acceptable if emotions were thoughts, behavior or actions constructed for specific goals, and if they were easily determined by conscious thinking. As we have emphasized, even though emotions are guided by thoughts, they should not be reduced to them, and they can't be judged for analytical quality. They express values that don't have a clear correlation with intelligence (you don't love or hate more according to your level of intelligence, or love the ocean if you are more or less intelligent).

On top of it, emotions are most commonly and primarily led by unconscious mental processes which are hard to judge for rationality or intelligence. For example, it is possible to think that we *should* have a certain emotion, and at the same time experience a very different one. Likewise, behavior does not always coincide with emotion. It is possible to be in love for years without doing anything about it, telling anybody, and/or showing any behavioral signs of it.

Therefore, it might be preferable to talk about "relational intelligence" instead of emotional intelligence ("R.Q." instead of "E.Q.").

This type of rationality implies thinking and forming the "right" relationships or treating various elements in one's environment appropriately.

Relational Intelligence could focus on judging relational thoughts, analysis, judgments, decisions, as well as relational actions and behavior. This way we use rationality for the elements it is meant for, namely cognitive processes and the actions that reflect them. At the same time, by looking at our relational decision making and behavior, we are judging the type of intelligence that is most relevant and closely associated with our emotional configuration.

According to this view, we would be better off not asking, for instance, whether intense love is rational, if a particular love is rational, or if it is rational to give up economic goals for an intense love. Instead, we could ask whether the loving person can still think rationally about this relationship and others, whether the partner merits such a sacrifice, ask if the intensity of the devotion is reciprocal, whether this way of relating really helps the lovers achieve their emotional goals (for example, expression of the love, greater closeness), how it will impact the rest of their lives, and so forth. Thus, we can learn relational capabilities and develop relational sophistication that can clearly help individuals and society as a whole. These relational skills, with a proper change of values and behavior, can also lead to a preferred emotional configuration.

Theories that identify dual mental systems in our analysis of the world and dealing with it, such as Epstein's (1984, 1999) Cognitive/ Rational Vs Experiential systems (CEST), and later Kahneman's (2011) *Thinking, Fast and Slow*, don't always rely on the traditional division between rationality and emotions. However, unless the basic understanding of emotions and their relations with rationality changes, the tendency for most people will be to view these theories and their findings as a continuation of the traditional dichotomy between these two. Namely, most people still hold on to the familiar tension between rationality and emotions which was emphasized in Greek philosophy and continued throughout the ages (see Carl Jung's [1961] distinction between thinking and feeling).

This dichotomous view often persists as an underlying or hidden necessity, assumption or outcome in most theories of emotions today, regardless of their attempts to rebottle this tension. Although these various approaches are helpful in bridging some of the competition between emotions and rationality, they still tend to view emotions in a way that is largely cognitive and instrumental; and, since in most cases they shy away from a deep theoretical reconfiguration, they typically end up either perpetuating or hiding the traditional conflict between emotions and rationality.

After briefly discussing the general question of whether emotions as a whole are rational, we will now turn to the question of whether particular emotions can be judged for rationality.

Emotions are better not judged for rationality. Instrumental or procedural rationality have been developed to judge cognitive and behavioral process, and they are less useful when applied to emotions, ways of relating that are mostly subconscious.

Instead of forcing rationality on emotions in various ways, it might be more helpful to view emotions and rationality as incompatible, incomparable categories, as we did with cognition. Rationality is closely associated with cognition, efficiency, and instrumentality, while emotions are relational configurations expressing directives and values. Therefore, while we can propose that rationality and emotions should not be viewed as mutually exclusive, or as the opposing ends of one continuum, we can nonetheless view them as distinct concepts or functions which in most cases and for most purposes should not be mixed together or applied to each other. It would be as if asking if being white or black, playing music, or driving a blue car is rational or efficient.

From this perspective, it is better not to utilize cognitive or behavioral procedural descriptions—the language of procedural rationality—for emotions (for example, efficiency). Namely, rationality should not be used to judge emotions or as a means of contrast, since it was created to evaluate purely cognitive processes or actions as the means of attaining ends and goals. It is more of a *technique, a standard or a social norm* for assessing cognitive or behavioral efficiency, effectiveness, and social conformity.

Rationality was designed and is primarily used today to judge and rate decision-making processes (such as determining a good escape from a burning house). Such evaluations are possible because of the underlying assumption of free will, choice, and the possibility of having some say in the various possible options. (We don't judge the rationality of a person who has fainted and been taken out of a burning house by fire fighters on a stretcher). For the same reason, people also attribute a sense of volition and choice to much of our behavior and actions, since they assume that they depend on and are an outcome of the cognitive or mental processes that led to them (to run away from a burning house, for example). Thus, judging behavioral rationality actually implies evaluating cognitive rationality. Following closely behind is the reason why in most cases cognitive processes and behavior incur a certain accountability as well: they imply free will and cognitive choice, partial awareness and control (as required, for example, to help your spouse to escape the fire).

Emotions, on the other hand, have frequently been seen as out-of-control phenomena. In the past, they were seen as imposed by some internal or external spiritual phenomena. Today, in somewhat of a similar manner, they are seen as an outcome of primarily subconscious processes. This is also why they have often been excluded from accountability and frequently assumed to interfere with rationality as an unmanageable inner desire or urge (as in the case of temporary insanity). This intuitive reading is not so far from current assessments, but the explanation might be more apparent and clear according to the relating theory suggested here. We have proposed here that emotions express, manifest, and can be seen as extensions of our life's drives, values or elected directions, and that they are mostly subconsciously framed. Therefore, they represent our goals and are hard to change or control consciously or quickly. Accordingly, it is uncommon to attribute volition to them or judge them for efficiency (which is what rationality does). We might tell people, for instance, to change their perception, actions, and treatment of their parents if they are difficult in their old age or unappreciative. However, it would remain difficult to tell people that it is irrational to love their parents in their old age.

Similarly, we don't ask if being tall or being born a Jew is rational, since it is not up to a person to decide those. However, we can contemplate whether it is rational to reveal your ethnicity in certain circumstances (for example, during the inquisition or in Nazi Germany), since this can in fact be decided. In the same manner, we don't judge a prisoner for rationality if they are following orders and have no say in the matter.

We claimed before and will argue later that emotions can be changed, and that we should be accountable for our emotions to a certain degree. However, we also suggested that it is probably easier and more effective to change our beliefs, habitual thought patterns, perceptions, values, and actions, as an intermediate step toward changing our emotions, instead of trying to change them directly (for example, trying to love someone more or hate them less). From this perspective, emotional accountability basically ends up a matter of being accountable for our values, perceptions, and actions.

Instead of assessing emotions in relation to rationality, specific emotions, like particular values, could perhaps be assessed and judged for a certain morality and consistency with a person's or a community's other values, overarching philosophy, and accepted norms and goals. For instance, do these emotions and values increase or decrease suffering for this person, for the community or for others around them? Are they consistent with the individual's other goals, stated values, with the community around them, and so forth.

In other words, saying an emotion is rational or irrational is like saying that emotions are reflective, analytical, functional, efficient, or that they must fit strict social norms. These are concepts that were developed to describe thinking techniques, processes, and behavior, and they are not necessarily applicable for emotions. Even though a connection may exist between emotion and rationality, ***emotions are not "irrational thoughts,"*** and calm emotions do not guarantee rationality. Emotions are a completely different "animal" which merits its own terminology and should not be confused with or reduced to internal cognitive processes or actions.

We can perhaps appraise the rationality of the cognitive aspects of emotions, but not the emotional phenomenon as a whole. Saying that "a person's love for the ocean is irrational" communicates very little. Any attempt to judge or contrast emotions with rationality, or even to judge a specific emotion, leads to a form of reductionism or universalism, since, as noted earlier, it presupposes a certain universal standard by which to judge values.

Similar views are suggested by Solomon (1992, 1977) who states that emotions provide both *the substance of a good life and the ends*. De Sousa says similarly that since emotions ". . . are concerned with the determination of ends, they remain, on this view, beyond the pale of rationality" (1979, Introduction).

Thus, in our example above, a person's love for the ocean or music cannot be judged to be rational or irrational. It is a basic preference, proclivity, value or direction in a person's life, and not a tool, instrument, or way of getting something or somewhere.

This view fits well with growing objections to rationality as a guiding criterion for social and philosophical development. It also matches growing resistance to the idea of universal objectivity and rational standards that are supposed to judge everything and everybody in life. It is not the case that values are primary only in such areas as art, morality, and politics, where a normative freedom has traditionally been more accepted. Rather it is increasingly recognized that values, relationships, and therefore emotions, act as building blocks, initiation points, and a framework for most other conceptual structures, including systems of categorization, language, ontology, and social structures. Emotions shape both the personal and social universe with their particular biases and preferences, within which rationality operates and is judged. In this sense, Solomon's (1992) and de Sousa's (1979, 2013) argument that "emotions are the framework of rationality" gets a whole new and deeper meaning.

Emotions Shape the Framework of Rationality

Emotions, as an extension of values, could be said to shape the framework of rationality. Whether we attribute our preferences, goals or directions in life to our drives, values or to the emotions that express them relationally, they end up shaping the world we live in personally or socially, and determine what is important or unimportant to us. This is why it is argued that they also shape the world or determine the framework within which we judge what is rational.

For instance, some of our stronger drives are for survival and reproduction, and these often end up as central values in our life. As an extension of reproduction, one of the obvious primary values is raising and protecting of our children. Accordingly, we tend to relate to our children in a manner that is commonly described as love. This is often said to be "natural" or "functional," as we suggested before (not necessarily rational, since most of us don't seem to have much cognitive say in it). Namely, we tend to care what happens to them, have empathy for them, wish them the best, are happy when they succeed, and are committed to them. Therefore, we typically also undertake the associated actions and behavior that attempt to protect them, help them, keep us close to them, and so forth.

If we assume that the end goal in this example is reproduction, and that love is an extension or expression of that goal, then rationality is framed within these goals, preferences, and biases. In other words, what is significant for us pulls and pushes us, shapes our universe, and becomes our goals and preferences; is not only a matter of survival and reproduction, but also the survival, success and well-being of our children. Rationality will have to be judged within this framework; it could evaluate, for instance, the cognitive manner in which we analyze, plan, and decide how to achieve these goals and preferences, including the best behavior and course of actions to protect and advance our children and our relationships with them.

Difficult Theoretical Options and Ease of Readers' Comprehension

As with any other attempt to profoundly change basic common concepts, it is difficult for this essay to decide how much to change the concept of emotions, to what extent to modify related concepts (such as cognition and rationality), and how to reconfigure a novel configuration for them all by spelling out their new relations, relative positions, interdependency, and so forth.

This is not only a question of theoretical and practical benefits, but also a question of creating a view that is easy for potential audiences to understand and accept, whether they are expert read-ers or interested non-specialists. Extreme modifications are not only hard to accept, but are often hard to understand. They require a whole new terminology, language, imagery, metaphors, and con-ceptual constellations that extend to larger and larger perceptual domains. On top of it, as we remind ourselves repeatedly, our life processes are all connected and flow into each other regardless of our arbitrary distinctions and linguistic categories. Thus, for in-stance, it is not so clear where the dividing line falls between our drives and values, mental processes, the cognitive conscious and sub-conscious portions, our emotional ways of relating, and our associ-ated actions and behavior. As a first step, this essay assumed that it would be more beneficial and more accessible for readers to change their view of emotions to a relational one, which necessitated the discussion of their interaction with cognition, rationality, and even behavior. However, it was decided not to over-extend this effort and attempt to change those actual domains beyond what is necessary for emotions. This decision makes the essay less ambitious, but, the author hopes, more comprehensible. Depending on emerging goals and definitions, this decision could be changed in the future—for instance, if research suddenly made clear just how cognitive pro-cesses participate in emotional formation, so that we could control them and our emotions to a high degree.

In summary, this essay proposes that if particular emotions are associated more with cognitive, elective processes, and related choic-es of behavior and actions, they could possibly also be judged for rationality. However, as long as we prefer to view emotions more as a relational stance that expresses our basic values and directions in life—aspects that are primarily subconscious and are less di-rectly consciously controlled—it is not beneficial to judge them for rationality.

Examples From Our "Foreign Policy" Analogy

If we revisit our ongoing foreign policy metaphor, we can draw some interesting parallels. Much of a country's foreign policy is functional and non-emotional, and thus very goal-oriented, so that actions in pursuit of these policies can be judged rational or irrational. For example, goals such as national security, increase in power and territory, and access to global resources are clear objectives in which the rationality of actions can be judged. However, when it comes to more emotional relationships, such as those that involve loyalty (for example between the U.S. and Great Britain), hatred (such as that between Germany and Russia in WWII), and especially ethnic hatred like that of the Germans for the Jews in WWII, it is hard to judge whether these emotions are rational or not. Certain values led to the intense hatred of the Jews (belief in "Aryan" superiority and purity). The horrifying actions that followed can be assessed as immoral and unethical, but it is unfortunately hard to judge whether they were necessarily irrational, like many other actions driven by hatred or love. Stalin probably killed many Russians without much emotional intensity and with undisturbed, calm rationality. In these cases, emotions are ways of relating, or a special type of relationship that expresses and facilitates the values and goals of these nations or leaders, and thus they are hard to judge according to standards of rationality.

One might argue that some of these intense emotional relationships are a good example of a rushed and less rational decision-making process in turbulent times, and that they therefore represent a lower quality of procedural rationality. For example, some argue that the Nazi's extreme, terrible conduct led to the early immigration of many Jewish scientists, who later helped the Americans build the first atomic bomb ahead of the Germans. Likewise, Hitler's insistence on conquering Stalingrad, which was seen by many as a strategic mistake (including many of his generals), may have been the result of his personal hatred for Russians and for Stalin in particular. However, while this explains the irrational results of these emotions, it remains impossible to judge actually whether these emotions themselves were rational or not. How is it possible to judge the rationality of one's love for Chinese food and hatred for licorice?

The phenomena and ideas discussed above are rather complicated and somewhat challenging. Nevertheless, this discussion is important because it shows the complexity of concepts, and how a change in the understanding of one concept can radically modify the relative positions of all. Recognition of these dynamics is critical to the way we treat these ideas in therapy, science, education, politics—or even in court, when judging "temporary insanity" for example. A few basic conclusions can be drawn from the discussion thus far to act as a platform for starting and developing future discourse:

1. A person tends to have a narrower, less conventional picture of reality and highly determined, biased goals in times of intense emotion. These goals are not necessarily irrational in themselves, but they are often considered so by others.
2. A person *can* have a less rational or lower quality thought *process* (according to the standards of procedural rationality) when experiencing an intense emotional state. This lapse often has to do with a narrowing of focus and lack of time to process a situation rather than an inability to process it.
3. Rationality can play an important part in the more cognitive aspect of emotions or in related behaviors. This capacity, often categorized as emotional rationality or intelligence, is better described as relational intelligence. Nevertheless, the

Notions on Emotions

fact that rationality can play a role in emotions does not, by itself, indicate whether emotions are rational or not.

4. From an evolutionary, utilitarian point of view, emotions could be considered a rational phenomenon, because they seem to serve the development of the species. However, we might better think of the role of emotions in human development as instrumental, functional or useful, rather than rational.

5. Particular emotions are better not judged for rationality since they manifest values, goals, and desired ends. We can only use the standard of rationality to assess the efficiency and effectiveness of the conscious thought processes and actions used to reach these goals (according to instrumental rationality).

Blaise Pascal's aphorism perhaps captures this chapter best: "The heart has its reasons which reason does not know."

8

Emotions and Objectivity

Objectivity, another loaded concept central to Western tradition, is in many ways closely associated with cognition, rationality, and emotions. Even more than rationality, objectivity has been seen in direct opposition to emotions, and objectivity is often defined by the absence of emotions—as a judgment "uninfluenced by emotions, surmise, or personal prejudice" (*American Heritage Dictionary* 1976). As with cognition and rationality, the scope of this essay does not allow for comprehensive examination of this topic, so we will only briefly suggest some implications that the new view of emotions might have for the idea of objectivity and its relation with emotions.

When it comes to objectivity and emotions, we will refrain from complex philosophical debate with the traditional definitions, views, and counterviews. Instead, we will try to look at this concept in more practical terms and within concrete social contexts. We will continue to use political and other analogies to demonstrate in a more familiar and visual manner the relations among these various terms and the phenomena they connote.

Contexts in which objective behavior is required, or at least desired, are abundant. We can consider judges in the legal system, referees in sports, administrators in the government, or scientists with their empirical work. We can also see ample examples of this relational technique and ideal when people in business are making judgments between employees, scenarios, outcomes or ideas, or in general assessments of "reality."

The main function of objectivity in most cases is to devise a principle, or a process, that will guarantee *equal or unbiased treatment* for different specified elements or options in a particular situation. Since such judgment has often been undertaken by people (now it is often relegated to computers), the context has usually been divided in two ways: On one hand, there is a presumed (or desired) distance between the judge or observer and the judged or observed. Namely, a judge is supposed to be detached from the judged, emotionally, socially, and even physically. On the other hand, there is some assumed connection (an association or resemblance) among the observed elements, independently of the observer. For example, the members of the control group in research share some common traits. Most importantly, it is usually specified that the observer should not be dependent on the outcome or on the observed, and therefore should have no biases or preferences. For example, referees are not supposed to be affected by the outcome of the event, and therefore should not care which team wins. If they do have a vested interest in the outcome of the game, they are considered unfit, biased or corrupt.

The best way to achieve this aim of neutrality, according to common wisdom, is for the observer to relate equally to all the relevant elements. This could be achieved by maintaining equal emotional relationships—for example, judging a game among equally loved children, or, more typically, by having no emotional relationships, thus being indifferent to what is observed and to the result (for example, experimenting on mice).

The preferred approach to ensure that a person can deal dispassionately with a group of elements under observation and remain indifferent to them at the same time is by having only *utilitarian or reflective relationships* with them. As defined above, these types of relationships tend to be limited to an exchange of utility or information and are handled with indifference. The belief is that this type of relationship, unlike the emotional way of relating, lacks the basic dimensions of emotional relationships, namely motivational direction, interdependence, specificity, and sensation (as discussed before).

The absence of motivation guarantees a lack of preference, since the judges or observers have no specific investment in a particular development in the element being observed or in their relationship with it. This lack of motivation contrasts with, say, the motivation for profit should one of the elements win, or the satisfaction of seeing close family members succeed. Observing professionals are not expected to perceive interdependence with their objects, or to hold any a priori opinion that would cause them to view any of the observed objects as special or better.

It is therefore clear that in situations that demand objectivity, one of the main objections to emotional relationships derives from the traditional intuitive recognition that with emotions come specific motivations, preferences, biases, a state of interdependence and specific care for some of the elements involved. These are the exact conditions that objectivity is hoping to avoid.

As we will explain soon, objectivity is rarely perfect and fluctuates to a large degree depending on the situation, the underlining relationships, the capacity and will of the "judge," and so forth.

At times, awareness can help to offset these biases to some extent, since we can correct for our emotional "gravity" if we are very determined, and perhaps excuse ourselves or ask for external advice (as an honest judge will do). However, considering the goal at hand (equal and unbiased treatment), it seems that the principle of objectivity does indeed conflict with many essential dimensions of emotions. Therefore, it makes sense to discourage emotional relationships between the observer/judge and the observed/judged. The challenge is knowing how to combine them, or practice either an emotional or an objective relationship without eliminating one or the other, or experiencing an ongoing conflict between them, something we will discuss shortly.

Another Common Usage of Objectivity: "A Realistic Reading of Reality"

Another type of procedural rationality that is closer to objectivity is the ability to read the "reality" around us "objectively." We will put aside the complex psychological question of what might be considered a *normal* or valid view of reality. In any event, emotions are often associated with strong biases and therefore are cited as an important source of interference in an individual's ability to be "objectively rational" or "in touch with reality."

Instead of judging or treating equally a group of objects in science, court or sports, we are here assumed to judge elements around us in an unbiased, objective way and to have a rational perception of the surrounding environment. Like rationality, this capacity is also judged by society or an external observer (for example, a psychiatrist) and has much to do with conformity.

In discussing rationality above, it was not all that clear whether a person is actually less rational in intense times or simply adopts new, less conventional, and more focused goals. Unless we have an extreme pathological case, such as hallucination or a biological inability to read external, environmental input, it could be that one's reading of reality simply changes in intense times, and thus seems highly subjective and irrational to outsiders.

In fact, individuals are subjective and biased all the time. However, when extremely angry, in a panic or passionately in love, we tend to adopt a different outlook on our situation according to our urgent, fresh, and specific goals. Thus, when people are madly in love, it is not so clear whether they are less objective about reality or simply care less about what other people think, about their income or future career. It is not easy to judge whether gaining the love of a lover, or saving a friend or a child, is more important than personal wealth. Yet again, these actions may have less to do with the inability to perform an objective reading of reality and more to do with a change of values, concentration on specific values, and indifference to conformity. Thus, we have to be very cautious when considering changes in people's perceptions of reality, and be especially careful about labeling these as either pathological mental inabilities or a change of values.

For similar reasons, it is important to keep in mind that this particular type of objectivity often has wider social and political dimensions. It is also used as a standard to evaluate the match between an individual's reading of reality and that of the surrounding society. Society typically defines what is considered to be normal, and what that means for a particular place and time. This phenomenon is well known and is described by many anthropologists and psychologists. Some even depict it as an intermediate, social type of objectivity and call it "inter-subjectivity" (see Harari 2015). However, in a sense it also forces the individual to match his or her reading to the social, "normal" standard, and fit in. This can be seen as a useful, cohesive, social force or a form of coercion, depending on the particular context, the specific details of each situation, and the values of the particular observer.

This discussion is not a call for wild, "free" emotional expressions, which can lead to a dysfunctional society and lack of mutual consideration. At the same time, it is not a claim for strengthening emotional and individual supervision and control, as practiced in some totalitarian cultures and regimes. These observations serve only as a reminder that this type of objectivity often has as much to do with conformity as it does with objectivity or reality.

What is important to recognize here is the idea that emotions are often an important part of what we consider to be our individuality, our personal constellation, or our uniqueness (including the distinctiveness of our community). They form and express our particular values and preferences in the face of public pressure for uniformity, homogeneity, and conformity. This is why evaluating this sense of objectivity or rationality can be very controversial (as Ken Kesey's [1962] *One Flew Over the Cuckoo's Nest* illustrates). Yet again we see the importance of understanding our emotions and their complex relations to intricate concepts such as rationality and objectivity. These considerations go beyond the personal therapeutic level and extend to the social and political arenas in which we have to consider the desires and preferences of individuals, as well as the needs and values of society as a whole.

Emotional Intensity and Objectivity

It is clear that the more intense the emotional experience is, the more it will affect our ability or willingness to be objective. Intense emotions will further focus the direction of our relationships, increase certain biases, and strengthen our commitment to them. (For example, if we fall in love with one of our employees or students, or fear one of them, it is clear that we would have a harder time being objective in judging them against the rest of the group.)

Intense emotional experience also results in "spill over" into other areas of life. Individuals who are charged with making dispassionate decisions, such as judges, for example, can be upset with their family members, or angry at their neighbors, as long as this emotion is "left at home." Their home affairs should not spillover and influence their behavior in court. But who would want a judge who just came out of a heated argument with his/her spouse?

Beyond the "spill-over" effect, we have noted that intense emotional situations also mean a lower level of cognitive control and a higher level of commitment to the emotional object. Thus, for example, while a slightly biased judge could enforce objective behavior in calm emotional times, it would be much more difficult in periods of intense emotions.

Finally, we have mentioned that powerful emotional events usually imply a high level of cognitive concentration, a tendency that limits the number of relationships we can consider, and focuses us on more immediate concerns instead of on the long term. However, these events can also decrease the capacity for reflective relationships and symbolic, theoretical, open-ended thinking. The problem is that one aspect of being objective is the ability to have reflective relationships with the elements under consideration. In other words, we must be able to separate and distance ourselves, as well as to relate to or manipulate those elements as anonymous, abstract symbols, instead of specific, unique particulars. For instance, the mice in the scientist's laboratory are treated as statistical, generic symbols, and not as particular "individuals." The same goes for citizens in IRS reviews or other governmental, official or corporate procedures.

As with cognition and rationality, objectivity and emotions are not mutually exclusive, but they do have a mutual influence that is more pronounced in times of intense emotional experience. However, if we view emotions as a way of relating, or a type of relationship, we must accept our earlier realization that we have emotions most of the time. This means that we can probably practice objectivity at the same time as we experience emotions. From this perspective, we can consider objectivity as a relational technique with specific rules and ideals—one that can coexist with emotions, but which deteriorates or is harder to perform if the judges are involved emotionally with the judged or when emotional intensity rises. Therefore, instead of contrasting objectivity with emotion, it may be better to contrast it with biased treatments or judgments, which are more likely at points of high emotional intensity.

Verbal Differences Between Emotions and Objectivity

Another route for verifying the inherent categorical differences and relations between emotions and objectivity is to pay attention to the profound differences in the way we describe, measure, and evaluate them.

As a procedure, objectivity can be evaluated in degrees of success, and not just according to "on/off" criteria. This is also true in the case of procedural rationality, which is reflected in the quality of our decision-making performance. Namely, as techniques, they are measured in terms of quality of practice (that is, how well an observer *can* practice rationality or be objective), and success can be measured (that is, how well *did* the observer practice it).

Emotions, on the other hand, can't be judged for success, since they signify our basic values and relationships. It is meaningless to ask "how well do I hate my neighbor"? In the odd cases when we attribute quality to emotions, it has less to do with the actual quality of emotions and more to do with the quality of our relationships, according to some personal or social standard. For example, we might say "I have a good, loving relationship with my son." While a judge may be expected to do his or her best to be objective, we can't expect a person to be in love with the ocean, or to do his/her best to love the ocean. For the same reason, we can say that the judge did a good job judging the case, managing to be highly objective. However, we can't say that a person did a good job of loving the ocean. The most common, measurable, quantitative element in emotions is their intensity, not the effectiveness of practicing them or the extent to which they achieve something. For example, we may ask how intense love is, but it is difficult to ask what love has accomplished or how well it has succeeded. This distinction is not just a verbal curiosity or a piece of trivia. As noted earlier, it captures our intuitive grasp of the categorical differences between emotions and cognition, rationality and objectivity. We intuitively sense that rationality and objectivity are forms of procedures, techniques, methods or standards, the quality of which can be measured. At the same time, like other cognitive procedures (such as judgments or conceptualizations), they are rarely measured for intensity (what does it mean to be intensely rational or objective?). Rationality and objectivity are thus profoundly different from emotions, which typically are not measured for quality of performance but are assessed for intensity (for example, it is possible to "hate him with a passion"). This is yet another example that demonstrates the categorical difference between objectivity and emotions. It confirms objectivity to be another type of cognitive behavioral method or standard, and emotions to be a relational style that expresses our drives, values, and motivations.

The Eternal Search for Ultimate Objectivity in Einstein's "Curved Space"

Martha Nussbaum (2001) offers a nice description of emotions in the introduction to *Upheavals of Thought*, stating that "Emotions shape the landscape of our mental and social lives." This image recalls the analogy of space travel presented previously in the context of Einstein's metaphor of curved space.

In Einstein's theory of relativity, he introduces the idea of "curved space," in which the gravity of different bodies contorts the fabric of space according to their relative mass. Analogous to Einstein's depiction of the forces of gravity, emotional relationships bias and stretch our picture or model of reality (past or present) according to their significance, preferences, and forces. Our space is never perfectly straight, flat, or uniform. It is always partially curved and contorted by the "gravity" of different emotional elements. We clearly experience our own gravity (the "self"), as well that of others around us, very much like the earth and other bodies around it with their corresponding gravitational fields. Namely, our emotions pull, push or otherwise force us closer to or away from elements around us, and make some of them feel tenfold bigger and more significant than others.

In space for example, as we approach a large body with enormous gravity, the pull of gravity goes up dramatically and overshadows most other forces. Similarly, if our relationship with a particular element suddenly becomes very intense, the motivational force it exerts will pull or push to such a degree that all other forces become negligible, so that our space becomes more curved, or differently curved.

This capacity to change the inner landscape or topography may also explain why emotions seem to confirm themselves or select whatever validates and fits their biases. If we hate a person, we will build our model of reality to fit and reinforce this view and the motivation that comes with it. Our reality, then, is always biased according to the "perceived size" of the elements around us and by the type and direction of the emotional forces that operate among us all.

Emotional "curved space" may be even more complex than what we know of outer space. It is affected by more considerations, different forces, and alternative scenarios, and it constantly changes. We are living organisms who change emotional relations often, and we deal with other living organisms that are active and partially unpredictable as well. Thus, we must improvise all the time in this highly intricate, contorted, and dynamic universe, and operate with probabilities instead of definite constant forces or outcomes.

Objectivity comes from accepting all these forces and biases, and trying as best we can to navigate among them all. Considering our success in outer space, this approach may be better than fighting with biases, ignoring emotions or attempting to achieve a universe (or occasions) without such distortions—something we have thus far assumed is possible. To increase objectivity using the curved space model, we would have to take into account the existing gravities of different entities (which we already do intuitively) and try to operate in areas where there is little or no gravity (as we do in outer space), or where "emotional gravity" doesn't directly interfere or compete with the judgment at hand. For instance, we try to not to judge other children against our child (high gravity). Luckily, we can also change some of these emotional gravities, unlike the gravity of the stars.

This analogy, helpful as it is, like all analogies is still not an exact depiction of our emotional system. However, it models rather well an emotional universe in which any attempt to be utterly rational or objective is at best an ideal that can be rarely reached by normal human beings. It could even be argued that in order to maintain our humanity, we should not even attempt to reach this questionable ideal (we have computers and psychopaths for that).

As is obvious by now, we are all always emotional, and we relate emotionally. Thus, we are always in a somewhat contorted, biased or curved cosmos. As suggested above, rationality and objectivity are not defined by the ability to navigate *without* emotions, but rather by the ability to navigate *within* the particular curved space of emotions. Rational and objective performance simply varies and goes up or down, depending on the time frame, context, and particular portion of the environment we are considering (best in non-emotional areas with less "gravity"), our cognitive and relational skills, and our emotional composition at the time.

This view might even be relevant to such arguments as Kahneman and Tversky's demonstration of people's irrationality (1979, 1992), or at least their imperfect rationality. These imperfections might also have to do with people's contorted universes, which are permanently curved by their emotions, even when they don't seem extremely emotional (or in our terms, when they relate in an emotionally calm manner).

This is yet another reason it is helpful to recognize our emotions as relational, and to accept their essential role and influence in our conceptual and social universe. It shows why it is not theoretically or practically beneficial to adopt a general policy that contrasts cognition, rationality or objectivity with emotions, or to view one as containing or dominating the other. It is clear that instead of combating the interactions between them and emotions, we need to accept their unique *coexistence* and figure out the best way to deal with it.

We can and should continue to apply our cognitive, rational, and objective capacities and practices, and improve them, in contexts where they are needed. Nevertheless, we should realize that these efforts are rarely perfect and actually facilitate and promote our emotional preferences, which essentially represent and express our values.

For instance, we can do our best to be objective in a scientific experiment, when judging in court and sports, or when ruling on cases as policemen, governmental employees or any other public function which requires it. However, the bottom line is that we ultimately perform these activities to promote our emotional goals, such as our dedication to our job, the love of our children or our commitment to helping others. It can also be done for the love of fame, power, and prestige, or out of a simple fear of punishment. These in turn, as we said before, express various survival values, drives for procreation and perpetuation, deep moral codes and beliefs in higher social and spiritual orders, and so forth.

Increasing rationality and objectivity to counter emotions, and trying to fight emotions or control them directly, will probably have very limited results. If we don't like the way people act or the way the world is going, we may need to understand better what emotions are all about, and change the guiding beliefs and values. We might also need to moderate the emotional intensity in some cases, improve the behavior that follows, and make sure that certain emotions don't lead to pure fanaticism.

9

Emotions and the Notion of Self

The idea of the Self is another complicated and controversial topic in psychology and philosophy, and it can't be covered sufficiently in this essay. Nevertheless, the modest hope here is to show how a relational view of emotions can shed some new light on various concepts, including notions of Self.

As noted earlier in this essay, emotions are almost always about something, which is to say that they are characterized by "intentionality," to use a term from the philosophy of emotions. We suggested that they express the way we relate to various specific elements in our environment and represent the manner in which we perceive our interdependence with them. We also mentioned that in addition to many external elements and notions, we can relate to ourselves as well.

This proposal might create a slight confusion regarding the notion of the "self" and the place it takes in our emotions. On one hand, we relate to more external elements we are somehow interconnected to—elements that did, do or will affect us—such as a sudden serious illness or our children. On the other hand, we also seem to be able to relate directly to ourselves, for instance, when we think about our self-image, our well-being, and so forth. On first impression, since we have been doing it for generations, it seems there is no problem in mixing the two. However, when we probe more deeply and come to the matter of emotions, it is not always completely clear what our emotions are about, and what or who they are related to. If we are always somehow concerned with ourselves, do we always relate to ourselves? Can we also relate to external elements like an illness, or do we relate to both?

One possible explanation for this ambiguity might be that we confuse two aspects or layers of being, of the sense of ourselves. Epstein (1999) and Kahneman (2011) distinguish between the Experiential Self and the Remembering or Narrative Self (or Analytical-Rational self for Epstein). It seems that the "first self" experiences sensations, and the "second self" connects them all and tells a plausible story of how they came about, why and where they are going.

To understand emotions better, we can make a slightly different distinction between a more *biological*, subconscious, intuitive sense of self and the more conscious *conceptual* image of ourselves. The two are clearly interconnected, but in order to comprehend the relational role of our emotions, it is worth distinguishing them.

On one hand, most of our actions, behavior, sensations, and emotions testify to some sort of inborn, involuntary, but ongoing, sense of self or of one's own being. This sense is what most of our drives, needs, motivations, and actions are designed to protect, advance, serve, contribute to or sacrifice. When we feel hungry or afraid, or say "I am hungry," we feel motivations to eat or otherwise feed and protect this "I" or "body." This sense of self is not very different from the one common to all organisms. It is perhaps somewhat closer to Kahneman's experiential self.

We might not be completely clear about this aspect of self, and it is probably less formulated or developed conceptually, since it doesn't require uniquely human conscious thought or awareness. Nevertheless, we constantly witness a multitude of processes and evidence which intersect in this "junction" and point to this "being." Like the deduction of a black hole, we assume the "gravity" and "existence" of such a self from the forces and the phenomena that surround it.

If we are trying to avoid the notion of the self or ego, as some Eastern traditions might, this sense of "one's own self" or "I" could be described as a "nexus of desires and relationships." For example, we see motivations and actions toward its protection and safety, reproduction of its genes, and advancement of its goals and values. Thus, for lack of a better term, we could describe this aspect of the self as the "biological self," "the present self" or "the personal nexus."

But for humans there is yet another aspect to the self. Because of their additional self-awareness and conscious ability, human beings seem to build also a conscious, cognitive concept, image or construct of who they are "individually." This "conceptual" self, of which we are at least partially aware, is being built and modified throughout life. It primarily consists of conscious information and images about our life which "construct" some kind of a "resume" or narrative about who we think we are. Therefore, it seems somewhat similar to Kahneman's Narrative self. Sources for this aspect of self might include personal memories and interpretations, as well as information we receive from other people and various sources around us. In many ways, this concept is not very different from the external concepts we have of other people, animals, and objects. For now, we can call it our "conceptual self."

In general, as many philosophers and psychologists will argue, when we relate to people, situations or institutions, we don't seem to be relating so much to these elements themselves, as to our concepts of them and their possible interactions with us. In this sense, the way we relate to the concept or image of ourselves, this "conceptual self," is rather similar to the way we relate to all other external concepts or elements we deeply care about or feel protective toward (such as our child or home).

When entertaining the subconscious scenarios of interdependence that precede emotional connections, we are concerned with how an external concept will interact with our "biological self." Sometimes we relate emotionally to an external element that can affect us directly (for example, fear of a bear that is chasing us). But at other times, it is possible to relate emotionally to something that can affect us indirectly (for example, fear of a bear that chases our child).

Our "conceptual self" is like our child or any other closely connected element. We view it as an extension of ourselves, and therefore love, protect it, and relate emotionally to any other element that might affect or endanger it (and thus, endanger us or our interest and goals, indirectly).

If we feel afraid of a bear, our "biological self" is afraid that the bear will *directly* harm it. Namely, the "biological self" relates with fear to the bear. Fear is our emotion, and the bear is the external concept which we are afraid of. This emotion is coming to serve and promote the safety and survival of the "biological self."

This is slightly different from feeling afraid of a client who might hurt our image as an intellectually respected professional. In this case, the "biological self" is afraid that the client will endanger the "conceptual self," an endangerment that can only *indirectly* affect also our "biological self." The "conceptual self" becomes another external element toward which we relate intensely, since we add it to the notion of our identity, and feel somewhat protective of it, as it tends to affect our "biological self." This is very similar to the way we relate to the well-being of our child, which we think might affect our "biological self".

In sum, if we think of emotions as primarily expressing and facilitating the drives and values that serve and promote the biological self, or our nexus of relationships, we can think of the "conceptual self" as another external concept, like our children, which the biological self protects as an extension of itself.

We mostly relate emotionally to external concepts (whether of ourselves or others), and at times these external factors can directly affect the biological self (injury). At other times, however, we relate emotionally to external concepts that affect the biological self only indirectly, by affecting closely connected elements, like an injury to our children or to our conceptual self.

10

Emotions and Relationships or Ways of Relating

The importance of relationships is not new, but the perspective offered in this study increases our appreciation for their amazing sophistication, complexity, and consequences. For example, we have suggested that rather than having many different relationships, we practice categorically different types of relating with different people, ideas or situations. We also proposed that, beyond the ability to relate uniquely to many particular elements, we are personally configured and affected by the way we relate to them. This essay has found people to have an amazingly intricate and dynamic set of relational capabilities with remarkable reciprocity. This line of thought and inquiry, with these surprising implications, could be relevant and useful to many other topics beyond emotions and psychology.

Relationships as Important and Basic as Tangible Entities

Here we are suggesting a shift to a more relational ontology in which relationships are considered as important and basic as tangible entities. Recently, there has been strengthening support for adding a theoretical formulation or perspective that will help us better understand the relational aspect of emotions, as well as the relational aspects of other human functions and natural processes. These attempts develop a supplementary outlook on the world in

which relationships are seen as central and basic, and in which entities—organisms, people, materials, and so forth—are seen as a
product of those relationships. In philosophical terms, these views
propose developing an ontology of relationships alongside the preva-
lent entity-based ontology.

In traditional Western ontology, entities like atoms, organisms,
people, materials, planets, and stars are the primary elements of reference, and relationships are seen to take place *between* these. This
perspective is particularly evident with regard to human beings and
the relationships among them.

By comparison, in a relational ontology, relationships (and possibly processes) are viewed as the primary elements, or at least they are
seen to be equally important and fundamental as supposedly independent, individual entities. From this perspective, people and other
entities are understood as a nexus of their relationships, as junctions
where all their relationships intersect, as a product or an outcome of
their interactions. This additional view could help us break through
a somewhat antiquated, and obviously limited, entity-based ontology. It will bring to light new, interesting, and helpful ways of understanding the world and its processes. It isn't necessary to give
up the old way of viewing the universe. We only need to entertain
the possibility of supplementary views, and benefit from the new
insights they bring.

***Relationships and relational ontology, Western versus Eastern
perspectives.*** Our visual impressions, intuitive sensations, and accordingly most of Western ontology, tend to place a strong emphasis
on entities and their individuality (such as objects and human beings). Thus, by default, relationships are viewed as external, secondary phenomena that take place *between* these otherwise *independent*

entities. This outlook marginalizes and limits historical focus on relationships and their importance and diversity.

It also adds a somewhat artificial, restrictive, and sometimes misleading dichotomy between external and internal processes and relationships. By considering all the processes and interactions between
supposedly autonomous entities as *external*, all other processes and
relationships, including emotional ones, come to be seen as *internal* by
default. These "inside" processes are assumed to be confined to our
"inner space," that is, within the entity, and so they are often taken as
personal, subjective processes or experiences which are secondary to
the importance of the entity and should be controlled by it.

In contrast, some Asian philosophies and other schools that emphasize more relational outlooks view relationships as equally important to entities, or even more primary. (See Hershock 1996, 1999,
2004, 2006, 2013, Mark and Ames 1995, and, indirectly, anthropologists such as White 2008, and others.) In such views, familiar
"entities" are actually a nexus or confluence of relational dynamics.
In more common but less precise terms they could be described as
a nexus or junction of relationships, or defined by a combination
of various relationships (as long as relationships are understood in
terms of their dynamic flow of interactions and energy and not simply as a static description of roles). For example, organisms can be
seen as products of the relationships between their parents and the
generations that led to them; with the food, water, and air they con-
sume and discharge; as the interaction between their various body
and mind components; in terms of the relationships they have with
their families, the children they have raised, friends, and co-workers;
as a product of the knowledge they receive from their social and
physical environment; as the actions, services, and goods they give
and take, and so forth.

Historically, the dominance of Western philosophy and science with its emphasis on discrete entities has made it difficult for those who live in a Western context, and for most Western scholars, to see the critical role of relationships and divide the world in other ways. A more relational world view might, for example, force us to see how entities that seem so complete, autonomous, and "whole," such as objects or people, are not only influenced by external relationships, but are critically dependent on them for their origin, energy, knowledge, and growth. This view not only reveals this vital dependency, but hopefully it will enable us to view entities as actually composed of their relationships, or as a temporary manifestation of their unique interactions and combinations. This is no different from the way we view a wave in the ocean or the hair on our heads, which we see as temporary manifestations of the elements around them instead of as separate entities.

Accordingly, phenomena which seem to be "contained" in these entities, such as genetic code, thoughts and desires, and particularly emotions, appear far from being autonomous, independent, and solely internal and cognitive. They might be seen as much more communal, relational, and interactional (as Wittgenstein noted about language, or White [2008] about emotions).

This perspective on the relational dimension of phenomena can also improve our understanding and view of processes that clearly continue beyond any particular entity or time frame, as observed in the infinite motion and transfer of energy in the universe. In "real life," processes are not sharply divided among entities, strictly external or internal, but are rather continuous. Any attempt to define them in this way is only one outlook among many. For the purpose of this essay and in the interest of the ideas we are exploring, adding a relational perspective can help clarify the view that emotions are a way of relating or channeling energy with diverse elements of the environment. This way, it is possible to see these various relationships as constituting who we are and what we are all about. This is somewhat similar to certain Chinese views that understand a person according to how they relate, as opposed to the epistemic view proposed by Descartes in which a person's being is primarily based on knowledge, namely "I think therefore I am." From a relational perspective, we don't have to envision a separate, independent person, ego or "I" that is influenced by relationships or decides whether to have them or not. *The person is, or could be seen as, the relationships that he or she engages in,* and we *are*, or could be seen as, the sum of our relationships, emotions, and how we feel and relate. This goes beyond the typical view that relationships influence social interactions and career development; it extends to the core of our well-being, and to the way we are instantly, constantly, and profoundly affected by how we relate to people, animals, objects, as well as to ideas and abstract notions that fill our personal universe.

In a comparable manner, to say that a person "is what they eat" is more than just a marketing statement. It is a recognition of the connection between the idea of "being" and the idea of "interactions" or "relationships." If we take this view a step further and realize that food is only one type of exchange, it is obvious that a person is also the outcome, expression or manifestation of other types of interactions and relationships. In addition to food, we can add other physical, social, and intellectual relationships such as birth from parents, giving birth and raising children, studying and learning, breathing, procreating, working, communicating, affecting and being affected by others, relating to things all around us, and so forth. Thus, this perspective demands a rather serious shift to a new outlook and emphasis.

The ability to perceive ourselves as a nexus of our relationships could help us change and improve our beliefs and values to reconstitute our relationships and what we are all about. It could be seen as yet another support for a more interactive, relational view of the connection between humankind and the environment. It is another reminder about the limits of our autonomous view of individuality, and reinforces a growing realization of our interdependence that extends to our emotional well-being. This view does not have to diminish individuality, uniqueness, and personal human rights. On the contrary, it points to new avenues for change through the alteration of our interactions and relationships and the conceptions and goals that underline them.

This last, somewhat complex, philosophical/psychological discussion presents a theoretical challenge that is difficult to carry out, and it is not crucial to fully embrace this view in order to appreciate the rest of the conceptual transformations suggested in this essay. Although full development of these intricate topics has been beyond the scope of our study, introducing them here may set the stage for future discussions to address the deeper, more fundamental philosophical and psychological questions and theories surrounding these issues. Such issues may be difficult to engage, but they could have a profound and lasting effect on how we view and treat our emotional universe.

Part D: Concluding Remarks

11

Concluding Discussion

Since we have provided a summary at the beginning of this essay, this chapter will look primarily at some possible implications of the relational view of emotion and project possible directions for future research, conversations and activities. Accordingly, this chapter will contain five main sections:

a. Emerging, general, working description of emotions
b. How changes in key related concepts might rejuvenate these notions and their interactions with the idea of emotions
c. A number of implications for the understanding of emotional problems and therapy
d. A chance for emotional improvement through public debate regarding new communal goals and ways of restructuring social, political, and economic values and objectives.
e. A renewed discussion and study of emotions based on this evolving new view, which we hope will lead to a more appropriate position for emotions in research, culture, and the pursuit of our various goals.

The Emerging Working Description of Emotions

The following summary provides a short, working description of emotions that emerges from the preceding discussions. It is designed to present a starting point for a range of future discussions and studies that might criticize, accept, change or incorporate some of its useful elements.

Working Description of Emotions

In the preceding discussion, we have proposed that emotions are, or can be seen as, a special category of *relational methods* that, while infinitely varied, are similar in style and share a number of characteristics. They enable us to relate *individually*, differently, and *dynamically* to *endless* elements—people, ideas, institutions, objects, and so forth. They allow for the constant and continuous customization and momentary adjustments of our relationships. They can also facilitate long-term connections and commitments to others. Emotions can vary dramatically and infinitely between positive, selfless, empathetic relational attitudes, negative, aggressive orientations, and a whole range of endless other ways of relating. Nevertheless, emotions represent a far more diversified, flexible, and focused relational method than those typical of pre-emotional, instinctual, limited, fixed, categorical, utilitarian or instrumental modes of relating. Emotions can be and often are combined with non-emotional relational techniques as needed. They express our beliefs, values, drives, and biases, and shape the unique personal "contorted conceptual space" in which every one of us lives and thinks.

We adopt and utilize emotions when relating to *specific* elements with which we sense or appraise some type of *interdependence*. Emotions differ from non-emotional ways of relating (such as instrumental or reflective) in their inclusion of a preference for a particular emotional element and commitment to its future destiny and our relationship with it. Like other "overall modes" or "states of being" (sleep, exhaustion, hunger), they comprise a particular configuration of our whole body/mind, including a wide array of specialized *body and mind preparations*. Emotions express or induce a *motivation* for action that facilitates or promotes the needs and goals involved. We partially sense and experience these ways of relating and the preparations which accompany them. As a result, we *feel* the way we perceive and relate, and we are affected by it. Emotion as a way of relating is marked by varying degrees of intensity that affect the level and style of our concentration, preparation, motivation, commitment, and sensation, according to the significance attached to the perceived interdependence.

In simple terms. In simpler terms, an emotion is a particular way of relating to individuals, situations, ideas, institutions or other elements of the environment with which we perceive a certain mutual dependency. We relate to these elements in an emotional manner because we think that they have affected us, do affect us, or somehow can affect us. We relate this way to an infinite number of elements assumed to facilitate or challenge our needs, goals, values, and well-being. Accordingly, we also care about and become invested in the future of these elements and in our relationships with them. Emotional styles are infinite in shades since they vary from person to person, and between each person and element. Most importantly, they constantly change according to our ongoing evaluations of our mutual interdependence with all the elements around us. Nevertheless, emotional modes of relating share common denominators, family resemblances, and repeated patterns that make it useful to group them together, partially recognize them, and name them.

We relate emotionally only to elements that have a particular identity for us, and we care what happens to them (for better or for worse). Namely, these elements are not exchangeable or easily replaced, their identity is essential and no longer accidental, and their destiny matters, in contrast to a purely utilitarian or reflective way of relating—say to a cashier in a large department store, to an ordinary hammer, or a distance random person or object. It is possible to relate emotionally not only to people and objects, but also to concepts, ideas, and communal terms (such as family, nation, state of affairs).

To relate in this manner, as part of the preparation for it and to best carry it out, we go through a wide range of physical as well as mental preparations or adjustments, which we only partially sense or are aware of. We also develop an inclination for particular actions or behaviors that can best deal with the anticipated effect of the element of our emotion (avoidance, seeking out or otherwise). Although emotions tend to lead to certain actions, for heuristic reasons and because of common traditional usage, those actions typically aren't included in what is considered an emotion.

Unlike purely cognitive processes such as thoughts or appraisals, emotions often have a dimension of force with intensity and arousal. The volume or level of intensity of an emotion changes the nature and force of the whole experience, the extent of the accompanying "preparations," the number and type of relationships we concentrate on, and the power of the motivation that emerges. This intensity is closely associated with the result of the appraisal process, the significance of the object of emotion, and its assumed effect. Because emotions are multifaceted phenomena, the depictions of emotion from a typical cognitive perspective—as an appraisal, evaluation or judgment—tend to be partial and somewhat deceptive.

Considering its comprehensive effect on our whole body and mind, emotion could also be depicted as a special relational *mode or state*, particularly when it is intense (for example, hypothermia, starvation, coma, orgasm). It is more apparent when we look at a person possessed with intense love or blinded by extreme anger. However, even a calmer emotion could be seen as a modality that incorporates a full body and mind relational method, policy, technique, style, strategy, approach, relationship, stance, position, bearing, orientation or attitude. It is important not to take these descriptions (for example, orientation) as purely cognitive or even solely mental, as some of traditional understandings have done. Emotional phenomena also include bodily processes, intensity, as well as personal preferences, biases, and other overall body and mind adjustments and configurations that are often absent from purely cognitive terms. This is why we stress the critical need for a whole *mind and body* outlook, and emphasize also the more "proactive," experiential, personal, and preparatory dimensions of emotions that extend beyond the current common connotations of appraisals, orientations, strategies, and so forth.

Emotions and Related Topics

Our last chapters discussed the concept of emotions and its interaction with a few, important related terms. In looking at the history of complex ideas, it is clear that the future position and treatment of emotions as a category is as dependent on its relations with related concepts and our understanding of them as it is on a strictly internal understanding of the concept. In the past, the concept of emotion has been dominated by the traditional contrast between emotions and cognition, rationality and objectivity; and recently, some attempts have tried to force emotions into cognition, or to equate emotions with elements of cognition, such as appraisals or judgments. The relating theory proposed here takes us out of these typical, tenuous dichotomies and offers a symbiotic connection between these concepts that may better explain their relationships and function. A relational approach maintains the differences between emotion and cognition while also explaining how they work together—without collapsing emotion into cognition, relying on a hierarchy or insisting upon conflict.

Cognition, Rationality, and Objectivity

Since cognition participates heavily in emotional dynamics and changes to accommodate them, some theories tend to label emotions as cognitive and view them as an aspect of cognition. However, cognition is involved in and reconfigured by many human functions and modes, and it is not useful to label all of them as cognitive or to collapse all these functions and modes into cognition.

There is a benefit in keeping emotions distinct from cognition while recognizing that they are highly interconnected. Maintaining this distinction emphasizes the unique, relational function of emotions apart from other cognitive functions and procedures.

We have offered an analogy that compares cognition to the government's decision- making bodies and process, while emotions are compared to the nation's foreign policies, the way the nation relates to other countries and issues, and how it prepares for them.

Likewise, we have tried to develop a different understanding of the connection between emotion and rationality. Traditionally emotions have been considered the main enemy of rationality, but upon reflection it seems that in most cases emotions cannot be judged as rational or irrational, since they express drives and values that articulate our choices and goals, and should not be viewed as means to an end (for example, love of music). It also became evident that conventional views of the irrationality of emotion may rest on the intensity of general human arousal expressed by emotion, and by the flouting of social conformity in these instances.

The wider implication of many of these discussions is the benefit of keeping certain human categories distinct while appreciating their close synergic interaction, mutual contribution, and influence. This demonstrates again the interconnectivity and complexity of our whole body/mind system, including its critical interdependencies with many elements around it. On one hand, this perspective pushes us further and further from traditional clear-cut Cartesian dualisms and other dualisms that split emotions and cognition or rationality. On the other hand, it forces us to deal with highly intricate, interconnected, multivariable, non-linear, dynamic systems that require complex theories and their evolving unique approaches and methods (See numerous studies on the subject from the Santa Fe Institute and other writings dedicated to this topic).

Despite attempts here to clarify slippery concepts like cognition and rationality in order to modify their conflicting relations with emotions, these concepts no doubt remain as mysterious and confusing as are concepts of emotion. We have a good intuitive sense of what these concepts mean and how they feel, but have a hard time defining them or even explaining them precisely. Understandably, this makes any transformation of their relations hard to comprehend for many people, difficult to accept, and even more difficult to experience in practice.

Nevertheless, the new relations between emotions and cognition suggested here have far-reaching positive implications for therapy, legal decisions, politics, and the evaluation of other people and cultures. For example, when judging whether people have been irrational during intense events, we must verify if they have been extremely emotional, have acted according to different values and goals, or actually have a pathological, continuous mental condition that makes it impossible for them to function properly. Emotions are not irrational thoughts but relational policies that express values within which rationality is judged. This careful configuration should extend to our judgment of organizations and nations that may seem to act in extreme and unacceptable ways because of different beliefs, religious fanaticism or atypical ideologies.

In addition to remaining aware of the difficulty of evaluating the rationality of other people and nations, we must be careful not to fall into the surprisingly common confusion among rationality, objectivity, and morality. A person or a nation can be rational but highly immoral, or highly moral but rather irrational. Judgments that involve assessment of rationality and morality are particularly complex and clearly call for more multidisciplinary analysis and research.

The important conclusion is that we must learn to navigate in a permanently curved universe where emotions *coexist* with cognition, rationality, and objectivity and *should be* closely connected to them. This interaction is a complex and dynamic process in which all these capacities constantly change and modify to facilitate and accommodate each other. We may have to abandon the futile, long-standing attempt to create a world or context clear of emotions. Instead, the challenge becomes how to accept, comprehend, and maneuver in such a complex landscape without uniting, negating or choosing one aspect at the expense of others. Hopefully, a perspective that views emotions as a relational phenomenon will help us with such tasks.

Drives and Values

This essay confirms the assumption that emotions manifest basic, long-term, and often subconscious, entrenched beliefs, drives, goals, and values that have been described here as directives. These directives express practiced values, rather than stated values, which is to say that they represent "more of what we want and believe in, instead of what we want to believe in."

What is less widely recognized is the idea that drives and values are a good place to look for an understanding of emotional choices and problems. It can be difficult to admit, but if we are not sure of our actual, practiced values, we can look at our emotions as a direct expression and indication of them. Accordingly, this study reiterates the idea that if we want a profound, lasting emotional change in ourselves or in the world (for example, less hatred, more love and compassion, more happiness), it is crucial to develop a better understanding of the connection between values and emotions. Such an understanding might enable a modification of values (or at least their scope and intensity) in such a way that they improve our situation as well as our emotional well-being, as we will suggest below.

This discussion also reinforces the reciprocal contribution between emotions and values, in which emotions are said to make morality and empathy possible, for example. What is unfortunately frequently forgotten is the hidden caveat that belief systems and values also determine what and how much is included or excluded from our sphere of empathy. Values and belief systems can thus result in less desirable attitudes of hatred and indifference.

We have asserted here that although belief systems and value configurations are hard to modify, they can change and so bring about an alteration of our emotional composition, either on the personal or communal level. At times, it takes a traumatic or profound event, but slow and even conscious adjustment can bring about a change as well—whether through therapy, spiritual practices, new ideologies and values, or behavioral modifications.

The Notion of the Self

The relational view of emotions also provides the possibility of a fresh look at the notion of Self. It suggests an emotional distinction to avoid a potential confusion between the biological and the conceptual selves. Though these ideas are only partially developed here, such new perspectives might help relieve some of the ongoing tension between various theories of ego and self. For instance, the fundamental difference between the Freudian Ego or the CBT sense of self, and the Buddhist philosophy of no self.

A Relational Ontology

Overall, a relating theory of emotions can lead us to entertain the possibility of an additional and much deeper and wider philosophical and psychological transition in the way we view emotions, the self, and the rest of our physical and social environment. The addition of a relational ontology gives priority to the relationships that supposedly create various familiar entities, and views them as combining or intersecting in specific formations, times, and places to constellate a wave, a storm or a person. From this perspective, such entities can be seen as temporary dynamic intersections, manifestations or nexuses of these relationships.

It is our hope that this fledgling proposal for a complex conceptual addition or transition may work as point of departure for further logical extension of a relational view of emotions and, in turn, shed light on other psychological mysteries as well as many additional phenomena.

Possible Changes in Understanding and Treating Emotional Problems

Even if this essay does not change anyone's overall view of emotions, it confirms that emotions are both highly flexible and complex. It emphasizes that this flexible complexity adds to their performance and our adaptability, but that it might, at the same time, contribute to the multitude of emotional pathologies, and to the difficulty of understanding and fixing emotional problems.

Unfortunately, even though this essay concentrates on emotions, it is obviously not a typical psychological or psychiatric article designed to resolve particular pathological emotional problems or to advance specific therapies. It is rather concerned with a general understanding of emotions and their overall role and place. Nevertheless, the new view of emotions proposed here can help in understanding emotional difficulties and possibly influence how they are treated.

Psychologists, psychiatrists, and therapists are by the nature of their profession good at understanding particular emotions, emotional problems, and theories regarding the formation and treatment of specific emotions and pathologies. However, many of them, along with most laypersons, are still puzzled by the overall phenomenon of emotions, about why we have them and how to categorize them. Fortunately, experts in a professional or scientific field can develop a very sound understanding and excellent skills at treating specific problems, even if the overall theory is incomplete. Neither the theory of relativity, nor even Newton's theory, are necessary to be familiar with gravity, to help a person who fell from the third floor, or to treat a person who is afraid of heights. You don't even need them to design a great elevator or airplane, or to trace the movement of some of the planets. Nevertheless, theoretical insights that improve our overall understanding can help join seemingly disconnected phenomena, explain them better, and open new avenues for treatment.

This essay will leave many questions about the therapeutic implications of the ideas presented here, and especially pathological considerations, for future studies and professional experts. It will only present a few examples to demonstrate how this change of outlook could be helpful to professionals and non-psychologists who are more interested in a theoretical understanding of emotions.

Greater Emphasis on the Relational Dimensions of Emotions

The first and most apparent impact on therapy would come from a more sophisticated view of the relational dimensions of emotions. While attention to relational elements in therapy is obviously not new or rare, the relational aspects are often seen as influencing emotions and not as an integral part of them. Seeing emotions as a specifically relational phenomenon brings a new perspective, and the classification of different types of relationships proposed here raises different questions and proposes new distinctions.

Therapists could, for example, pay more attention to people's interactions with, and perceptions of, their interdependence with the environment and the key elements within it. This perspective could encourage a more relational view in addition to analysis that is overly concentrated on internal contemplations of ego or past memories. The various dimensions of emotions described here, such as specificity, interdependence, force, and motivation, might assist understanding as well. We might first search to see what the emotion is "about" (that is, the intentionality of the emotion), how we perceive this element, and what form of interdependence exists between the two parties. We can try to figure out why this particular object of emotion is so special and significant, and determine why the person has developed an emotional relationship with this object (and not just utilitarian one, for example). We can also try to investigate if the emotional person perceives any personal investment and commitment, and how they want the object of the emotion or their relationships with them to develop. We might also look at which drives or values this emotion expresses or serves, and how they can possibly change if necessary. Although most professional therapists will already ask most of these questions, this particular approach to framing and focusing the questions and interpreting the answers could help therapists get a novel picture and a fresh angle on a situation.

A relating theory of emotions can shed light on the increasingly common and growing difficulties people now have with their personal relationships—the increase in divorce cases, growing urban alienation, and many other relational problems we have with people, situations, and ideas. It might even help the rising number of people who find themselves obsessively involved with a movie star, a fictional character, or imaginary personas on the Internet. The discussion of "emotional concentration" versus "multitasking," with the assistance of the military metaphor of alerts and focus, could possibly help with instances of emotional "over reaction" (panic attacks and anxiety, fits of rage and anger management, various obsessions and obsessive behavior, and so forth). Some even think that a more relational view of emotions will help explain cases of autistic spectrum disorder, in which emotional and relational problems are so closely linked. Finally, it could possibly improve our eternal search for happiness by clarifying how we relate to our own self-image and the environment as a whole.

Seeing emotions as a way of relating emphasizes accountability for our emotional constellation and suggests the possibility for change. As methods of relating, we have viewed our emotions more as our interfaces or foreign policies that can be partially selected and modified. This is different from some of the popular, traditional depictions of emotions as mysterious, out-of-control events or forces, or deep personal cognitive constructs. It is closer to approaches such as those of CBT that emphasize the tie between beliefs and emotions. However, this fresh outlook takes our emotional constitution and accountability a step further. We can now see emotions as expressions of our own values or ways in which we *opt* to relate to elements, and not just as something that "happens" to us (for example, "I went crazy and I could not control myself"; or "I just had to buy it").

It is true, as we discussed, that emotions are heavily influenced by our subconscious directives and beliefs, and thus not easy to quickly modify by simple thoughts and wishes. Nevertheless, they represent our values, aims, and beliefs, for which we are accountable and which we can modify and improve upon if we so choose. No longer can we simply blame an uncontrollable "spell" that fell on us, other people and situations, human nature or past history for every emotional problem. We can't push all the fault to the actions and qualities of external individuals and situations, saying for example that "all men are the same, they only want to take advantage of me," or that "women only want to get married and have somebody take care of them," or that "the world is cruel and I can't be happy in such a place."

The relating theory of emotions emphasizes the importance of our perception of interdependence with the object of our emotions. Although emotion is clearly influenced by the qualities of the object (such as a nice or nasty boss), it also has much to do with our own habitual and selected perceptions. This is why people sometimes end up in a world full of threats, jerks or indifference.

Amazingly enough, even though this dynamic is well-known among therapists, it is not so familiar to the general public. Most of us assume that we relate to individuals, situations or ideas primarily according to their qualities and their possible effect on us. For example, we hate the boss and feel angry strictly because he or she is "nasty" and treats us badly. This is also how we try to justify our emotions, and we work very hard to convince ourselves and others that our fears and anger are realistic, justified, and should be taken seriously. All in all, our personal emotional analysis seems to us very final, objective, and definite.

However, periodically, we notice that *other* people's perceptions of interdependence vary dramatically according to their personalities. For example, some people tend to be suspicious, fearful or angry, while others are more forgiving and cheerful. We also know that through the spillover effect mentioned before, intense emotions tend to color other situations, regardless of their inherent qualities (for example, getting angry at people at home after a bad day at work). Ironically, we also find in statistical studies that a poor village in Laos often has more "happiness" to go around than a rich neighborhood in L.A. It is therefore obvious that much of the difference has to do with different values, expectations, and perspectives rather than with material or physical conditions.

It is widely understood that emotional relationships are determined by the combination of the unique configuration we bring to the table and the unique qualities presented to us by different individuals or situations. What a more relational view demonstrates is an individual's responsibility for his or her emotional constellation and choices, and the possibility of changing them. Psychologists and therapists study these emotional configurations frequently and in depth, but many of us have a hard time genuinely accepting that we have some responsibility and can practice to change them.

Love, for example, often has as much to do with our ability and readiness to love as it does with how great or upsetting our spouse is, or how loveable some potential lovers are or with attributes of other ethnic groups. Contrary to the common view, one could argue that the qualities of the objects of our love are often less important than our ability and readiness to love. People are known to love abstract ideas such as God or spirits, ideology, pets, art, sick and dying people or even an abusing partner. It is obvious that some objects are easier to love than others (for example, a good dog). Nevertheless, as a way of relating, love (like most other emotions) is also the way we choose to relate to somebody or something. Thus, we can opt to amplify this emotion or orientation or make it scarce. This is not a song about "all we need is love." However, as mentioned before, this view may be part of what some spiritual leaders talk about when they suggest that we practice more love for happiness.

Motivation for Emotional Changes

A relational view offers additional explanation for the difficulty of emotional changes and suggests motivation for making them. Despite the benefits of being aware of and accountable for our emotional configurations, it is obviously not easy to change our emotions when we are overly upset about something or illogically afraid of someone. Changing our emotions basically calls for a change of values and beliefs, of who we are, what we stand for or believe in. Clearly, if we believe something, why would we change it? After all, we actually believe that that our view is true and right. Tautological as it sounds, an emotional change may require admitting being at fault or mistaken, recognizing that our values are wrong after all, or relinquishing fundamental beliefs in favor of a different point of view. If the change is small, such as making a rail stronger to dispel a fear of heights, or lowering your suspicion and dislike for a far-away ethnic group, it is easy to accept. But if you need to change your more profound life values, your children's lives, your sense of self-respect, or your understanding of the global social order and your place in it, the change is far harder. It requires a much greater level of personal sacrifice and a significant change in who you think you are, your practices, and what you mean and represent. Very few of us are ready to change that much or capable of it—we would rather suffer. Even if we do undertake such a change, it is hard to sustain the effort over time. On top of it all, we often are not even sure what to change in the complex web of our relationships, values, beliefs, and views. As much as we think that we know ourselves, this is not an easy map to decipher, and finding sophisticated external help is not easy or inexpensive.

The relating theory proposed here can't help with many of these difficulties (particularly not with finding a good therapist), but at least it can help us better understand the connection between our emotions and our beliefs and values. It can help explain why it may be necessary to change some of these beliefs and values to improve the way we feel.

A relational view doesn't only help us recognize our habitual practices, perceptions, and values. It also motivates us by demonstrating how we are personally affected by the way we relate to others and other elements. Thus, if we relate with constant anger, violence, and hatred to people around us, and destroy many living things and most of our environment, chances are that we will suffer emotionally and be unhappy. Even if the people surrounding us have such values and practices, we will suffer a similar hardship and emotional repercussions. Asking people to change their values for noble causes such as morality, the good of mankind or future generations, is often a hard sell. However, showing a clear personal emotional benefit and reciprocal gain from changing certain values and practices might be more convincing to many.

Incorporating Communal or Global Conditions
To improve therapy, we may need to increase our understanding and further incorporate communal or even global conditions and developments. Since global conditions, world views, culture, and values play an important part in emotional configuration, it follows that similar emotional difficulties may be common to many members of

the same community. In addition to considering relationships with parents, siblings, and other members of society, social psychology and anthropology also look at communal emotional dynamics and factors. Many studies in these fields portray us as social beings immersed in and strongly influenced by culture, communal moods and perspectives. This communal philosophical environment (spiritual, conceptual, relational) tends to influence our belief system, and the way we interpret otherwise private experiences and our emotional reactions to them. For example, the same hardship might be seen as a "positive challenge" or a "horrifying punishment," for people of different cultures or intentions.

White expresses it well, arguing that "The identification of emotion as a subject for strictly psychological research, and the disciplinary division of labor itself, are reflections of a Western folk psychology that conceives of persons primarily as autonomous individuals rather than as actors whose subjectivity is continually formed in and through interactions with others" (White 1993, 29). He goes on to show the importance of cultural and public environment in emotional formation, emphasizing the communal nature of emotion, rather than the traditional understanding of emotions as private, inner, subjective, unique experiences.

Not only are we influenced by the attitudes of the external communal culture, but as mentioned before, we actually form emotional relationships with communally conceived ideas, theories or ideological concepts embodied in nations, institutions, class systems, gender, and ethnic groups. These in turn, often affect us no less—and may even affect us more—than the actual, immediate people or items around us. Thus, for example, the sense of a "dying nation and culture" for a Tibetan, the notion of a "deteriorating empire" for a U.S. citizen, or a sense of a lost environmental battle for a "global citizen" can be as devastating as a personal fight with an angry father.

If more people are divorced and bitter and unhappy about the "other" gender, if a larger number of people feel neglected or even betrayed by their governments, if billions of people feel poor by comparison to the few rich, or left with a decaying environment, the global emotional map might be changing rapidly. With growing global connectivity, media, and culture, the emotional influence of these communal factors is increasing, and more and more people are deeply affected emotionally in the same manner (also see relevant studies in the history of emotions by Stearns [1993] and others).

However, most psychotherapies and the theories behind them concentrate on personal psychological problems and the ability of the individual to resolve their emotional problems by themselves (even if they need the help of a therapist, a group or a family).

Therefore, although personal therapy is important, its explanatory powers and effectiveness may diminish if it is limited to personal or even localized experiences. More and more, therapists may need to supplement individual analysis with a better understanding of communal and even global emotional challenges and difficulties. They may have to incorporate various public perspectives or even consider worldwide conditions, whether physical, economic, social, political, environmental, philosophical or spiritual, as we will discuss in our next section.

Emotions on the Public, Communal Level

Beyond theoretical and therapeutic applications, a new view of emotions could also help us on the communal, public level. First, many of our global difficulties are partially caused by emotions such as hate, envy or simple indifference. Second, as just noted, many of the emotional problems of individuals are widespread across their communities and clearly brought about by shared conditions, developments, institutions, cultures, and so forth. Third, it seems that we tend to have communal sentiments or moods beyond our individual ones.

Although these claims are not altogether novel, and have been studied by social psychology, anthropology or political science, research on some of the emotional aspects of these issues is rather limited, and the new approach to emotions proposed here might be helpful. As usual, we can't cover here all these multifaceted topics and questions, but it seems beneficial and important to at least introduce some of them shortly and give a few examples.

Utilitarian Relationships

Utilitarian relationships can be combined with emotional relationships, but they should not replace them or become a substitute. One realization that emerges from a relational point of view is what appears to be a shifting balance between emotional ways of relating and utilitarian approaches. In some cases, utilitarian relationships are altogether appropriate: relationships with the government, between large companies and their clients, with a cashier in the supermarket or the chicken we ate for lunch are largely utilitarian. Emotional relationships also typically include an element of utilitarian interdependency, as with a spouse, or even with children. However, in some situations, instead of being complementary, one style or relating tends to dominate at the expense of the other.

For example, under the influence of strong utilitarian cultures, as manifested in traditional Western orientations to nature and the environment, or in extreme forms of communism and capitalism, the tendency is to adopt an overly utilitarian, functional approach to life. Such an approach leads us to care primarily about the utility of the people and animals around us, and to forget their intrinsic value, the value of our emotional engagement with them, or our empathy. Communism, which calls for the sacrifice of personal ties for the sake of the state, might be disappearing, but extreme capitalism calls for a similarly impersonal view under the auspices of personal benefit and efficiency. As a result of this cultural climate, more and more people and institutions end up judging their educations, their spouses, friends, clients or even their kids in utilitarian terms. They may say, for example, "I'm not going to have kids since they are too expensive these days"; or assess relationships according to whether they are helpful or holding one back, useful for one's career or costing too much. Accordingly, people can give up the emotional dimension, dispense with relationships when they become inconvenient, and extinguish care for others (or limit it to imaginary relationships with celebrities). This utilitarian orientation and the behaviors that come with this attitude can easily extend to coworkers, other members of society in a big city, animals, various ethnicities, and to most other human beings and objects around the world. This leaves us with less and less empathy, and much more apathy and deep-seated alienation. This tendency toward relationships defined by utilitarian motives is particularly problematic on the public level. If more and more of life is run by larger and larger companies, big institutions, governments, and computers, as a result of the concentration of industry, exponential growth in population, high mobility, and tremendous technical development, this anonymous, utilitarian way of relating becomes a form of sociopathic orientation to nearly everyone and everything around. Such an attitude translates easily to aggression or usury. It is ingeniously presented in Bruce Springsteen's (1995) song "Youngstown": "Once I made you rich enough, rich enough to forget my name." This was very obvious in the past, in the regrettable treatment of slaves, for example. However, still today, it is a very common way of relating to the environment, food animals, and poor working people. This is not the place for a religious sermon about loving all people, a "tree hugging" call for adoring all animals and plants, or a demonstration against capitalistic efficiency. Nevertheless, this way of looking at relationships may make us more aware and cautious about extreme practices of utility and productivity, which have quite a lot in common with Social Darwinism.

Emotions as an Important Aspect of Communal Behavior and Interaction

The cultural-emotional tendency discussed above is just one example in a much wider field of critical questions. The idea that communities fight because they hate, fear, are jealous of each other or indifferent is as old as humankind and is almost taken for granted. However, we must ask: what are the emotional formations that facilitate these kinds of problems, and what can be done about them? Some public social programs are in place that are supposed to improve such emotional tendencies by educating people and changing their perceptions. For instance, there are various attempts to increase cooperation between Israelis and Palestinians in the arts, scientific research, business, and so forth. However, these attempts are typically limited and rare. On top of it, they have to overcome long years of established prejudice, and must counter the organized efforts of leaders and media to gather support by stimulating fear and hatred. This is why we clearly need more discussion and research into these types of questions and associations. If we study personal emotional pathologies carefully and condemn sociopathic behavior, why do we allow and even promote it on a national level?

It is striking to realize that we seem to have much greater interest in global happiness; we find many more serious studies of this than we find of global fear, envy, anger, and hatred. Unfortunately, these possibly harmful emotions can lead to suffering and aggression, which, among other things, clearly decrease happiness. They can reduce the conditions for happiness by inciting conflict and war, as well as by contradicting and diminishing happiness directly through an increase of fear and pain.

If we would take the association between drives, values, world views, and emotions more seriously, we might be able to figure out, for example, why it is so popular or easy to hate, and so rare or hard to love. What is it about these ways of relating that make them so common and perhaps even necessary for mankind? What do we need to do to reach a more tolerant or loving way of relating on a large scale? Perhaps, these destructive emotions are part of a genetic evolutionary tendency required for survival, which can only be controlled by strong law and order. It could also be that we have to change our value system and give up some elements of control, honor, respect, independence, competition, and raise the importance of values such as tolerance, interdependence, compromise, forgiveness, contribution, and cooperation. Whatever is required, progress in this area could, without exaggeration or doubt, help billions of people.

Extra Attention to the Emotional Consequences of Global Developments

We might pay extra attention to the emotional consequences of various global developments. The close association between emotions and public practices and developments is clearly a two-way street. On one hand, we outlined some of the social problems that seem to arise from certain emotional tendencies and configurations, including all the beliefs and values that lead to global developments (such as war). On the other hand, global developments and changes have important emotional consequences that we know little about. We have begun requiring an environmental impact study before approving a major development, but rarely do we wonder about the emotional consequences of major public decisions.

Some of the problems that probably affect more than half the population on earth, such as war, terrorism, lack of work, abuse of human rights, and poverty, are sadly familiar. However, beyond stark, obvious global problems, there are endless global developments that have direct emotional consequences but are far less clear. For instance, there are philosophical/spiritual problems that affect us emotionally, such as growing frustration with exaggerated economical expectations (see Hade's forthcoming monograph on this topic), spiritual vacuums, lower religious tolerance, and growing fanaticism. There are numerous economic developments with emotional implications including the growing disparity of income, exponential population growth, rising stress levels, and economic and political concentration of power in enormous, sociopathic conglomerates. The same could be said for social issues like the increase in the divorce rates and the weakening of the traditional family, or rising longevity that corresponds with growing neglect of older people. Political issues include the increase in control and intervention of "Big Brother," continued coercion, and lack of governmental responsiveness. We are all similarly familiar with examples from the physical environment, and can only imagine what it feels like to be living in a crowded slum with extremely polluted air. The area of health presents its own problems, such as improvement of the quality of healthcare with outrageous price tags, and longer life with low emotional quality. Last but not least, we have a multitude of examples of the profound emotional consequences of exponential progress in technological innovations, along with total dependency on technical tools and experts, and the constant need to study new technology, or arbitrarily imposed but critical formats.

It becomes increasingly clear that we don't understand the effects of our policies and developments, could care less about them, do little to offset them, or all of the above. Contrary to the widely-held belief in the correlation between economic development and happiness, it seems that the better-off, more developed part of the global population seems to have serious, though perhaps different, emotional difficulties as well, and that these difficulties actually correlate closely to our desire for success and progress. As we noted before, it is remarkable to see the high level of happiness in some poor village in a developing country in comparison to the extreme unhappiness in many of the rich neighborhoods in the U.S.A, Europe or Japan (see Hade's forthcoming monograph on Happiness).

Collective conditions and developments also affect our communal mood, spirit or sentiment. Similar to a person's general mood or disposition, which comes on top of his/her specific emotions, it seems that as a community we share some sort of a common attitude or orientation. Non-specific as it might sound, this type of pervasive public mood or sentiment seems to have far-reaching influence on the community and how it acts. Everybody that lived through diverse periods like the 60s and the 90s can tell how markedly different these periods felt and operated. Nevertheless, not too many people or even experts can actually explain these dynamics and their overall influence. (See research on the history of emotions by Stearns 1993 and others.)

Thus, the association between global conditions and our personal and communal emotional configurations is far from clear. Further study of this connection would not only help therapy but also advance changes in existing policies and the formulation of new directions for development.

The Difficulty and Risk in Changing Communal Emotional Practices

The importance of emotions is obviously clear to psychologists, but as we mentioned above, the importance of philosophy and worldview in emotional configuration is not so apparent (or is simply too complex and challenging to consider). While these global perspectives are often more familiar to philosophers, philosophers are rarely interested in emotional issues. The same is true for most other disciplines that consider global situations, such as political science and economics (both of which have recently tried to incorporate the impacts of irrational behavior). This segmentation of focus reflecting standard departmental divisions of labor (narrow and deep instead of wide and inclusive) is problematic in many areas, but particularly in the study of human interactions and relationships. A relational view of emotions shows the growing need for interdisciplinary knowledge and better cooperation among experts.

Even within psychology, most studies tend to concentrate on pathological and abnormal manifestations rather than on the education and challenges involved in the improvement of normal emotions. ("Positive Psychology" has been claiming recently to address this oversight.) Emotions are mostly treated on a personal level, or in small groups (that is, through group dynamics), and rarely on the public or global level. With modernity's concentration on individualism, this tendency has only intensified. When studied on a large scale, the science of emotions is mostly aimed at public manipulation (for example through advertising campaigns and politics), or on business efficiency in relation to productivity or production lines. Though the pursuit of happiness is a national priority, it is very rare to hear about national goals and budgets set to study and promote this objective or to help related emotions. (One exception is studies that have recently grown out of the "Gross National Happiness" concept of Bhutan). It means that although we declare the pursuit of happiness as a national goal and recognize the negative impact of many global developments (even in wealthy countries), we don't think or do much about these developments and their negative emotional impacts. (See the website GNH grossnationalhappiness. com, bhutanstudies.org.bt, Otsubo 2016, and others).

This problem is even more evident at public institutions where emotions have traditionally been excluded as a private, individual, unpredictable phenomenon. Law, government, economics, and medicine, for example, are defined by logical, rational, objective, and utilitarian quantitative goals (such as economic progress, physical health, and longevity). Emotions have been excluded from official practice and thus forgotten as a public variable and neglected as a focus for study, consideration or policy.

Unlike a shift of emotion on the personal level, a change of public emotional configuration requires more than just alteration of sentiments and beliefs. At the outset, it necessitates a major battle with powerful forces and wealthy parties that benefit from the existing configuration and will try to preserve it. On top of that, it demands an immense effort to alter powerful, formalized institutions.

Institutional Emotional Patterns

The ability to form emotional connections with communal concepts such as company, country, and various institutions, suggested throughout this essay, is an aspect of emotion that is often underestimated. This emotional tendency is not new, but today more than ever, most of us work, live, tightly interact, or are controlled by one or more of these social structures—a company, an institution, a government body or a nation. These structures can be viewed as formalized sets of relationships that are embedded with specific values, require particular behavior, and accordingly promote certain values and emotions. Most structures include explicit or implicit but clear guidelines or preferences about how their members ought to feel and relate to others (whether, for example to be aggressive or accommodating, suspicious or trusting) and to the institution itself (love, loyalty); and how those who deviate from the norm or non-members should feel (for example, fear or shame). These types of expectations may be more obvious in a terrorist organization, a cult or a totalitarian nation, but are also apparent in governmental bodies, aggressive corporations, and most other institutions and organizations. Because these communal values and emotions often overpower personal emotions—we think "I must do my job and I can't let my own preferences interfere"—they tend to dominate much of our global behavior and emotional composition.

It is well-established, and we have asserted here, that emotions require a larger mental capacity, and that this makes them unique and novel among more evolved species. The presence of emotions helps to differentiate more decentralized, adaptable societies of "larger brain" organisms like human beings, from less flexible more centralized "smaller brains" societies like social insects. Unfortunately, the enormous concentration of human populations combined with overpowering institutions that are larger, more centralized, and more homogeneous will probably only lower this capacity for diversity, individuality, and adaptability.

Studying the Emotional Impact of Public Policies and Developments

This essay is not a call for Romanticism, a New Age, "touchy-feely" policies or self-centered sentiments about "getting in touch with your feelings." Such attempts are often rather impractical and ineffective on a large scale. We are rather presenting a simple and practical argument for the consideration of the emotional impact of various communal goals, policies, institutions, actions, and developments. Recently we have learned to add the environmental bottom line to the financial one, and we might want to do the same with regard to the emotional impact of public policies. After all, what good is economic and environmental success in a miserable, depressed, anxious, lonely society.

A search for emotional improvement, happiness, and love, which obsess and elude so many of us, seems to plague our modern, individualistic society. Unfortunately, this widespread discontent may have more to do with cultural values, global perspectives, and the type of progress we promote so stubbornly, than with our physical situation or "emotional genetics." Even if emotional difficulties are partially an extension of survival instincts and can't be changed biologically, it is definitely possible to change ourselves conceptually, behaviorally, and organizationally.

Although changing values and world views is not an easy task, it may nevertheless be the main long-term solution for emotional improvement. There are many examples of individuals and communities, both secular and spiritual, which have succeeded in shifting world views throughout history. We can think of the incredible changes that were brought about by all the major religions and religious movements, by the leading ideologies such as democracy and communism, by political movements like the Civil Rights Movements, or even by certain individuals and/or particular books such as Mother Teresa, Nelson Mandela, and the Bible.

Such vast and profound changes typically take a major commitment, sacrifice, effort, energy, discipline, and persistence to succeed and last. Some claim that in most cases we don't suffer sufficiently to seek major changes, and that it will take apocalyptic or revolutionary conditions to really bring a profound transformation. It could also be that *the people who suffer can't change the system and that the ones who could bring about change don't suffer*—or at least not enough. However, it is important to remember that we don't have to solve all the world's problems before we can resolve some widespread emotional problems and increase global well-being. A slower or more gradual approach, in which we modify our values to a degree without undertaking a complete transformation, can also bring about change. We can also remind ourselves and others of changing priorities, and alter some of our practices to promote new values and emotions. The bottom line is that we must simply be very patient and persistent.

This essay clearly doesn't have all the solutions for emotional transformation. Nevertheless, realizing the close tie between emotions, relationships, values, and global conditions at least leads us in a helpful direction (if we are determined to change). If it is any consolation, at least it clarifies why it is so hard for most of us, including psychologists, psychiatrists, philosophers, and even scholars of emotions (this writer included), to modify their emotions or emotional tendencies.

The Risk of Public Policies Regarding Emotions.

Exploration of public policies regarding emotions entails a serious risk. While it is important to consider how public emotions affect the overall well-being of those affected by them, *we must be extremely careful not to move toward some form of social or public emotional engineering, or emotional coercion of the sort immortalized in Orwell's 1984.* Such programs often arise from, or lead to, dogmatic domination by fanatical ideologies, totalitarian regimes, intolerant religious practices or megalomaniac leaders. *We have to be exceptionally cautious not to hand over our emotional configurations and decisions to private corporations, religious institutions, governments or any other such controlling, and often self-serving, organization.* Lots of this is already being done by governments and private corporations through their various policies and advertising campaigns, which tell us how to live and feel. However, at least they are not as coercive as totalitarian regimes or institutions and thus let us maintain our illusion of free will. We should be exceedingly cautious not to make it worse by trying to make it better!

A Call to Re-position Emotions in Research and Culture

Throughout this essay, different theories, models, and analogies related to emotions have been presented in hope of rejuvenating how emotions are viewed and studied. We traced a transition from the idea that emotions are private and internal to the view that they are, in fact, interactive and relational. By identifying some of the singular characteristics of emotions and comparing them to other ways of relating, we have demonstrated their essential components and asserted their uniqueness. We witnessed the importance of how we interface with various aspects of the environment and the diversity of ways to interface with it, particularly whole body/mind configurations or "modes" of relating, and the reciprocal effect exerted by relationships. This exploration calls for a better theory of the function of emotional skills and their development in the human evolutionary process. By modifying the way emotions are understood in relation to other key phenomena, such as drives, values, cognition, rationality, objectivity, self, and relationships, this essay has undertaken a fundamental, psycho-philosophical conceptual reconfiguration of emotions that could have substantial consequences.

Beyond the immediate intellectual contribution of this study, the hope is that some of the innovative ideas and insights will stimulate further discussion, research, and treatment. Surprisingly few studies exist of emotions as a general category, and any new ideas or discussions could advance the understanding of this phenomenon and our interactions with it. Considering the central role emotions play in all areas of our life, and their importance to our physical, social, and personal well-being as individuals and a community, we understand very little about them and invest even less to improve our understanding. By comparison, numerous discussions of happiness have emerged recently, and psychological studies of emotional pathologies continue to proliferate. Many of these analyses are undertaken without a sufficient understanding of the general theory of emotions, a good theory of what they are all about, their exact function, or their unique characteristics and requirements.

Outside the emotional realm, we devote an incredible amount of time and resources to figure out how to prolong life, alleviate physical pain and suffering, and increase economic comfort. Yet, though we are very familiar with emotional suffering and are constantly impacted by it, outside of psychology and pathology, we make a surprisingly small effort to alleviate it. We pay particularly little attention to the increase in emotional pain caused by our personal and communal values, behavior or policies.

Clearly, this essay lacks many of the answers, and is probably not completely correct in all its analysis and details. However, this should not stop readers from further discussing and studying these issues. First, the realization of the limited studies in this area should already motivate more people to concentrate on the subject. Second, even if readers identify only a few interesting and innovative elements among the many offered here, their efforts could support and continue this debate. They could criticize the views presented here, use them as a base to build on, or take them as triggers for new ideas.

Beyond the therapeutic contribution of such future deliberations and study, an improved understanding of emotions could help our personal and communal well-being as well as many other global issues. For example, if it is the case, as we considered here, that emotions enable morality and express our drives and values, they may play an important role in hatred, aggression, and wars, or in love, compassion, and peace. They obviously contribute to many types of crime, such as crimes of passion, jealousy or simple indifference, or social acts of contribution and support. General relating theory could help in comparing, assessing, and balancing different relational styles and methods. These theories could also be used to analyze job satisfaction, productivity, and the anonymous indifference that leads large organizations to develop exploitative, usurious practices toward their employees or citizens. In the realm of technology, a better understanding of emotions and other ways of relating could assist in better simulations and service to humankind. In the absence of emotions, we remain very far from what it means to be human. As we advance technologically, it will be important to ensure that our methods and techniques are more humane and helpful—hopefully more than the way we currently treat our food animals. The benefits of productive, continuous research about emotion extend to many areas—the education of our children for a better "EQ" or "ER," better relationships and greater happiness, artificial intelligence, or the development of desirable culture and beautiful art.

In a conference about innovation, a speaker once talked about the combination of suitcases and wheels. While both have been around for thousands of years, for some odd reason these technologies only merged in the last 30 or 40 years. For some, wheels on suitcases probably seemed odd at first, while for others it may have seemed completely inevitable, as if the idea had been around for centuries. Amazingly enough, for most of us today, it seems an unsurprising, obvious combination that doesn't suggest much innovation or creativity. This example is not presented to suggest that this essay deserves the sole credit for innovation or creativity, nor do we propose a patent on emotional understanding—even though companies already patent our genes and most of our wisdom. Rather, the example is presented to show that a seemingly slight change of view can bring about a major change of understanding and practice. It is also offered to warn against the tendency to trivialize or ignore subtle philosophical and psychological insights and reconfigurations that are nonetheless critical. Occasionally, they can bring about a major shift in research and social goals.

The goal of this essay is to stimulate a good, open dialogue—not to start a new "school," dogma or cult, as is sometimes the fate of good ideas. Hegel's ideas ended up both in fascism and communism; Nietzsche's inspired both fascism and capitalism; and Jesus's teaching was claimed both by saints and the inquisition. One would hope to avoid a dogmatic, fanatical following as much as anonymity. The goal is to stimulate, inspire, and refresh, not to die in oblivion or live in control. Ideas are not nations, and they should not demand blind loyalty. They flourish best through a moderate, honest interest, continued debate and reflection, occasional reorganization, and some applications if possible.

Bibilography

Alford, Brad and Aaron Beck. 1997. *The Integrative Power of Cognitive Therapy.* New York: Guilford Press.

Aristotle. 1987. *The Nicomachean Ethics.* Amherst, MA: Prometheus Books.

Aquinas, Thomas. 2002. Summa Theologica, Authentic Classics, Translated by Father of the English Dominican Province

Arnold, B. Magda. 1960. *Emotion and Personality*, Vols. 1 and 2. New York: Columbia University Press.

Barrett, L. Feldman. 2016. *How Emotions are Made: The New Science of the Mind and Brain.* Boston, MA: Houghton Mifflin Harcourt.

_____, Mesquita, Ocsner, and Gross. 2007. "The Experience of Emotion." Journal Review of Psychology 58: 373-403.

_____ and Russell, eds. 2015. *The Psychological Construction of Emotion.* New York: Guilford Press.

Beck, Aaron, John Rush, Brian Shaw and Gary Emery. 1979. *Cognitive Therapy of Depression.* New York: Guilford Press.

Beck, Julie. 2015. "Hard Feelings: Science's Struggle to Define Emotion." The Atlantic, Feb.24.

"Bhutan Studies."www.bhutanstudies.org.bt.

Ben-Zeev, Aaron. 2000. *The Subtlety of Emotions.* Cambridge, MA: MIT Press.

Bok, Sissela. 1995. *Common Values.* Columbia, MO: University of Missouri Press.

Bonger, B. and L. Beutter, eds. 1995. *Comprehensive Textbook of Psychotherapy Theory and Practice.* Oxford, UK: Oxford University Press.

Calhoun, C. and C.R. Solomon. 1984. *What Is an Emotion?* Oxford, UK: Oxford University Press.

Cannon, W.B. 1927. "The James-Lange Theory of Emotions: A Critical Examination and an Alternative Theory." *American Journal of Psychology* 39:106-124.

Carse, P. James. 2012. *Finite and Infinite Games.* New York: Free Press.

Clark, David and Aaron Beck. 2010. *Cognitive Therapy and Anxiety Disorder.* New York: Guilford Press.

Csikszentmihalyi, M. 1990. *Flow: The Psychology of Optimal Experience.* New York: Harper and Row.

Damasio, Antonio. 1994. *Descartes' Error: Emotion, Reason, and the Human Brain.* New York: Putnam's Sons.

_____. 1999. *The Feeling of What Happens.* New York: Harcourt Brace Inc.

_____. 2003. *Looking for Spinoza-Joy, Sorrow, and the Feeling Brain.* New York: Harvest Books Harcourt, Inc.

_____. 2010. *Self Comes to Mind-Constructing the Conscious Brain.* New York: Pantheon Books.

Descartes, Rene. 1964. *Philosophical Essays.* London: The Library of Liberal Arts, Macmillan Publishing Co.

de Sousa, Ronald. 1979. "The Rationality of Emotions." *Dialogue* 18 (1): 41-63

_____. 1990. *The Rationality of Emotion.* Cambridge, MA: The MIT Press.

_____. 2011. *Emotional Truth.* Oxford, UK: Oxford University Press.

_____. 2013. "Emotion." In the *Stanford Encyclopedia of Philosophy, https: //plato.stanford.edu/entries/emotion, accessed Sept. 15, 2016*

Dewey, John. 1958. *Experience and Nature.* Mineola, NY: Dover Publications, Inc.

Donaldson, M. 1992. *Human Minds: An Exploration.* London: Penguin Press.

Ekman, Paul and Richard Davidson. 1994. *The Nature of Emotion: Fundamental Questions.* Oxford, UK: Oxford University Press.

Ekman, P. 2007. *Emotions Revealed.* New York: Owl Books.

Ellis, Albert. 1994. *Reason and Emotion in Psychotherapy-Revised and Updated.* New York, Toronto: Carol Publishing Group.

Ellsworth, C. Phoebe and Klaus Scherer. 2009. "Appraisal processes in emotion." In *Handbook of Affective Sciences,* edited by Davidson, Goldsmith, and Scherer. New York and Oxford: Oxford University Press.

Ellsworth, C. Phoebe. 2013. "Appraisal Theory: Old and new questions." *Emotion Review* 5 (2): 125-131.

Elster, Jon. 1998. *Alchemies of the Mind: Rationality and the Emotions.* Cambridge, UK: Cambridge University Press.

Epicurus, *Stanford Encyclopedia of Philosophy,* 2005, revised 2014, accessed May 28, 2016. http//www. plato.stanford.edu/entries/epicurus/.

Epstein, Seymour. 1984. "Controversial Issues in Emotion Theory." *Review of Personality and Social Psychology* 5: 64-88.

_____. 1999. "The Relation of Rational and Experiential Information Processing Styles to Personality, Basic Beliefs, and the Ratio-bias Phenomenon." *Journal of Personality and Social Psychology* 76: 972-987.

Fiske & Pavelchak. 1986. "Category-based versus piecemeal-based affective responses: Developments in schema-triggered affect." In *Handbook of Motivation and Cognition,* edited by R. M. Sorrentino and E. T. Higgins, 167-203. New York: Guilford Press.

Frijda, H. Nico. 1986. *The Emotions*. Cambridge, UK: Cambridge University Press.

_____. 2007. *The Laws of Emotion*. Mahwah, NJ: Lawrence Erlbaum Associates Inc.

Goldie, Peter. 2010. *The Oxford Handbook of Philosophy of Emotion*. Oxford, UK: Oxford University Press.

Goleman, Daniel. 2005. *Emotional Intelligence*. New York: Bantam Dell, a division of Random House Inc.

Gordon, M. Robert. 1987. *The Structure of Emotions-Investigations in Cognitive Philosophy*. Cambridge, UK: Cambridge University Press.

Graham, C. Michael. 2014. *Facts of Life: Ten Issues of Contentment*. Denver, CO: Outskirts Press.

"Gross National Happiness" (GNH). http://www. grossnational-happiness.com.

Haes, J., B. Pennink, and K. Welvaart. 1987. "The Distinction Between Affect and Cognition." *Social Indicators Research* 19: 367-378.

Hagen, Anne Hilde Vessbo, with Leslie Greenberg. Accessed May 2016. "Alfred and Shadow-A Short Story about Emotions." Institute for Psychological Counseling, htttp.//www.ipr.no, Norwegian Institute of Emotion Focused Therapy, http.//www.nieft.no.

Harari, Y.N. 2014. *Sapiens/A Brief History of Humankind*. London: Harvill Secker.

_____. 2015. *The History of Tomorrow*. Israel: Kinneret, Zmora-Bitan, Dvir-Publishing House Ltd.

Harlow, F. Harry. 1958. "The Nature of Love." *American Psychologist* 13: 573-685.

Heidegger, Martin. 1962. *Being in Time*. New York: Harper and Row.

_____. 1972. *On Time and Being*. New York: Harper and Row.

_____. 1993. "The Question Concerning Technology." In *Martin Heidegger Basic Writings*, Second edition, Revised and Expanded, edited by David Farrell Krell. New York: Harper Collins.

Hershock, D. Peter. 1996. *Liberating Intimacy*. Albany, NY: SUNY Press.

_____. 1999a. "Disorienting Premises and Technical Missteps: A Buddhist Perspective on the Nature-Nurture Debate and the Meaning of Emotion." Unpublished manuscript.

_____. 1999b. *Reinventing the Wheel*. Albany, NY: SUNY Press.

_____. 2003. "Renegade Emotion: Buddhist Precedents for Returning Rationality to the Heart." 53(2): 251-70.

_____. 2004. *Chan Buddhism*. Honolulu, HI: University of Hawaii Press.

_____. 2006. *Buddhism in the Public Sphere: Reorienting Global Interdependence*. London: Routledge Publishing.

_____. 2013. *Valuing Diversity: Buddhist Reflection on Realizing a More Equitable Global Future*. Albany NY: SUNY Press.

Hilgard, R. Ernest. 1980. "Consciousness in Contemporary Psychology." *Annual Review of Psychology* 31:1-26

Hogan, Colm Patrick. 2003. *The Mind and Its Stories*. Cambridge, UK: Cambridge University Press.

Hockenbury, D.H. and S.E. Hockenbury. 2007. *Discovering Psychology*. New York: Worth Publishers.

Hume, David. 1977. *An Enquiry Concerning Human Understanding*. Indianapolis, IND: Hackett Publishing Co, Inc.

Husserl, Edmund. 1960. *Cartesian Meditations-An Introduction to Phenomenology*. Translated by Cairns. Berlin/Heidelberg, Germany: Springer.

Izard, Carroll. 1991. *The Psychology of Emotions*. New York: Plenum Press.

_____. 2007. "Basic Emotions, Natural Kinds, Emotion Schemas, and a New Paradigm." *Perspectives on Psychological Science* 2 (3): 260-280.

_____. 2009. "Emotion Theory and Research: Highlights, Unanswered questions, and Emerging Issues." *Annual Review of Psychology* 60:1-25.

James, William. 1890. *The Principles of Psychology*. New York: Henry Holt and Company.

———— and Carl Lange. 1922. *The Emotions*. Baltimore: William & Wilkins.

————. 1950. "The Emotions." In *Principles of Psychology*, Vol 2. New York: Dover Publications.

Johnson-Laired and Keith Oatley. 1989. "The Language of Emotions: An Analysis of a Semantic Field." *Cognition and Emotions* 3 (2): 81-123.

Jung, C. G. 1961. *Memories, Dreams, Reflections*. New York: Random House, Inc.

Kahneman, Daniel and Amos Tversky. 1979. "Prospect Theory: An Analysis of Decision under Risk." *Econometrica* 47(2): 263.

Kahneman, Daniel. 2011. *Thinking, Fast and Slow*. New York: Farrar, Straus and Giroux.

Kalupahana, J. David. 1976. *Buddhist Philosophy- a Historical Analysis*. Honolulu: University of Hawaii Press.

Kazdin, Alan, ed. 2000. *Encyclopedia of Psychology*. American Psychological Association.

Kesey, Ken. 1962. *One Flew Over the Cuckoo's Nest*. New York: Viking Press.

Kierkegaard, Soren. 1992. *Either/Or.* Edited by Eremita and translated by Hannay, London: Penguin Books.

Lachman, Roy, Janet Lachman, and Earl Butterfield. 1979. *Cognitive Psychology and Information Processing.* Mahwah, NJ: Lawrence Erlbaum Publishing.

Lakoff, George and Mark Johnson. 1980. *Metaphors We Live By.* Chicago, IL: University of Chicago Press.

_____. 1999. *Philosophy in the Flesh.* New York: Basic Books.

Lazarus, S. Richard. 1991a. *Emotion and Adaptation.* Oxford, UK: Oxford University Press.

_____. 1991b. "Progress on a Cognitive-Motivational-Relational Theory of Emotion." *American Psychologist* 46(8): 819-834.

_____. 2006. *Stress and Emotion: A New Synthesis.* Heidelberg/Berlin, Germany: Springer Publishing Co.

Lazarus, S. Richard and Bernice N. Lazarus. 1994. *Passion and Reason: Making Sense of Our Emotions.* Oxford, UK: Oxford University Press.

LeDoux, E. Joseph. 1996. *The Emotional Brain.* New York: Touchstone Books.

Lewis, Thomas, M.D., Fari Amini, M.D., and Richard Lannon, M.D. 2000. *A General Theory of Love.* New York: Vintage Books.

Lewis, Michael, Jeannette Haviland-Jones, and Lisa Feldman Barrett, eds. 2008. *Handbook of Emotions*, third edition. New York: Guilford Press.

Lutz, Catherine and Geoffrey M White. 1986. "The Anthropology of Emotions." *Annual Review of Anthropology* 15: 405-436.

Lutz, Catherine. 1986. "Emotion, Thought, and Estrangement: Emotion as a Cultural Category." *Cultural Anthropology* 1(3): 287-309.

Manstead T., S.R. Antony, Nico Frijda, and Agneta Fischer, eds. 2004. *Feelings and Emotions, The Amsterdam Symposium.* Cambridge, UK: Cambridge University Press.

Marks, J. and R. Ames. 1995. *Emotions in Asian Thought.* Albany, NY: SUNY Press.

Mascolo, F. and S. Griffin, eds. 1998. *What Develops in Emotional Development?* New York: Plenum Press

Maslow, H. Abraham. 2013. *A Theory of Human Motivation.* Eastford, CT: Martino Publishing.

_____. 1970. *Motivation and Personality*, 2nd ed. New York: Harper & Row.

McDougall, William. 1960. *An Introduction to Social Psychology*, 23rd ed. Methuen, MA: University Paperbacks.

Mead, Margaret. 1999. *Continuities in Cultural Evolution.* New Brunswick, NJ: Transaction Publishers.

Merleau-Ponty, Maurice. 1968. *The Visible and the Invisible*. Evanston, IL: Northwestern University Press.

Merriam-Webster.com (Encyclopedia), definition of emotion, accessed Jan. 20, 2016

Meyer W., R.Reisenzein, and A. Schutzwohl. 1997. "Toward Process Analysis of Emotions: The Case of Surprise." *Motivation & Emotion* 21(3):251-274.

Michalos, Alex. 1985. "Multiple Discrepancies Theory." *Social Indicators Research* 16(4): 347-413.

Mill, John Stuart. *Utilitarianism*. Reprinted from *Fraser's Magazine*, 7th ed. London: Longmans, Green and Co., 1879. Ebook #11224, released Feb. 22, 2004. Project Gutenberg EBook.

Moisi, Dominique. 2009. *The Geopolitics of Emotion-How cultures of fear, humiliation, and hope are reshaping the world*. New York: Doubleday.

Moors, Agnes, Phoebe Ellsworth, Klaus Scherer, and Nico Frijda. 2013. "Appraisal Theories of Emotion: State of the Art and Future Development." *Emotion Review* 5:119-124.

Myers, D.G. 2004. *Theories of Emotions*, 7th ed. New York: Worth Publishers.

Neisser, Ulrich. 1967. *Cognitive Psychology*. Englewood Cliffs, NJ: Prentice Hall.

_____. 1976. *Cognition and Reality*. New York: Freeman Publishing.

Neu, Jerome. 2000. *A Tear Is an Intellectual Thing*. Oxford, UK: Oxford University Press.

Nietzsche, Friedrich. 1997. *Beyond Good and Evil*. Mineola, NY: Dover Publications.

Nussbaum, C. Martha. 1994. *Therapy of Desire*. Princeton, NJ: Princeton University Press.

_____. 1999. "Precis of *The Therapy of Desire*." *Philosophy and Phenomenological Research* 59 (3): 785-786.

_____. 2001. *Upheavals of Thought-The Intelligence of Emotions*. Cambridge, UK: Cambridge University Press.

Oatley, Keith. 1992. *Best Laid Schemes, The Psychology of Emotions*. Cambridge, UK: Cambridge University Press.

Orwell, George. 1949. *1984*. London: Harvill Secker.

Otsubo, Shigeru Thomas. 2016. *Globalization and Development*, Vol. 3. 2016. London: Routledge Press.

Panksepp, Jaak. 1982. "Toward a general psychological theory of emotions." *Behavioral and Brain Sciences* (5)3: 407-422.

_____. 2004. *Affective Neuroscience-The Foundation of Human and Animal Emotions*. Oxford, UK: Oxford University Press.

_____. 2005. "Affective consciousness: Core emotional feelings in animals and humans." *Consciousness and Cognition* 14(1): 30-80.

Parkinson B., A. Fischer, and T. Manstead. 2005. *Emotions in Social Relations: Cultural, Group, and Interpersonal Processes.* Hove, UK: Psychology Press.

Parrott, Gerrod, ed. 2001. *Emotions in Social Psychology-Essential Readings.* Hove, UK: Psychology Press.

Plutchik, Robert. 1980. *Emotion: A Psychoevolutionary Synthesis.* New York: Harper & Row.

_____. 2002. *Emotions and Life.* American Psychological Association.

Prinz, J.Jesse. 2004. *Gut Reactions-A Perceptual Theory of Emotion.* Oxford, UK: Oxford University Press.

Redding, Paul. 1999. *The Logic of Affect.* Ithaca, NY: Cornell University Press.

Reisenzein, Rainer. 2006. "Arnold Theory of Emotion in Historical Perspective." *Cognition and Emotion* 20 (7): 920-951.

Ricard, Mattheiu. "The Habit of Happiness," TED 2004 20:54;https://www.ted.com/talks/matthieu_ricard_on_the_habits_of_happiness, Filmed Feb. 2004.

Rorty, Amelie, ed. 1980. *Explaining Emotions.* Los Angeles, CA: University of California Press.

Roseman, Ira. 1984. "Cognitive Determinants of Emotion: A Structural Theory." *Review of Personality and Social Psychology* 5: 11-36.

_____. 2013. "Appraisal in the Emotion System: Coherence in Strategies for Coping." *Emotion Review* 5 (2): 141-149.

Russell, A. James. 1991. "Culture and the Categorization of Emotion." *Psychological Bulletin* 110: 426-450.

Sabini, John and Maury Silver. 1996. "On the Possible Non-Existence of Emotions: The Passions." *Journal of Theory of Social Behavior* 26 (4): 375-398.

_____. 1997. "Volcan Redux." *Journal of Theory of Social Behavior* 27(4): 499-502.

Sartre, Jean-Paul. 1957. *Existentialism and Human Emotions*. New York: Philosophical Library, Inc.

Schachter, S. and J.E. Singer. 1962. "Cognitive, Social and Physiological Determinates of Emotional States." *Psychological Review* 69 (5):379-399.

Scheler, Max and McAleer Graham. 2008. *The Nature of Sympathy*. New Brunswick, NJ: Transaction Publishers.

Scherer, Klaus, Angela Schorr, and Tom Johnstone, eds. 2001. *Appraisal Processes in Emotion-Theory, Method, Research*. Oxford, UK: Oxford University Press.

Scherer, Klaus and Paul Ekman, ed. 2009. *Approaches to Emotion*. Hove, UK: Psychology Press.

Scherer, Klaus. 2009a "Emotions are emergent processes: they require a dynamic computational architecture." *Philosophical Transactions* 364 (1535): 3459-3474.

Scherer, Klaus, Tanj Banziger, and Etienne Roesch, eds. 2010. *Bluprint for Affective Computing.* Oxford, UK: Oxford University Press.

_____. 2013. "Emotions induced by music: The role of the listening context and modality of presentation." Conference paper, June 2013.

Salovey, Peter and John Mayer. 1990. *Emotional Intelligence.* Amityville, NY: Baywood Publishing.

Schopenhauer, Arthur. 1969. *The World as Will and Representation.* Mineola, NY: Courier Dover Publications.

Smith, Craig and Richard Lazarus. 1999. "Emotion and Adaptation." In *Handbook of Personality: Theory and Research* edited by Pervin and John, 609-637. New York: Guilford Press.

Smith, Craig and Leslie Kirby. 2009. "Putting appraisal in context: Toward a relational model of appraisal and emotion." *Cognition and Emotion* 23 (7): 1352-1372.

Solms, Mark and Oliver Turnbull. 2002. *The Brain and the Inner World: An Introduction to the Neuroscience of the Subjective Experience.* New York: Other Press.

Solomon, C. Robert. 1977. "The Rationality of the Emotions." *The Southwestern Journal of Philosophy* 8(2): 105-114.

_____. 1992. "Existentialism, emotions, and the cultural limits of rationality." *Philosophy and the West* 42(4):597-621.

_____. 1995. "Some Notes on Emotion, East and West." *Philosophy East and West* 45(2): 171-202.

_____. 1997a. "In Defense of the Emotions (and Passions too)." *Journal for the Theory of Social Behavior* 27(4): 489-497.

_____. 1997b. "Beyond Ontology: Ideation, Phenomenology and the Cross-Cultural Study of Emotion." *Journal for the Theory of Social Behavior* 27(2-3): 289-303.

_____, ed. 2003. *What Is an Emotion? Classic and Contemporary Readings*, 2nd edition. New York, Oxford, UK: Oxford University Press,

_____. 2016. "Emotion." *Encyclopedia Britannica*.

Sorrentino, Richard and Edward Higgins, eds. 1996. *Handbook of Motivation and Cognition*. New York: Guilford Press.

Springsteen, Bruce. 1995. "Youngstown," on the Album "The Ghost of Tom Joad."

Stearns N. Peter. 2008. "History of Emotions: The Issue of Change." In *Handbook of Emotions*, edited by Lewis, Haviland, and Barrett. New York: Guilford Press.

Thoits, A. Peggy. 1989. "The Sociology of Emotions." *Annual Review of Psychology* 5: 317-342.

Tugate, Michele, Michelle Shiota, and Leslie Kirby, eds. 2014. *Handbook of Positive Emotions*. New York: Guilford Press.

Turski, George. 1994a. *Toward a Rationality of Emotions: An Essay in the Philosophy of Mind*. Athens, Ohio: Ohio University Press.

_____. 1994b. "Emotions and the Self." *Philosophy Today* 38(1): 3-17.

Tversky, Amos and Daniel Kahneman. 1992. "Advances in prospect theory: Cumulative representation of uncertainty." *Journal of Risk and Uncertainty* 5(4): 297-323.

Verywell.com. "Theories of Emotions" by Kendra Cherry, updated Aug. 1, 2017, accessed Sept. 10, 2017.

White, M. Geoffrey. 2008. "Emotions Inside Out: The Anthropology of Affect." In *Handbook of Emotions*, edited by Lewis, Haviland, and Barrett. New York: Guilford Press.

Wikipedia, s.v. "Emotion," accessed Jan. 20, 2016, https://en.wikipedia.org/wiki/Emotion.

William, Morris, ed. 1976. *The American Heritage Dictionary of the English Language*. New York: Houghton Mifflin Co.

Wittgenstein, Ludwig. 2001. *Philosophical Investigations*. Translated by Anscombe. Hoboken, NJ: Blackwell Publishing.

Wollheim, Richard. 1999. *On the Emotions.* New Haven, CT: Yale University Press.

Zajonc, R. B. 1980. "Feeling and Thinking Preferences Need No Inferences." *American Psychologist* 35(2): 151-175.

Acknowledgements

I wish to thank all the people that helped me with this book as well as those who freed my time to work on it. In particular I would like to thank my wife, my sons, and the rest of my family and friends for their patience and advice, Harriette Grissom for a great editing job, Peter Hershock and Russell Alfonso for their original ideas and suggestions, and Kamea Hadar for his beautiful art work.